广视角·全方位·多品种

权威·前沿·原创

皮书系列为
"十二五"国家重点图书出版规划项目

权威报告　热点资讯　海量资源

当代中国与世界发展的高端智库平台

皮书数据库　www.pishu.com.cn

　　皮书数据库是专业的人文社会科学综合学术资源总库,以大型连续性图书——皮书系列为基础,整合国内外相关资讯构建而成。该数据库包含七大子库,涵盖两百多个主题,囊括了近十几年间中国与世界经济社会发展报告,覆盖经济、社会、政治、文化、教育、国际问题等多个领域。

　　皮书数据库以篇章为基本单位,方便用户对皮书内容的阅读需求。用户可进行全文检索,也可对文献题目、内容提要、作者名称、作者单位、关键字等基本信息进行检索,还可对检索到的篇章再作二次筛选,进行在线阅读或下载阅读。智能多维度导航,可使用户根据自己熟知的分类标准进行分类导航筛选,使查找和检索更高效、便捷。

　　权威的研究报告、独特的调研数据、前沿的热点资讯,皮书数据库已发展成为国内最具影响力的关于中国与世界现实问题研究的成果库和资讯库。

皮书俱乐部会员服务指南

1. 谁能成为皮书俱乐部成员?

- 皮书作者自动成为俱乐部会员
- 购买了皮书产品(纸质皮书、电子书)的个人用户

2. 会员可以享受的增值服务

- 加入皮书俱乐部,免费获赠该纸质图书的电子书
- 免费获赠皮书数据库100元充值卡
- 免费定期获赠皮书电子期刊
- 优先参与各类皮书学术活动
- 优先享受皮书产品的最新优惠

3. 如何享受增值服务?

(1) 加入皮书俱乐部,获赠该书的电子书

第1步　登录我社官网(www.ssap.com.cn),注册账号;

第2步　登录并进入"会员中心"—"皮书俱乐部",提交加入皮书俱乐部申请;

第3步　审核通过后,自动进入俱乐部服务环节,填写相关购书信息即可自动兑换相应电子书。

(2) 免费获赠皮书数据库100元充值卡

100元充值卡只能在皮书数据库中充值和使用

第1步　刮开附赠充值的涂层(左下);

第2步　登录皮书数据库网站(www.pishu.com.cn),注册账号;

第3步　登录并进入"会员中心"—"在线充值"—"充值卡充值",充值成功后即可使用。

4. 声明

解释权归社会科学文献出版社所有

皮书俱乐部会员可享受社会科学文献出版社其他相关免费增值服务,有任何疑问,均可与我们联系

联系电话:010-59367427　企业QQ:800045692　邮箱:pishuclub@ssap.com.cn

欢迎登录社会科学文献出版社官网(www.ssap.com.cn)和中国皮书网(www.pishu.com.cn)了解更多信息

城市生活质量蓝皮书

BLUE BOOK OF
QUALITY OF LIFE IN CITIES

中国城市生活质量报告(2013)

REPORT ON THE QUALITY OF LIFE IN CHINESE CITIES (2013)

生活质量：指数平稳，挑战严峻

中国经济实验研究院

社会科学文献出版社
SOCIAL SCIENCES ACADEMIC PRESS (CHINA)

图书在版编目(CIP)数据

中国城市生活质量报告.2013,生活质量：指数平稳,挑战严峻/中国经济实验研究院著.—北京：社会科学文献出版社,2014.1
（城市生活质量蓝皮书）
ISBN 978-7-5097-5573-0

Ⅰ.①中… Ⅱ.①中… Ⅲ.①城市-生活质量-指数-研究报告-中国-2013 Ⅳ.①D669.3

中国版本图书馆CIP数据核字（2014）第012898号

城市生活质量蓝皮书
中国城市生活质量报告（2013）
——生活质量：指数平稳，挑战严峻

著　　者 / 中国经济实验研究院
英文翻译 / 王宏彧

出 版 人 / 谢寿光
出 版 者 / 社会科学文献出版社
地　　址 / 北京市西城区北三环中路甲29号院3号楼华龙大厦
邮政编码 / 100029

责任部门 / 经济与管理出版中心 (010) 59367226　责任编辑 / 陈凤玲 于 飞
电子信箱 / caijingbu@ssap.cn　　　　　　　　　责任校对 / 程雷高
项目统筹 / 恽 薇　　　　　　　　　　　　　　 责任印制 / 岳 阳
经　　销 / 社会科学文献出版社市场营销中心 (010) 59367081 59367089
读者服务 / 读者服务中心 (010) 59367028

印　　装 / 北京季蜂印刷有限公司
开　　本 / 787mm×1092mm　1/16　　　　　　 印　张 / 15
版　　次 / 2014年1月第1版　　　　　　　　　 字　数 / 210千字
印　　次 / 2014年1月第1次印刷
书　　号 / ISBN 978-7-5097-5573-0
定　　价 / 59.00元

本书如有破损、缺页、装订错误，请与本社读者服务中心联系更换
▲ 版权所有 翻印必究

中国经济实验研究院

本报告执笔人 　张连城　赵家章　张自然

专项研究执笔人 　张　平　吴　伟　汪红驹

最 终 定 稿 　张连城　张　平　杨春学

组织和策划本次调研的人员

　　　　　　　　　张　平　张连城　杨春学
　　　　　　　　　纪　宏　刘霞辉　郎丽华
　　　　　　　　　徐　雪　王　诚　张晓晶
　　　　　　　　　田新民　袁富华　张自然
　　　　　　　　　赵家章　王　银　马　力

中国经济实验研究院简介

改革开放以来，特别是社会主义市场经济体制建立以来，中国经济发展已经进入一个崭新的阶段。中国已经成为世界第二大经济体，人均国民收入已经达到中等收入国家的水平；同时，中国改革正在从"浅水区"进入"深水区"，改革所面临的形势将更为艰巨和复杂，中国改革必须从"摸着石头过河"的"实践试错"向着利用现代手段进行政策模拟和评估的"实验试错"转变。与此同时，从学科发展的角度看，经济学发展到今天，科学研究正在向协同研究和交叉学科研究的方向发展。这在客观上要求我国的高等院校、研究机构要打破学科界限、打破单位界限，整合一切可利用的资源，精诚合作，不断创新，才有可能应对中国社会所面临的新挑战。在这种背景下，经过长期调研、论证和精心准备，首都经济贸易大学与中国社会科学院经济研究所合作，共同成立了"中国经济实验研究院"。

早在2006年，首都经济贸易大学与中国社会科学院经济研究所就组建了"中国经济增长与周期研究中心"，并且联合香港经济导报社从2007年开始，成功举办了6届"中国经济增长与周期论坛"。目前，"论坛"已经成为国内研究宏观经济的著名学者进行学术交流的重要平台。2010年，首都经济贸易大学与中国社会科学院经济研究所又组建了"中国城市生活质量研究中心"，经过对城市生活质量指数体系的深入研究和几个月的调研，在2011年举办的第五届"中国经济增长与周期论坛"上，首次发布了中国30个省会城市的生活质量指数，在国内引起了很大的反响，并引起了国际同行和世界银行等国际机构的关注。中国经济实验研究院就

是在上述研究机构的基础上成立的。

目前，研究院设有"中国经济增长与周期研究中心""中国城市生活质量研究中心""数量经济研究中心"和"WTO研究中心"，并且设有经济运行与国际贸易实验室、经济预警实验室、经济数据处理与计算机仿真实验室和数字化调查中心。

中国经济实验研究院成立以后，在对原有机构和实验室进行整合的基础上，拟设如下机构：

1. 中国经济实验研究院专家委员会
2. 中国经济增长与周期研究中心
3. 中国城市生活质量研究中心
4. 数量经济研究中心
5. 博士后流动站
6. 中国经济增长与周期论坛
7. 北京经济转型发展研究中心
8. 经济运行与经济预警实验室、计算机仿真实验室

中国经济实验研究院成立以后，近期的主要任务是：

第一，将进一步深入开展中国经济增长与经济周期的研究；继续办好"中国经济增长与周期论坛"，并且将逐步实现国际化；

第二，进一步扩大生活质量指数研究的覆盖面，使其逐步从省会城市扩展到全国中等城市、从国内扩展到国际，同时实现指数发布的常态化。此外，生活质量只是经济增长质量的一部分内容，研究院成立后，将逐步把经济增长质量的研究纳入自己的研究视野，争取获得一批高质量的科研成果。

第三，研究院成立以后，将不断拓展经济实验研究的范围，开展经济改革实验、政策效应实验、经济增长压力实验等，为中国改革、政府机构及相关部门提供可量化的决策支持，并且努力服务社会。

第四，成立具有国际化特色的研究生指导团队，同时开展与国外大学

的紧密合作，共同指导硕士和博士研究生，招收博士后，为首都经济贸易大学的人才队伍建设做出贡献。

第五，中国经济实验研究院目前与国外 20 多所高校有着紧密的合作关系。研究院成立以后，将以此为基础，开展广泛的国际合作和国际学术交流，共同进行科学研究，协同创新，构造研究院的国际化特色。

中国经济实验研究院的宗旨是：推动经济实验研究，繁荣经济科学，为推进我国的经济体制改革、提高经济增长质量、促进经济发展服务。中国经济实验研究院的目标是：在未来，经过我们的不懈努力，争取把中国经济实验研究院建设成为这一领域的具有国际一流水平的高度开放的研究机构。

摘 要

继2011年和2012年发布中国城市生活质量指数之后,为进一步推进对我国经济增长和居民生活质量的研究,中国经济实验研究院城市生活质量研究中心于2013年3~5月对中国35个城市的生活质量进行了调查,通过统计分析计算出了2013年城市生活质量的主观满意度指数和客观经济指数。

本次调查仍然采用国际通用电脑辅助电话调查(CATI)方法,固定电话前3位或4位电话号码保证空间分布的广泛性,尾号4位随机抽样,总共拨打了298590个电话,其中257150个固定电话用户,41440个手机用户,产生有效随机样本12759个。整体主观满意度指数的标准误差从2012年的0.24缩小到2013年的0.19,使本次调查的可靠性进一步增强。本次调查除了对城市居民生活质量满意度指数进行了调查外,还安排了两项专项调查。一是关于城市房价预期的专项调查,二是关于食品安全满意度的调查,其中后一项调查是本次新增的专项调查,这对于深入了解城市居民生活质量具有重要意义。

调查显示,全国35个城市的生活质量主观满意度指数平均值为50.87,与2012年的平均值50.88基本一致,越过了50分满意与不满意的临界点,进入了满意区间,但仍旧偏低。主观满意度指数超过50分的有26个城市,比2012年多3个城市。在城市生活质量主观满意度指数的5个分指数中,生活水平和生活成本满意度比2012年有所提升,人力资本、社会保障、生活感受满意度略有下降。尽管生活成本满意度有所上升,但居高不下的生活成本仍旧是拉低城市居民生活质量满意度的最重要的原因。

通过本次对35个城市生活质量的调查，我们发现与2012年的调查结果相比，2013年的城市生活质量客观指数有所提高，主观满意度指数基本持平，总体态势平稳，客观指数的提升主要得益于中央民生工程的继续深入实施。但是居高不下的生活成本，普遍存在的房价上涨预期，居民对食品安全、社会治安和空气质量的担忧，这一系列因素形成了极为严峻的挑战。政府应采取有效的措施，改变房价长期上涨的心理预期，加强对食品安全的监管力度，以转型升级为主线，以提高居民生活质量为目标，加大民生投入，切实提高居民对生活质量的满意度。

关键词： 城市生活质量　主观满意度指数　客观经济指数　食品安全　房价预期

目 录

BⅠ 总报告

B.1 2013：提高城市生活质量面临严峻挑战 …………………………… 001

BⅡ 综合篇

B.2 对2013年城市生活质量调查的说明 …………………………………… 007

BⅢ 观测篇

B.3 2013年中国35个城市生活质量指数 …………………………………… 010

B.4 2013年中国35个城市生活质量分指数 ………………………………… 023

BⅣ 结论与对策篇

B.5 结论和启示 …………………………………………………………… 078

BⅤ 专题研究篇

B.6 中国与国际房地产价格动态比较…………………………083

B.7 参考文献……………………………………………………103

皮书数据库阅读使用指南

总报告

B.1 2013：提高城市生活质量面临严峻挑战

1.1 引言

在2011年举办的第五届"中国经济增长与周期论坛"上，中国经济实验研究院城市生活质量研究中心首次发布了中国30个城市生活质量总指数和各个分指数。2011年的综合分析结果表明，我国经济高速增长过程中存在"两大反差"：一是高速的经济增长与居民生活质量的提高存在反差；二是居民实际生活质量与居民主观感受存在反差。2011年的调查给了我们非常重要的启示，对了解和把握城市居民生活质量总体状况，具有非常重要的意义。

为了更客观、全面、准确地反映城市生活质量，2012年，课题组对城市生活质量指标体系进行了完善和局部调整，并增加了城市样本数，从而使该次调查能够更全面、更准确地反映我国城市居民生活质量水平。具体

包括以下几个方面。第一，增加了调查城市数。第二，使用了城市的常住人口数。第三，扩大了主观问卷调查样本量。第四，调查的精确度进一步得到提高。95%的置信度下主观指数的绝对估计误差从±0.27以内缩小到±0.24以内。第五，增加了房价预期专项调查。2012年的调查结果表明：城市生活质量主观满意度总体水平比2011年有所提高，但两个"反差"依然存在；高生活成本拖累了城市生活质量满意度的提高；房价上涨预期普遍存在，并成为城市生活成本继续上升的隐忧；城市规模过大可能不利于生活质量的提高；东部地区的城市生活质量客观指数总体上要高于中西部地区。政府应有效遏制城市生活成本上升、稳定房价和物价水平、管理好通货膨胀预期、控制过大的城市规模，这些都是提高生活质量的关键。上述调查结果给我们的启示在于：中央民生工程的深入实施有利于居民生活质量的提高，但城市居民的生活成本仍旧偏高，只有进一步有效地遏制城市房价过快上涨、稳定物价总水平、管理好通货膨胀预期，才能进一步提高城市居民生活质量；地方政府在重视经济快速发展的同时，更要重视民生建设、加大民生方面的投入、保障和改善民生的制度性安排，在城市居民生活实实在在改善的同时，使城市居民对生活质量的满意度不断提高。

中国经济实验研究院城市生活质量研究中心继2011年和2012年发布中国城市生活质量指数之后，于2013年3~5月对中国35个城市的生活质量进行了第三次年度调查，并通过统计分析和计算得出了2013年城市生活质量的主观满意度指数和客观经济指数，该指数在2013年第七届"中国经济增长与周期论坛"发布。本报告是2013年度中国35个城市生活质量指数的调查结果。

1.2 主要结论

本次调查结果显示，全国35个城市生活质量主观满意度指数平均值为50.87，与2012年的平均值50.88基本一致，越过了50分满意与不满意的

临界点，进入了满意区间，但仍旧偏低。主观满意度指数超过50分的有26个城市，比2012年多3个城市。城市生活质量主观满意度指数的五个分指数平均值分别为：人力资本（58.89）、社会保障（56.64）、生活感受（55.07）、生活水平（52.51）、生活成本（31.22）。与2012年相比，居民对生活水平和生活成本的主观满意度有所提升，对人力资本、社会保障、生活感受的主观满意度略有下降。虽然居民对生活成本的满意度有所上升，但居高不下的生活成本仍旧是阻碍城市居民生活质量满意度进一步提高的最重要原因。

调查结果显示，在被调查的35个城市中，生活质量满意度（主观）指数排名前10位的城市是：济南（1）、青岛（2）、厦门（3）、长春（4）、合肥（5）、西宁（6）、宁波（7）、石家庄（8）、福州（9）、杭州（10）。其中有7个东部城市，2个中部城市，1个西部城市。排名后10位的城市分别是：大连（26）、太原（27）、南宁（28）、哈尔滨（29）、贵阳（30）、广州（31）、武汉（32）、昆明（33）、深圳（34）、兰州（35）。其中有3个东部城市，3个中部城市，4个西部城市。

房价预期的专项调查结果显示：35个城市房价预期指数平均值为64.65，比2012年上升了17.6%。这不仅表明房价上涨预期普遍存在，而且2013年房价预期上升的幅度比2012年更大。房价预期指数较高的10个城市依次为：广州（68.64）、西宁（68.33）、乌鲁木齐（67.37）、南昌（66.73）、郑州（66.60）、合肥（66.07）、上海（65.97）、深圳（65.96）、银川（65.93）、南京（65.92）。预期2013年比2012年房价上涨幅度较大的10个城市依次为青岛（37.9%）、杭州（33.2%）、济南（31.4%）、北京（26.3%）、长春（24.4%）、合肥（23.7%）、上海（23.7%）、宁波（22.6%）、长沙（22.1%）、福州（22%）。①

食品安全满意度的调查结果显示：全国35个城市的居民对食品安全的

---

① 括号中百分比的计算方法是：用2013年的得分减去2012年的得分，然后再除以2012年的得分。

满意度指数平均为41.67，这个平均值没有进入满意区间。在这35个城市中，高于50分的仅有厦门一个城市。整体上看，城市居民对于食品安全的满意程度较低，或者说，除厦门市外，其他34个城市的居民对食品安全均不满意。食品安全满意度指数较高的10个城市是：厦门（53.06）、西宁（49.44）、海口（46.98）、重庆（45.67）、银川（45.05）、贵阳（44.49）、成都（44.39）、宁波（44.03）、北京（43.55）、深圳（43.25）。食品安全满意度较低的10个城市是：武汉（36.47）、太原（36.87）、长沙（36.90）、郑州（37.08）、沈阳（38.49）、石家庄（38.51）、兰州（38.84）、上海（39.12）、福州（39.24）、哈尔滨（39.24）。另外，调查结果还显示，从性别角度看，男性受访者对食品安全的满意度（43.61）高于女性受访者的满意度（39.46）；从年龄段来看，20~30岁受访者对食品安全的满意度最高（43.68），41~60岁受访者的满意度最低（39.56）。

2013年35个城市生活质量客观指数（社会经济数据指数）的平均值为57.75，比2012年的54.56有所提高。生活质量客观指数得分在50分及以上的城市有33个，比2012年多2个。城市生活质量客观指数5个分指数的平均值分别是：生活水平（63.39）、生活成本（58.67）、人力资本（57.78）、社会保障（55.26）、生活感受（53.67）。跟2012年相比，这5个客观分指数均有不同程度的提高。生活质量客观指数较高的10个城市依次为：北京（69.80）、广州（66.85）、南京（66.65）、西安（64.65）、深圳（63.93）、呼和浩特（62.22）、厦门（61.89）、上海（61.78）、宁波（61.47）、沈阳（59.99）。生活质量客观指数较低的10个城市依次为：重庆（47.83）、西宁（49.29）、南宁（50.00）、郑州（50.54）海口（51.50）、哈尔滨（51.86）、贵阳（52.45）、福州（52.66）、南昌（53.03）、乌鲁木齐（54.59）。东部地区的生活质量客观指数整体上要高于中西部地区。

中国经济实验研究院城市生活质量研究中心本次对35个城市生活质量调查的结论有：与2012年的调查结果相比，城市生活质量客观指数有

所提高，主观满意度指数基本持平，总体态势平稳；我国经济发展过程中的"两大反差"依然存在；生活成本过高仍然是影响生活质量满意度提高的主要因素；房价上涨预期趋强，未来房价还有进一步上升的趋势；食品安全形势严峻。当前，不断增加的生活成本，普遍存在的房价上涨预期，居民对食品安全、社会治安和空气质量的担忧，对居民生活质量的提高构成了极为严峻的挑战。面对上述挑战，必须进一步推进经济体制改革，加快经济转型，打造中国经济升级版，这需要政府政策在以下几方面做出调整：第一，应当改变对传统经济增长方式的过度依赖，从要素驱动、投资驱动向创新驱动、消费驱动过渡；从过度依赖人口红利、土地红利，转向依靠改革来形成制度红利。第二，以经济转型升级为主线，以提高居民生活品质为目标，加大投资、统筹发展、加强生态环境建设。第三，继续深入推进民生工程，完善社会保障制度建设。

1.3 框架安排

本书的第二部分是对2013年城市生活质量调查方法、对本次调查指标体系设置和调整以及样本选取所做的说明。

第三部分是2013年对中国35个城市生活质量指数调查的总体情况、排序以及相应的说明，其中包括35个城市生活满意度指数和客观指数（社会经济数据指数），此外还包括城市住房价格指数和食品安全满意度指数，即两个专项调查的结果。为了便于分析各城市的生活质量状况，本部分将各个城市生活质量总指数的评分和排序逐个列出，并通过与2012年和2011年的总指数进行比较，动态分析城市生活质量的变化。

第四部分是中国35个城市生活质量指数（包括主观满意度指数和客观指数）的各项分指数的调查结果。各个城市生活质量的主观满意度指

数和客观指数的高低和变化都可以从各项分指数中得到说明。在这一部分中，我们给出了35个城市生活质量的各项分指数及排序的结果，也给出了35个城市的生活质量一级指标的雷达图，并进行了动态比较。

第五部分是本次调查的主要结论和启示。

最后，在本次调查的同时，进行了"中国与国际房地产价格动态比较"的专项研究，作为本书的第六部份。

综合篇

B.2 对2013年城市生活质量调查的说明

为了保证调查结果的连续性和可比性，2013年我们在调查方法、指标体系设置以及样本的选取方面延续了2012年的做法，同时在局部做了细微的调整和完善。

2.1 对本次调查的整体说明及调整

2013年选取的城市样本仍旧是35个城市，包括4个直辖市、26个省会城市和5个计划单列城市。为了获取这35个城市生活质量的主观满意度指标，我们继续采用国际通用的电脑辅助电话调查的方法（CATI），固定电话号码的抽取仍旧采用分层二阶段随机抽样方法。第一阶段按照被调查的城市分布分层，第二阶段在每个城市行政区内，按照电话局号码分层，保证调查在城市空间分布上的广泛性，同时用随机尾数拨号法抽取后

四位电话号码，以保证抽取样本的随机性。与2012年的主观调查不同的是，本次调查增加了针对移动电话用户的调查。对移动电话用户的调查同样遵循了城市间空间分布的广泛性和样本抽取随机性原则。本次调查总共拨打了298590个电话，其中包括257150个固定电话用户，41440个移动电话用户，最后共产生有效随机样本12759个。此次调查的可靠性进一步增强，整体主观指数的标准误差缩小到0.19。

在客观指标方面，与2012年最大的不同是我们在计算某些与人均相关的客观指数时全面使用了全市的常住人口数，而2012年有些城市使用的是市辖区人口数。常住人口数以全国第六次人口普查的结果为准。全面使用城市常住人口数据，能更准确地评价一个城市生活的质量水平，但可能使某些城市的客观指标发生一些技术性变化。

2.2 主客观指标体系的构建和专项调查

2013年度中国城市生活质量指数（QLICC）[①] 体系仍然包括两个部分：主观满意度指标体系和客观指标（社会经济数据指数）体系。主观满意度指标体系和客观指标体系的构建均延续了2012年的做法。QLICC的主观指标体系包括以下5项分指数：生活水平满意度指数、生活成本满意度指数、人力资本满意度指数、生活保障满意度指数、生活感受满意度指数。其中生活水平满意度指数被细分为收入现状满意度指数和收入预期满意度指数，两个细分指数各占50%的权重；社会保障满意度指数被细分为医疗保障和安全状况两个细分指数，两个细分指数也各占50%的权重；生活感受满意度指数被细分为生活节奏和生活便利两个细分指数。这样，对生活质量主观满意度的调查就生成了8个主观问题，通过向受访者询问这些主观问题，我们得到"很满意""满意""一般""不满意""很不满意"

---

① "中国城市生活质量指数"2013年以前的英文缩写为"CCLQI"，自2013年起改为"QLICC"。

对2013年城市生活质量调查的说明

等5个不同的答案,并根据不同的答案给出不同的赋值,进而得出主观满意度指数。就我国经济发展的现阶段而言,上述8项指标不仅涉及人们的收入状况和生活成本,还包含城市的宜居性以及人们所承受的生活压力,基本上可以反映现阶段我国城市居民对所在城市生活质量的主观感受。①

此外,在本次主观满意度的电话调查中,除了继续对城市住房价格预期进行专项调查外,我们还增加了关于食品安全的专项调查。住房预期价格指数的调查是通过询问受访者对所居住城市的房屋价格(在今后1~2年)是涨还是跌的主观问题,得到"大涨""上涨""不涨不跌""下跌""大跌"等5个不同的答案,并将每种答案给出不同的赋值,得出住房价格预期指数。食品安全状况的专项指数的构建是通过询问受访者对所居住城市的食品安全状况是否满意,得到"很满意""满意""一般""不满意""很不满意"等5个不同的答案,并根据不同的答案给出不同的赋值,进而得出食品安全主观满意度指数。尽管这两个专项调查结果并不进入QLICC体系,但这些结果可以佐证居民对生活质量的满意度。

QLICC的客观指标体系包括以下5项分指数:生活水平客观分指数、生活成本客观分指数、人力资本客观分指数、生活保障客观分指数和生活感受客观分指数。5项分指数又由8个一级指标和20个二级指标构成。在20个经济指标的基础上,运用归一化平权方法计算出反映城市生活质量的8个一级指标,再将一级指标的数据求平均值得到5个客观分指数,最后按照功效系数法进行调整,使之能够与主观满意度指数对接②。需要说明的是,35个城市的20个二级指标的客观数据是从官方文件中选取的,通过计算所得出的客观指数反映的是2012年的经济状况。

---

① 具体指标体系可参考:张连城等《高生活成本拖累城市生活质量满意度提高——中国35个城市生活质量调查报告(2012)》,《经济学动态》2012年第7期;详见《中国城市生活质量报告(2012)》蓝皮书,社会科学文献出版社,2013。
② 未包含5个计划单列城市的排序。35个城市全国平均值的计算方法是:根据调查样本的分布情况,将35个城市的分指数加权平均。这种计算方法也适用于下面所有主观满意度分指数中全国平均值的计算和专项调查中全国平均指数的计算。

观测篇

B.3
2013年中国35个城市生活质量指数

表3-1和表3-2列出了本次调查得出的中国35个直辖市、省会城市和计划单列城市的生活质量指数(包括主观满意度指数和客观指数)以及排序情况。

3.1 2013年城市生活质量主观满意度指数

2013年城市生活质量主观满意度指数的调查结果及排序情况显示在表3-1中。

表3-1 中国35个城市生活质量主观满意度指数

城 市	2013年得分	2013年排序	2013年上升位次	2012年得分	2012年排序	2012年排序*	2011年排序	2012年上升位次
济南市	53.68	1	3	53.78	4	4	4	0
青岛市	53.05	2	6	52.31	8	—	—	—
厦门市	53.00	3	6	52.3	9	—	—	—

2013年中国35个城市生活质量指数

续表

城　市	2013年得分	2013年排序	2013年上升位次	2012年得分	2012年排序	2012年排序*	2011年排序	2012年上升位次
长春市	52.34	4	-3	54.51	1	1	10	9
合肥市	52.34	5	0	53.2	5	5	6	1
西宁市	52.21	6	8	51.57	14	11	9	-2
宁波市	52.17	7	0	52.51	7	—	—	—
石家庄市	52.17	8	-5	53.86	3	3	21	18
福州市	52.06	9	-3	52.6	6	6	11	5
杭州市	52.05	10	-8	54.04	2	2	3	1
海口市	51.80	11	12	50.05	23	19	1	-18
南京市	51.70	12	4	50.75	16	13	16	3
成都市	51.40	13	-1	52.13	12	9	7	-2
天津市	51.35	14	-1	52.07	13	10	17	7
郑州市	51.28	15	0	50.76	15	12	19	7
沈阳市	51.25	16	10	49.73	26	22	18	-4
西安市	51.16	17	0	50.4	17	14	14	0
银川市	51.07	18	-8	52.29	10	7	5	-2
重庆市	51.01	19	-8	52.28	11	8	8	0
上海市	50.53	20	0	50.24	20	16	23	7
乌鲁木齐市	50.38	21	0	50.23	21	17	13	-4
呼和浩特市	50.37	22	0	50.14	22	18	29	11
南昌市	50.35	23	10	48.41	33	28	28	0
北京市	50.16	24	4	49.47	28	24	20	-4
长沙市	50.15	25	-6	50.29	19	15	24	9
大连市	50.10	26	-8	50.37	18	—	—	—
太原市	49.90	27	2	49.38	29	25	27	2
南宁市	49.81	28	-1	49.6	27	23	22	-1
哈尔滨市	49.79	29	2	48.78	31	26	12	-14
贵阳市	49.58	30	5	47.33	35	30	15	-15
广州市	49.21	31	-6	49.74	25	21	25	4
武汉市	49.07	32	-8	49.95	24	20	30	10
昆明市	48.73	33	-1	48.72	32	27	26	-1
深圳市	48.68	34	-4	49.16	30	—	—	—
兰州市	48.57	35	-1	47.95	34	29	2	-27
全国平均	50.87①			50.88			49.71	

* 未包含5个计划单列城市的排序。

① 35个城市全国平均值的计算方法是：根据调查样本的分布情况，将35个城市的分指数加权平均。这种计算方法也适用于下面所有主观满意度分指数中全国平均值的计算和专项调查中全国平均指数的计算。

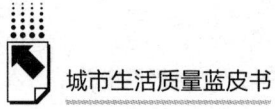

表 3-1 显示，2013 年，全国 35 个城市生活质量主观满意度指数加权平均值为 50.87，与上年的加权平均值 50.88 基本一致，越过了 50 分满意与不满意的临界点，进入了满意区间。生活满意度指数超过 50 分的有 26 个城市，比 2012 年多 3 个城市。其中 5 个计划单列城市中有 4 个超过 50 分，与 2012 年的调查结果类似；深圳市得分没有超过 50，并且排名下降了 4 位，位居第 34 位。直辖市和省会城市中有 22 个城市超过 50 分。而在 2011 年的调查中，主观指数超过 50 分的城市只有 11 个。这说明 2013 年城市生活质量满意度指数在整体上与上年基本持平，比 2011 年有所提高。

2013 年城市生活质量主观满意度指数的五个分指数平均值分别为：人力资本（58.89）、社会保障（56.64）、生活感受（55.07）、生活水平（52.51）、生活成本（31.22）。与 2012 年相比，生活水平和生活成本满意度有所提升，人力资本、社会保障、生活感受满意度略有下降。①

2013 年生活质量满意度（主观）指数排名前 10 位的城市为：济南（1）、青岛（2）、厦门（3）、长春（4）、合肥（5）、西宁（6）、宁波（7）、石家庄（8）、福州（9）、杭州（10）。排名后 10 位的城市分别是：大连（26）、太原（27）、南宁（28）、哈尔滨（29）、贵阳（30）、广州（31）、武汉（32）、昆明（33）、深圳（34）、兰州（35）。从地区分布来看，与 2012 年的分布基本一致。前 10 位的城市中，有 7 个东部城市，2 个中部城市，1 个西部城市。生活质量满意度指数排名后 10 位的城市中，有 3 个东部城市，3 个中部城市，4 个西部城市。排名前 10 位的城市基本上都属于中等规模的城市，没有北京、上海、广州这样的大城市，说明城市规模可能会对居民生活质量满意度产生了负面影响。这点与 2012 年的结论一致。

仅从排序上看，济南、合肥、长春已经连续两年排名在前 5 位，兰州、深圳、昆明连续两年排名在后 5 位。海口（12）、沈阳（10）、南昌

---

① 下文将对分指数进行详细分析。

(10)、西宁(8)等城市的排名上升比较明显。① 海口的排名上升最为明显，从 2012 年排名第 23 位上升到 2013 年的第 11 位，这可以从分指数中得到解释：海口市生活成本满意度指数发生了较大变化，从 2012 年的排名第 29 位上升到 2013 年的第 8 位。这点还可以从海口市房价预期满意度指数得到进一步解释，该城市的房价预期指数排名第 33 位，房价上涨预期较低，可能对生活成本指数有一定影响。另外，海口市的食品安全满意度指数在全国排名第 3，这在一定程度上也提高了该城市的居民生活满意度指数。

沈阳市生活质量满意度指数的排名也有较明显地上升，从 2012 年排名的第 26 位上升到 2013 年的第 16 位，上升了 10 位。通过分析分指数，沈阳排名的上升主要得益于社会保障 (7)、生活水平 (7)、生活成本 (5) 满意度指数的提升。② 另外，沈阳市的房价上涨预期也较低，排名第 30 位。食品安全满意度指数排名第 31 位，处于较低水平。

南昌市的排名上升也较为明显，从 2012 年的第 33 位上升到 2013 年的第 23 位。南昌市的排名上升得益于生活水平 (9)、人力资本 (9)、社会保障 (5) 满意度指数的大幅提升。③ 生活成本和生活感受的排名上升幅度较小，生活成本主要是受房价上涨预期的拖累，因为房价上涨预期比 2012 年上升了 10 位。

西宁市的主观满意度指数排名上升的幅度也比较明显，从 2012 年的第 14 位上升到 2013 年的第 6 位。这同样可以从细分的主观满意度指数中寻找可能的解释：该市人力资本满意度指数的排名提升了 11 位，生活水平满意度指数的排名提升了 8 位。

此外，其他排名的上升幅度比较大的城市还有青岛和厦门两个计划单列城市，均上升了 6 位。青岛市排名的上升主要是由于生活水平 (8)、

---

① 括号内的数字代表上升的位次。
② 括号内的数字代表上升的位次。
③ 括号内的数字代表上升的位次。

人力资本（4）、社会保障（6）满意度指数的大幅提升。① 厦门市排名的上升主要是由于生活水平（10）满意度指数的大幅提升。

排名下降幅度比较明显的城市有杭州（-8）、银川（-8）、重庆（-8）、大连（-8）、武汉（-8）、长沙（-6）、广州（-6）。② 其他城市的排序变化不大。

杭州市生活质量主观满意度指数排名从 2012 年的第 2 名下降到 2013 年的第 10 名，排名的大幅度下降主要是由于生活水平（-9）、生活成本（-8）、人力资本（-10）满意度指数的下降，社会保障和生活感受满意度指数排名有所下降，但幅度不大。杭州市生活水平满意度指数排名的大幅下降主要是由于收入预期满意度指数排名的大幅下降，排名从 2012 年的第 2 位下降到 2013 年的第 23 位，下降了 21 位。生活成本满意度指数排名的下降可能是受房价预期指数排名上升的影响。

银川市生活质量满意度指数排名从 2012 年的第 10 位下降到 2013 年的第 18 位，下降了 8 位。排名下降主要是被人力资本和生活成本满意度指数的排名大幅下降所拖累，人力资本满意度指数排名下降了 14 位，生活成本满意度指数排名下降了 9 位。生活水平满意度指数排名略有下降。生活成本满意度指数排名的下降可能主要是受房价上涨预期趋强的影响，房价预期指数排名上升了 8 位。

重庆市生活质量满意度指数排名从 2012 年的第 11 位下降到 2013 年的第 19 位，下降了 8 位。排名的下降主要是被社会保障（-19）和生活水平（-15）满意度指数的排名下降所拖累，生活成本（-4）、人力资本（-7）③也有一定程度的下降，仅有生活感受满意度指数的排名略有提升。

大连市生活质量满意度指数的排名从 2012 年的第 18 位下降到 2013 年的第 26 位，下降了 8 位。排名的下降主要被生活水平（-10）、生活

---

① 括号内的数字代表上升的位次。
② 括号内的数字代表下降的位次，例如"-8"代表下降了 8 位，下同。
③ 括号内的数字代表下降的位次。

感受（-8）、社会保障（-3）满意度指数的排名下降所拖累①，生活成本（1）、人力资本（7）满意度指数的排名有所上升。②

武汉市生活质量满意度指数的排名从2012年的第24位下降到2013年的第32位，下降了8位。排名的下降主要是受5个分指数下降的影响，生活水平（-5）、生活成本（-5）、人力资本（-5）、社会保障（-6）、生活感受（-3）满意度指数都有所下降。③

长沙市生活质量满意度指数排名从2012年的第19位下降到2013年的第25位，下降了6位。排名的下降主要被生活感受（-14）和人力资本（-12）满意度指数的排名下降所拖累。④

广州市生活质量满意度指数排名从2012年的第25位下降为2013年的第31位，下降了6位。排名的下降主要是由于人力资本（-14）、生活成本（-9）满意度指数的排名大幅下降。其他分指数的排名没有太大的变化。

3.2 2013年城市生活质量客观指数（社会经济数据指数）

与2012年相同，城市生活质量客观指数是通过计算35个城市的20个二级客观经济指标，然后运用归一化平权方法计算出反映生活质量的8个一级指标，再将一级指标求平均值得到5个客观分指数，最后将5个客观分指数求平均值计算出每个城市的客观总指数，即每个城市的社会经济数据指数（具体指标见张连城，2013）。⑤ 2013年城市生活质量客观总指数的计算结果显示在表3-2中。

---

① 括号内的数字代表下降的位次。
② 括号内的数字代表上升的位次。
③ 括号内的数字代表下降的位次。
④ 括号内的数字代表下降的位次。
⑤ 客观指数的全国平均值是按照第六次人口普查中35个城市的人口规模比重加权平均计算得出的，此种计算方法也适用于下面5个客观分指数全国平均值的计算。

表 3-2 中国 35 个城市生活质量客观指数及排序

城 市	2013 年得分	2013 年排序	上升位次	2012 年得分	2012 年排序
北京市	69.80	1	0	68.72	1
广州市	66.85	2	0	64.87	2
南京市	66.65	3	2	62.38	5
西安市	64.65	4	2	61.59	6
深圳市	63.93	5	-2	64.24	3
呼和浩特市	62.22	6	1	59.55	7
厦门市	61.89	7	2	58.86	9
上海市	61.78	8	-4	62.72	4
宁波市	61.47	9	3	55.21	12
沈阳市	59.99	10	1	56.59	11
长春市	59.64	11	8	52.29	19
杭州市	59.54	12	-4	59.09	8
武汉市	58.93	13	-3	56.61	10
长沙市	58.36	14	2	53.53	16
昆明市	58.05	15	-1	54.08	14
银川市	57.68	16	2	52.45	18
济南市	56.84	17	0	53.22	17
合肥市	56.73	18	8	50.92	26
成都市	55.96	19	5	51.15	24
大连市	55.64	20	1	52.00	21
太原市	55.45	21	-1	52.15	20
天津市	55.42	22	-9	54.3	13
兰州市	55.22	23	8	50.08	31
石家庄市	54.78	24	4	50.49	28
青岛市	54.76	25	-10	54.05	15
乌鲁木齐市	54.59	26	6	49.73	32
南昌市	53.03	27	7	49.03	34
福州市	52.66	28	-6	51.37	22
贵阳市	52.45	29	-4	50.98	25
哈尔滨市	51.86	30	-1	50.44	29
海口市	51.50	31	-8	51.17	23
郑州市	50.54	32	-2	50.26	30
南宁市	50.00	33	-6	50.69	27
西宁市	49.29	34	1	45.21	35
重庆市	47.83	35	-2	49.40	33
全国平均		57.75①		54.56	

①客观指数的全国平均值是按照第六次人口普查中 35 个城市的人口规模比重加权平均计算得出的，此种计算方法也适用于下面 5 个客观分指数全国平均值的计算。

表 3-2 显示，2013 年全国 35 个城市生活质量客观指数加权平均值为 57.75，比 2012 年的全国平均值 54.56 有所提高。得分 50 分以上的城市有 33 个，得分 55 分以上的城市有 23 个，超过 60 分以上的城市有 9 个。城市生活质量客观指数 5 个分指数的平均值分别是：生活水平（63.39）、生活成本（58.67）、人力资本（57.78）、社会保障（55.26）、生活感受（53.67）。跟 2012 年相比，五个客观分指数均有不同程度的提高。生活质量客观指数排名前 10 位的城市是：北京（1）、广州（2）、南京（3）、西安（4）、深圳（5）、呼和浩特（6）、厦门（7）、上海（8）、宁波（9）、沈阳（10）。排名后 10 位的城市是：乌鲁木齐（26）、南昌（27）、福州（28）、贵阳（29）、哈尔滨（30）、海口（31）、郑州（32）、福州（-6）、南宁（33）、西宁（34）、重庆（35）。东部地区生活质量客观指数整体上要高于中西部地区。城市生活质量客观指数排名前 10 的城市中有 8 个东部城市，2 个西部城市。排名后 10 位的城市中，有 2 个东部城市，3 个中部城市，5 个西部城市。东部地区生活质量客观指数整体上要高于中西部地区。

生活质量客观指数排名上升比较明显的城市有：长春（8）、合肥（8）、兰州（8）、南昌（7）、乌鲁木齐（6）、成都（5）。① 排名下降比较明显的城市有：青岛（-10）、天津（-9）、海口（-8）、福州（-6）、南宁（-6）。② 北京、广州、南京、深圳等四个城市已经连续两年排名前 5 位；而西宁、重庆两个城市已经连续两年排名后 5 位。

长春市生活质量客观指数排名从 2012 年的第 19 位上升到 2013 年的第 11 位，上升了 8 位。排名的上升受益于人力资本（13）、社会保障（7）、生活水平（4）客观指数排名的上升，③ 生活感受（-3）和生活成

---

① 括号内的数字代表上升的位次。
② 括号内的数字代表下降的位次。
③ 括号内的数字代表上升的位次。

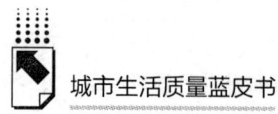

本(0)客观指数排名变化幅度不大。[①]

合肥市生活质量客观指数排名从2012年的第26位上升到2013年的第18位,上升了8位。排名的上升主要受益于生活感受客观指数排名的上升,从2012年的第31位上升到2013年的第16位,上升了15位。其他4个细分客观指数的排名,生活水平(3)、生活成本(3)两个客观指数排名有所上升,而社会保障(-6)、人力资本(-1)客观指数排名均有不同程度的下降。

兰州市生活质量客观指数排名从2012年的第31位上升到2013年的第23位,上升了8位。排名的上升主要受益于生活水平客观指数排名的大幅上升,较2012年提升了17位,社会保障客观指数排名下降了5位,其他3个细分客观指数排名变化不大。

南昌市生活质量客观指数排名从2012年的第34位上升到2013年的第27位,上升了7位。排名的上升主要受益于生活水平客观指数排名的大幅上升,较2012年提升了10位。其他几个细分的客观指数排名变化不大。

青岛市生活质量客观指数排名下降较为明显,较2012年下降了10位。排名下降的主要原因是生活水平客观指数排名的大幅下降,从2012年的第8名下降到了2013年的第28名,下降了20位。其他几个细分客观指数排名变化不大。

天津市生活质量客观指数排名从2012年的第13位下降到2013年的第22位,下降了9位。天津排名下降的主要原因是生活水平、人力资本客观指数排名的大幅下降,分别下降了10位、9位,生活成本和社会保障客观指数排名下降幅度不是特别明显,生活感受客观指数排名没有变化。

海口市生活质量客观指数排名从2012年的第23位下降到2013年的第31位,下降了8位。海口市排名下降的主要原因是人力资本客观指数排名的大幅下降(下降了18位)。其他几个分指数排名变化不大,生活

---

① 括号内的数字代表下降的位次。

水平客观指数排名下降了 2 位，社会保障客观指数排名上升了 2 位，生活成本和生活感受客观指数排名没有发生变化。

南宁市生活质量客观指数排名从 2012 年的第 27 位下降到 2013 年的第 33 位，下降了 6 位。南宁市排名下降的主要原因是生活水平客观指数排名的大幅下降（下降了 12 位），人力资本和生活感受客观指数排名略有下降，分别下降了 5 位和 3 位。社会保障客观指数排名则大幅上升，上升了 12 位，生活成本客观指数上升了 1 位。

3.3 专项调查

3.3.1 房价预期调查

表 3 - 3 是 2013 年房价预期专项调查的结果。这是通过询问受访者所居住城市的房价今后（1~2 年）是涨还是跌，并根据答案赋值得到的。

表 3 - 3　35 个城市房价预期指数*

城　　市	2013 年得分	2013 年排序	2012 年得分	2012 年排序	上升位次
广州市	68.64	1	58.55	7	6
西宁市	68.33	2	63.89	2	0
乌鲁木齐市	67.37	3	55.26	15	12
南昌市	66.73	4	55.28	14	10
郑州市	66.60	5	55.24	16	11
合肥市	66.07	6	53.42	25	19
上海市	65.97	7	53.35	26	19
深圳市	65.96	8	56.55	9	1
银川市	65.93	9	55.21	17	8
南京市	65.92	10	54.36	22	12
北京市	65.71	11	52.04	28	17
济南市	65.68	12	50	33	21
武汉市	65.40	13	54.41	21	8

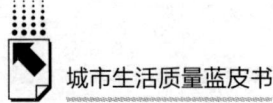

续表

城　市	2013年得分	2013年排序	2012年得分	2012年排序	上升位次
昆明市	65.38	14	55.77	13	-1
石家庄市	65.19	15	54.13	23	8
厦门市	65.14	16	59.59	5	-11
青岛市	64.57	17	46.82	35	18
太原市	64.53	18	57.18	8	-10
重庆市	64.46	19	55.84	12	-7
福州市	64.45	20	52.75	27	7
兰州市	63.98	21	59.94	4	-17
长春市	63.70	22	51.2	30	8
南宁市	63.66	23	58.8	6	-17
西安市	63.64	24	55.1	18	-6
长沙市	63.39	25	51.9	29	4
天津市	63.18	26	53.65	24	-2
成都市	63.06	27	54.53	20	-7
贵阳市	62.99	28	60.48	3	-25
杭州市	62.85	29	47.17	34	5
沈阳市	62.43	30	56.35	10	-20
宁波市	62.15	31	50.68	31	0
大连市	62.13	32	54.91	19	-13
海口市	61.26	33	64	1	-32
呼和浩特市	61.26	34	56.07	11	-23
哈尔滨市	60.99	35	50.39	32	-3
全国平均	64.65		全国平均	54.99	

* 该指数越高说明该城市房价上涨预期的幅度越大，越低说明该城市房价下降预期的幅度越大。

表3-3的调查结果显示，2013年，房价预期指数的加权平均值为64.65，比2012年的54.99高出9.66，上升了17.6%。在调查的35个城市中，房价预期指数全部超过了60。这意味着35个城市的居民均存在对房价上升的预期，并且除海口市外，其他34个城市2013年房价预期上升的幅度均比2012年大。其中预期2013年比2012年房价上涨幅度较大的10个城市依次为青岛（37.9%）、杭州（33.2%）、济南（31.4%）、北

京 (26.3%)、长春 (24.4%)、合肥 (23.7%)、上海 (23.7%)、宁波 (22.6%)、长沙 (22.1%)、福州 (22%); 比 2012 年预期房价上涨幅度较小的城市有海口 (-4.3%)、贵阳 (4.2%)、兰州 (6.7%)、西宁 (6.9%)、大连 (7.2%)、南宁 (8.3%)、呼和浩特 (9.3%)、厦门 (9.3%) 等 8 个城市; 其余 17 个城市的上升幅度都在 10.8% ~21.9% 之间。①

从排序上看, 2013 年 35 个城市中排序上升位次较大的城市有济南 (21)、上海 (19)、合肥 (19)、青岛 (18)、北京 (17)、乌鲁木齐 (12)、南京 (12)。② 有意思的是, 海口市去年房价预期上涨最大, 排名第 1, 2013 年排名下降到了第 33 位; 2012 年房价预期看跌的青岛市和杭州市以及房价预期看平的济南市, 2013 年不仅全部看涨, 并且看涨的幅度名列前茅。

3.3.2 食品安全满意度调查

食品安全问题直接关系到居民的生存和身体健康, 居民的食品安全需求在多大程度上得到了满足, 是评价政府民生工程的重要方面。因此, 针对我国近两年较为突出的食品安全问题, 本次调查新增了对食品安全满意度的调查。我们通过电话调查询问受访者对所居住城市的食品安全状况是否满意, 然后根据答案赋值得到表 3-4。③

根据表 3-4 显示的调查结果, 2013 年, 全国 35 个城市居民对食品安全满意度指数的加权平均值为 41.67 分, 没有越过满意和不满意的临界值 50 分, 处于不满意区间。在 35 个城市中, 高于 50 分的仅有厦门一个城市。

---

① 括号中百分比的计算方法是: 用 2013 年的得分减去 2012 年的得分, 然后再除以 2012 年的得分。
② 括号内的数字为上升的位次。
③ 该表中的答案赋值方法与生活质量主观满意度指数的答案赋值方法相同。

表3-4 食品安全满意度指数

城 市	得分	2013年排序	城 市	得分	2013年排序
厦门市	53.06	1	济南市	40.77	19
西宁市	49.44	2	呼和浩特	40.50	20
海口市	46.98	3	杭州市	40.35	21
重庆市	45.67	4	广州市	40.28	22
银川市	45.05	5	南京市	40.01	23
贵阳市	44.49	6	西安市	39.40	24
成都市	44.39	7	天津市	39.35	25
宁波市	44.03	8	哈尔滨市	39.24	26
北京市	43.55	9	福州市	39.24	27
深圳市	43.25	10	上海市	39.12	28
乌鲁木齐市	43.08	11	兰州市	38.84	29
合肥市	42.86	12	石家庄市	38.51	30
昆明市	42.69	13	沈阳市	38.49	31
青岛市	42.51	14	郑州市	37.08	32
长春市	42.16	15	长沙市	36.90	33
南宁市	42.11	16	太原市	36.87	34
南昌市	41.00	17	武汉市	36.47	35
大连市	40.83	18	全国平均	41.67	

整体而言，城市居民对食品安全的满意程度较低。食品安全满意度指数排名前10位的城市是：厦门（1）、西宁（2）、海口（3）、重庆（4）、银川（5）、贵阳（6）、成都（7）、宁波（8）、北京（9）、深圳（10）。排名后10位的城市是：哈尔滨（26）、福州（27）、上海（28）、兰州（29）、石家庄（30）、沈阳（31）、郑州（32）、长沙（33）、太原（34）、武汉（35）。食品安全满意度指数排名前10位的城市中，东西部城市各有5个；排名后10位的城市中，东部城市有4个，中部城市有5个，西部城市有1个。值得注意的是，低于40分的城市多达12个。另外，调查结果还显示，从性别角度看，受访者中男性对食品安全的满意度（43.61）要高于女性的满意度（39.46）；从年龄段来看，20~30岁的受访者食品安全满意度最高（43.68），41~60岁的受访者满意度最低（39.56）。

B.4
2013年中国35个城市生活质量分指数

城市生活质量主观满意度指数和客观指数的高低变化及排序情况,均可以从分指数中得到解释。与2012年一样,支撑35个城市生活质量总指数的分指数包括生活水平指数、生活成本指数、人力资本指数、社会保障指数和生活感受指数。每个分指数都包括主观满意度指数和客观指数(社会经济数据指数)。

4.1 生活水平指数

生活水平指数包括生活水平主观满意度指数和客观指数(社会经济数据指数)。前者是根据电话调查并结合答案赋值得到的,后者是通过对35个城市的社会经济指标计算得出的。

4.1.1 生活水平主观满意度指数

表4-1列出了本次调查得出的35个城市生活水平的主观满意度指数和排序情况以及与2012年的比较。

表4-1 中国35个城市生活水平满意度指数

城 市	2013年得分	2013年排序	2013年上升位次	2012年得分	2012年排序*	2011年排序	2012年上升位次
海口市	56.46	1	2	54.75	3	1	-2
青岛市	55.81	2	8	52.59	10	—	—
厦门市	55.69	3	10	52.18	13	—	—
西宁市	55.00	4	8	52.31	12	19	9

续表

城 市	2013年得分	2013年排序	2013年上升位次	2012年得分	2012年排序*	2011年排序	2012年上升位次
福州市	54.64	5	-1	53.76	4	7	3
宁波市	54.62	6	2	52.77	8	—	—
呼和浩特市	54.31	7	17	50.36	24	28	9
济南市	54.29	8	9	51.43	17	5	-8
合肥市	54.14	9	-7	55.76	2	4	2
杭州市	54.10	10	-9	56.49	1	6	5
乌鲁木齐市	54.10	11	9	50.99	20	8	-8
西安市	53.88	12	19	48.79	31	21	-5
贵阳市	53.74	13	15	49.4	28	24	1
长沙市	53.44	14	11	50.29	25	9	-11
成都市	53.30	15	3	51.39	18	12	-2
长春市	53.07	16	-11	53.74	5	14	9
昆明市	52.84	17	-6	52.32	11	16	7
上海市	52.59	18	-3	51.65	15	17	6
南京市	52.34	19	10	49.23	29	23	-1
广州市	52.32	20	1	50.97	21	10	-7
天津市	52.24	21	-2	51.27	19	15	0
北京市	52.19	22	1	50.37	23	11	-7
南昌市	52.18	23	9	48.27	32	20	-7
重庆市	52.11	24	-15	52.64	9	13	5
石家庄市	51.79	25	-19	53.38	6	29	23
深圳市	51.65	26	-12	52.08	14	—	—
沈阳市	51.54	27	7	46.95	34	30	1
南宁市	51.48	28	-12	51.47	16	22	10
银川市	51.10	29	-2	49.74	27	18	-4
太原市	50.42	30	3	48.27	33	26	-2
武汉市	50.39	31	-5	49.95	26	27	6
大连市	50.28	32	-10	50.69	22	—	—
哈尔滨市	49.86	33	-3	48.89	30	3	-22
兰州市	49.72	34	1	46.88	35	2	-28
郑州市	48.00	35	-28	52.86	7	25	18
全国平均		52.51			51.28	51.76	

* 未包含5个计划单列城市的排序。

表4-1显示，2013年，35个城市生活水平满意度（主观）指数的加权平均值为52.51分，比2012年全国平均水平51.28分略高。35个城市中，有32个城市的生活水平满意度指数超过50分，均进入了满意区间。城市生活水平满意度指数排名前10位的城市是：海口（1）、青岛（2）、厦门（3）、西宁（4）、福州（5）、宁波（6）、呼和浩特（7）、济南（8）、合肥（9）、杭州（10）。排名前10位的城市中，有7个东部城市，1个中部城市，1个西部城市。排名前10位的城市中，除杭州、合肥和福州外，其他城市的排名较2012年都有了较大幅度的提升。排名后10位的城市是：深圳（26）、沈阳（27）、南宁（28）、银川（29）、太原（30）、武汉（31）、大连（32）、哈尔滨（33）、兰州（34）、郑州（35）。排名后10位的城市中，有3个东部城市，4个中部城市，3个西部城市。排名后10位的城市中，深圳、南宁、大连、郑州的排名降幅较大。

与2012年的调查结果相比，排名上升幅度较为明显的城市有：西安（19）、呼和浩特（17）、贵阳（15）、厦门（10）、南京（10）、济南（9）、乌鲁木齐（9）、南昌（9）、青岛（8）、西宁（8）、沈阳（7）。① 排名下降幅度较为明显的是：郑州（-28）、石家庄（-19）、重庆市（-15）、深圳（-12）、南宁（-12）、长春（-11）、大连（-10）。② 其中郑州和石家庄下降的幅度最为明显。

生活水平主观满意度指数是由收入现状和收入预期满意度指数加权平均获得的。因此，生活水平主观满意度指数排名的变化可以由收入现状和收入预期满意度的变化得到解释。我们通过询问受访者对目前收入状况以及收入预期的满意程度，结合答案赋值，分别得到收入现状满意度指数和收入预期满意度指数。

表4-2和表4-3给出了2013年35个城市收入现状满意度指数和收

---

① 括号内的数字代表上升的位次。
② 括号内的数字代表下降的位次。

入预期满意度指数及排序情况,并给出了2013年和2012年城市的排名及排名位次变化的情况。

表4-2 中国35个城市收入现状满意度指数

城 市	2013年得分	2013年排序	2013年上升位次	2012年得分	2012年排序	2012年排序*	2011年排序	2012年上升位次
海口市	56.87	1	1	57.5	2	2	1	-1
青岛市	56.58	2	8	53.18	10	—	—	—
厦门市	56.39	3	12	52.03	15	—	—	—
福州市	56.39	4	0	54.19	4	4	8	4
杭州市	56.25	5	-4	58.25	1	1	5	4
宁波市	55.21	6	0	53.65	6	—	—	—
长春市	54.52	7	-2	54.01	5	5	13	8
西宁市	54.44	8	5	52.78	13	11	14	3
合肥市	54.42	9	-6	55.04	3	3	6	3
乌鲁木齐市	54.38	10	-1	53.29	9	8	3	-5
济南市	54.15	11	3	52.11	14	12	7	-5
成都市	53.82	12	7	50.88	19	15	18	3
呼和浩特市	53.80	13	16	48.21	29	24	26	2
南京市	53.42	14	17	48.08	31	26	22	-4
西安市	53.25	15	13	48.3	28	23	24	1
昆明市	53.17	16	0	51.76	16	13	17	4
广州市	52.94	17	4	50.57	21	17	9	-8
长沙市	52.62	18	12	48.1	30	25	11	-14
上海市	52.60	19	-2	51.43	17	14	15	1
天津市	52.15	20	0	50.79	20	16	21	5
贵阳市	51.98	21	11	47.86	32	27	16	-11
石家庄市	51.85	22	-14	53.43	8	7	28	21
沈阳市	51.75	23	11	46.57	34	29	29	0
北京市	51.65	24	-2	50.1	22	18	10	-8
重庆市	51.38	25	-18	53.45	7	6	12	6
银川市	51.37	26	-15	53.13	11	9	20	11
南宁市	51.20	27	-4	50	23	19	27	8
南昌市	51.18	28	-2	48.58	26	21	19	-2
深圳市	51.12	29	-11	51.39	18	—	—	—
大连市	50.46	30	-6	49.69	24	—	—	—

2013 年中国 35 个城市生活质量分指数

续表

城市	2013年得分	2013年排序	2013年上升位次	2012年得分	2012年排序	2012年排序*	2011年排序	2012年上升位次
武汉市	50.39	31	-6	49.68	25	20	23	3
哈尔滨市	49.33	32	1	47.78	33	28	4	-24
兰州市	48.87	33	2	44.6	35	30	2	-28
郑州市	48.42	34	-22	53.1	12	10	25	15
太原市	48.32	35	-8	48.51	27	22	30	8
全国平均		52.54			51.20			

* 未包含 5 个计划单列城市的排序。

表 4-2 显示，2013 年，35 个城市收入现状满意度指数加权平均值为 52.54，比 2012 年有所提升。城市收入现状满意度指数排名前 10 位的城市是：海口（1）、青岛（2）、厦门（3）、福州（4）、杭州（5）、宁波（6）、长春（7）、西宁（8）、合肥（9）、乌鲁木齐（10）。排名前 10 位的城市中，有 6 个东部城市，2 个中部城市，2 个西部城市。排名前 10 位的城市中，青岛、厦门较 2012 年有了较大幅度的提升。杭州、合肥较 2012 年有了较大幅度的下降。排名后 10 位的城市是：银川（26）、南宁（27）、南昌（28）、深圳（29）、大连（30）、武汉（31）、哈尔滨（32）、兰州（33）、郑州（34）、太原（35）。排名后 10 位的城市中，有 2 个东部城市，5 个中部城市，3 个西部城市。排名后 10 位的城市，银川、深圳、大连、武汉、郑州、太原较 2012 年有较大幅度的下降。

收入现状满意度排名上升比较明显的城市有南京（17）、呼和浩特（16）、西安（13）、厦门（12）、长沙（12）、沈阳（11）等城市，① 排名下降比较明显的城市有郑州（-22）、重庆（-18）、银川（-15）、石家庄（-14）等城市。② 海口居民的收入现状满意度近年来保持了较高的排名，2011 年排名第 1，2012 年排名第 2。

---

① 括号内的数字代表上升的位次。
② 括号内的数字代表下降的位次。

表4-3 中国35个城市收入预期满意度指数

城 市	2013年得分	2013年排序	2013年上升位次	2012年得分	2012年排序	2012年排序*	2011年排序	2012年上升位次
海口市	56.04	1	13	52	14	11	1	-10
西宁市	55.56	2	16	51.85	18	14	24	10
贵阳市	55.51	3	20	50.95	23	18	26	8
青岛市	55.04	4	9	52	13	—	—	—
厦门市	55.00	5	7	52.33	12	—	—	—
呼和浩特市	54.82	6	4	52.5	10	9	27	18
西安市	54.50	7	22	49.27	29	24	17	-7
济南市	54.43	8	16	50.75	24	19	3	-16
长沙市	54.26	9	2	52.49	11	10	5	-5
宁波市	54.03	10	6	51.89	16	—	—	—
合肥市	53.85	11	-10	56.47	1	1	4	3
乌鲁木齐市	53.81	12	19	48.68	31	26	21	-5
南昌市	53.18	13	20	47.97	33	28	23	-5
福州市	52.90	14	-9	53.32	5	5	8	3
重庆市	52.84	15	4	51.82	19	15	20	5
成都市	52.78	16	-1	51.9	15	12	6	-6
北京市	52.74	17	8	50.63	25	20	11	-9
上海市	52.57	18	-1	51.88	17	13	22	9
太原市	52.51	19	13	48.02	32	27	10	-17
昆明市	52.50	20	-13	52.88	7	7	15	8
天津市	52.34	21	-1	51.75	20	16	13	-3
深圳市	52.18	22	-14	52.78	8	—	—	—
杭州市	51.94	23	-21	54.72	2	2	9	7
南宁市	51.76	24	-18	52.93	6	6	12	6
石家庄市	51.74	25	-21	53.33	4	4	28	24
广州市	51.71	26	-4	51.38	22	17	14	-3
长春市	51.62	27	-24	53.48	3	3	18	15
沈阳市	51.33	28	6	47.34	34	29	30	1
南京市	51.26	29	-3	50.38	26	21	25	4
银川市	50.82	30	5	46.35	35	30	16	-14
兰州市	50.56	31	-1	49.15	30	25	7	-18
哈尔滨市	50.39	32	-4	50	28	23	2	-21
武汉市	50.39	33	-6	50.21	27	22	29	7
大连市	50.09	34	-13	51.69	21	—	—	—
郑州市	47.58	35	-26	52.62	9	8	19	11
全国平均		52.48			51.36			

*未包含5个计划单列城市的排序。

2013 年中国 35 个城市生活质量分指数

表4-3显示，2013年，35个城市收入预期满意度指数加权平均值为52.48分，较2012年略有提升。除郑州外，其他34个城市的得分都超过了50分，比2012年多6个城市，2012年，有28个城市的得分超过50分。但排名第1的城市得分比2012年略有下降，2012年收入预期满意度指数排名第1的合肥市得分为56.47分，而2013年排名第1的海口市的得分为56.04分。收入预期满意度指数排名前10位的城市是：海口（1）、西宁（2）、贵阳（3）、青岛（4）、厦门（5）、呼和浩特（6）、西安（7）、济南（8）、长沙（9）、宁波（10）。排名前10位的城市中，有5个东部城市，2个中部城市，3个西部城市。排名前10位的城市中，绝大多数城市的排名较2012年都有较大幅度的提升。排名后10位的城市是：广州（26）、长春（27）、沈阳（28）、南京（29）、银川（30）、兰州（31）、哈尔滨（32）、武汉（33）、大连（34）、郑州（35）。排名后10位的城市中，有4个东部城市，4个中部城市，2个西部城市。排名后10位的城市中，长春、武汉、大连、郑州较2012年有较大幅度的下降。

收入预期满意度排名上升比较明显的城市有西安（22）、贵阳（20）、南昌（20）、济南（16）、乌鲁木齐（19）、西宁（16）、海口（13）、太原（13）等城市。排名下降比较明显的城市有郑州（-26）、长春（-24）、大连（-13）、杭州（-21）、石家庄（-21）、南宁（-18）等城市。

4.1.2 生活水平客观指数（社会经济数据指数）

表4-4列出了本次调查得出的35个城市生活水平客观指数（社会经济数据指数）的计算结果和排序情况以及与2012年的比较。与2012年相同，生活水平客观指数由收入水平指数和生活改善指数两个一级指标构成，其中又包括消费率、人均财富、人均可支配收入、人均消费增长、人均财富增长、人均可支配收入增长6个二级指标。前3个二级指标用以说明一级指标中的收入水平指数；后3个二级指标用以描述一级指标中的生活改善指数。

表4-4 中国35个城市生活水平客观指数

城　　市	2013年得分	2013年排序	2013年上升位次	2012年得分	2012年排序
南京市	80.00	1	5	66.33	6
厦门市	79.22	2	21	52.4	23
深圳市	78.91	3	4	64.78	7
西安市	78.59	4	11	56.07	15
北京市	77.84	5	-4	80.03	1
上海市	73.93	6	-4	77.84	2
杭州市	73.83	7	-4	76.79	3
宁波市	72.47	8	-3	68.7	5
济南市	72.27	9	3	57.43	12
成都市	72.13	10	1	58.8	11
广州市	70.24	11	-7	72.14	4
海口市	69.40	12	-2	59.8	10
呼和浩特市	68.67	13	3	55.87	16
合肥市	67.04	14	3	55.75	17
兰州市	65.59	15	17	46.3	32
长春市	63.27	16	4	53.67	20
福州市	61.51	17	-8	60.75	9
郑州市	61.40	18	-4	56.11	14
大连市	61.23	19	10	47.14	29
长沙市	60.91	20	4	50.97	24
南昌市	60.59	21	10	46.6	31
武汉市	60.51	22	3	50.81	25
天津市	60.42	23	-10	57.02	13
银川市	60.00	24	9	45.55	33
石家庄市	58.80	25	-4	53.09	21
乌鲁木齐市	58.61	26	2	47.54	28
沈阳市	57.82	27	-1	48.84	26
青岛市	56.06	28	-20	64.76	8
昆明市	55.27	29	5	40.76	34
西宁市	54.92	30	5	40	35
太原市	52.32	31	-1	46.87	30
贵阳市	49.09	32	-5	47.86	27
哈尔滨市	49.04	33	-15	55.47	18
南宁市	41.04	34	-12	52.98	22
重庆市	40.00	35	-16	53.9	19
全国平均		63.39		56.28	

2013 年中国 35 个城市生活质量分指数

表4-4显示，2013年，35个城市生活水平客观指数的加权平均值为63.39，比2012年的全国平均值56.28有了较大幅度提升。得分超过75分的城市有5个，比2012年多了2个；超过60分的城市有24个，比2012年多了15个；得分超过50分的城市有31个，比2012年多了6个。从单个城市看，北京、广州、南京、深圳连续两年排名前5位；西宁、重庆连续两年排名后5位。无论从平均值还是分城市来看，生活水平的客观指数都有了较为明显的提高。

城市生活水平客观指数排名前10位的城市是：南京（1）、厦门（2）、深圳（3）、西安（4）、北京（5）、上海（6）、杭州（7）、宁波（8）、济南（9）、成都（10）。其中，有8个东部城市，2个西部城市。排名前10位的城市中，厦门、西安、南京较2012年有了较大幅度提升。城市生活水平客观指数排名后10位的城市是：乌鲁木齐（26）、沈阳（27）、青岛（28）、昆明（29）、西宁（30）、太原（31）、贵阳（32）、哈尔滨（33）、南宁（34）、重庆（35）。其中，有2个东部城市，3个中部城，5个西部城市。排名后10位的城市中，青岛、哈尔滨、南宁、重庆较2012年有较大幅度的下降。整体上看，东部城市生活水平客观指数高于中西部城市。

城市生活水平客观指数排名上升比较明显的城市有厦门（21）、兰州（17）、西安（11）、大连（10）、南昌（10）、银川（9）。排名下降比较明显的城市有福州（-8）、天津（-10）、青岛（-20）、哈尔滨（-15）、南宁（-12）、重庆（-16）。[①]

4.2 生活成本指数

同其他分指数一样，生活成本指数也包括主观满意度指数和客观指数

---

① 括号内的数字代表上升或下降的幅度。

（社会经济数据指数），前者是根据电话调查并结合答案赋值得到的，后者是通过对35个城市的社会经济指标计算得出的。

4.2.1 生活成本主观满意度指数

表4-5列出了35个城市生活成本主观满意度指数得分以及排序情况。与前两年的调查一样，生活成本指数越高，说明该城市生活成本越低，居民满意度越高；反之则相反。

表4-5 中国35个城市生活成本满意度指数

城市	2013年得分	2013年排序	2013年上升位次	2012年得分	2012年排序	2012年排序*	2011年排序	2012年上升位次
石家庄市	39.13	1	3	34.27	4	4	8	4
沈阳市	36.31	2	5	31.73	7	7	12	5
济南市	36.16	3	-1	35.39	2	2	9	7
长春市	36.02	4	-1	34.36	3	3	1	-2
郑州市	35.03	5	3	31.67	8	8	10	2
合肥市	34.40	6	-5	35.43	1	1	4	3
太原市	34.22	7	4	30.94	11	11	7	-4
海口市	33.96	8	21	26	29	26	26	0
福州市	33.65	9	0	31.21	9	9	18	9
南宁市	33.45	10	14	27.16	24	23	15	-8
天津市	33.32	11	-6	32.62	5	5	6	1
南昌市	33.18	12	2	28.66	14	14	17	3
西安市	33.03	13	-7	31.92	6	6	3	-3
重庆市	32.94	14	-4	30.98	10	10	23	13
成都市	32.41	15	-3	30.92	12	12	16	4
厦门市	32.36	16	-1	28.49	15	—	—	—
哈尔滨市	32.06	17	0	28.38	17	16	2	-14
武汉市	31.96	18	-5	30.57	13	13	13	0
长沙市	31.08	19	2	27.63	21	20	27	7
呼和浩特市	30.85	20	8	26.43	28	25	11	-14
南京市	30.10	21	-2	27.95	19	18	22	4
昆明市	30.00	22	-4	28.04	18	17	19	2

续表

城 市	2013年得分	2013年排序	2013年上升位次	2012年得分	2012年排序	2012年排序*	2011年排序	2012年上升位次
贵阳市	29.38	23	7	25.71	30	27	5	-22
杭州市	29.10	24	-8	28.42	16	15	25	10
宁波市	29.03	25	2	26.62	27	—	—	—
西宁市	28.89	26	-3	27.31	23	22	14	-8
青岛市	28.78	27	-2	27.12	25	—	—	—
乌鲁木齐市	28.53	28	6	24.67	34	29	20	-9
广州市	28.46	29	-9	27.79	20	19	24	5
兰州市	27.82	30	-4	26.7	26	24	11	-13
银川市	27.47	31	-9	27.6	22	21	21	0
大连市	27.04	32	1	25.15	33	—	—	—
深圳市	26.56	33	-1	25.3	32	—	—	—
北京市	26.13	34	1	23.06	35	30	28	-2
上海市	25.59	35	-4	25.45	31	28	30	2
全国平均		31.22			28.91		32.7	

*未包含5个计划单列城市。

2013年，35个城市生活成本满意度指数的加权平均值为31.22分，高于2012年的28.91分，但低于2011年的32.70分。尽管比上年有所改善，但生活成本满意度指数仍旧偏低。35个城市的得分均低于40分，排名最高的石家庄市的得分（39.13）高于2012年排名第1的合肥市的得分（35.43）。排名最低的上海市的得分（25.59）也高于2012年排名最低的北京市的得分（23.06）。生活成本主观满意度指数排名前10位的城市是：石家庄（1）、沈阳（2）、济南（3）、长春（4）、郑州（5）、合肥（6）、太原（7）、海口（8）、福州（9）、南宁（10）。其中，有5个东部城市，4个中部城市，1个西部城市。排名后10位的城市是：西宁（26）、青岛（27）、乌鲁木齐（28）、广州（29）、兰州（30）、银川（31）、大连（32）、深圳（33）、北京（34）、上海（35）。其中，有6个东部城市，4个西部城市。北京、上海、深圳、大连等东部大城市生活成

本满意度偏低，说明这些城市的生活成本偏高。这也从下文的生活成本客观指数得到进一步印证，这些大城市的生活成本客观指数排名均比较低。

生活成本主观满意度指数较2012年上升比较明显的城市有海口（21）、南宁（14）、呼和浩特（8）、乌鲁木齐（6）、贵阳（7）等城市。① 生活成本满意度指数上升说明这些城市的生活成本下降，居民对生活成本的满意度有所提高。生活成本主观满意度下降比较明显的城市有银川（-9）、杭州（-8）、西安（-7）、天津（-6）、武汉（-5）等城市。② 生活成本满意度指数下降说明这些城市的生活成本上升，居民对生活成本的满意度下降。

4.2.2 生活成本客观指数（社会经济数据指数）

生活成本客观指数由房屋销售价格指数、通货膨胀率、房价收入比3个二级指标构成。表4-6给出了35个城市生活成本客观指数及其排序情况。

表4-6显示，2013年，35个城市生活成本客观指数加权平均值为58.67分，比2012年的平均值56.10分有所提升。得分超过70分的城市有3个，比2012年多1个；得分超过60分的城市有18个，比2012年多6个；得分超过50分的城市有31个，比2012年多3个。城市生活成本客观指数排名前10位的城市是：昆明（1）、呼和浩特（2）、长沙（3）、石家庄（4）、西宁（5）、西安（6）、银川（7）、南昌（8）、济南（9）、青岛（10）。其中，有3个东部城市，2个中部城市，5个西部城市。排名后10位的城市是：福州（26）、宁波（27）、天津（28）、太原（29）、广州（30）、上海（31）、杭州（32）、深圳（33）、北京（34）、海口（35）。其中，有9个东部城市，1个中部城市。整体上看，东部地区城市生活成本要高于中西部地区。

---

① 括号内的数字代表上升的位次。
② 括号内的数字代表下降的位次。

表4-6　中国35个城市生活成本客观指数

城　市	2013年得分	2013年排序	上升位次	2012年得分	2012年排序
昆明市	80.00	1	1	74	2
呼和浩特市	77.96	2	-1	79.97	1
长沙市	71.79	3	0	69.57	3
石家庄市	66.75	4	0	64.74	4
西宁市	66.05	5	5	60.51	10
西安市	65.27	6	3	61.38	9
银川市	65.18	7	7	59.38	14
南昌市	64.81	8	-3	63.36	5
济南市	64.59	9	7	59.19	16
青岛市	63.40	10	-2	62.34	8
重庆市	63.36	11	-5	63.34	6
沈阳市	62.89	12	-1	60.11	11
武汉市	62.61	13	0	59.68	13
郑州市	62.30	14	-7	63.02	7
成都市	61.68	15	-3	60.06	12
贵阳市	61.67	16	1	58.21	17
厦门市	60.70	17	-2	59.22	15
南宁市	60.61	18	1	54.24	19
兰州市	59.93	19	3	52.63	22
长春市	59.57	20	0	53.58	20
哈尔滨市	58.67	21	2	52.46	23
乌鲁木齐市	58.33	22	7	46.58	29
合肥市	58.17	23	3	51.49	26
大连市	57.15	24	-6	56	18
南京市	55.70	25	-1	52.18	24
福州市	55.43	26	1	51.01	27
宁波市	55.19	27	3	46.16	30
天津市	54.63	28	-3	51.83	25
太原市	53.84	29	2	46.09	31
广州市	53.15	30	-9	53.24	21
上海市	50.00	31	1	44.5	32
杭州市	48.73	32	1	42.5	33
深圳市	45.82	33	-5	50.14	28
北京市	45.17	34	0	40.8	34
海口市	40.00	35	0	39.97	35
全国平均		58.67			56.10

城市生活质量蓝皮书

4.3 人力资本指数

人力资本指数由主观满意度指数和客观指数（社会经济数据指数）构成，前者是根据电话调查并结合答案赋值得到的，后者是通过对35个城市的社会经济指标计算得出的。

4.3.1 人力资本主观满意度指数

表4-7给出了2013年35个城市人力资本主观满意度指数的调查结果，包括每个城市的得分及排序情况。人力资本主观满意度指数是通过询问受访者对自己或子女受教育状况的满意程度，并结合答案赋值得出的。

表4-7显示，2013年，35个城市的人力资本主观满意度加权平均值为58.89分，比2012年的59.42分有所降低。其中，得分超过60分的城市有10个，比2012年少2个。所有城市的得分均超过了50分，整体仍处于较高的水平。排名前10位的城市是：青岛（1）、济南（2）、乌鲁木齐（3）、大连（4）、郑州（5）、合肥（6）、呼和浩特（7）、上海（8）、宁波（9）、西宁（10）。其中，有5个东部城市，2个中部城市，3个西部城市。排名后10位的城市是：沈阳（26）、重庆（27）、广州（28）、哈尔滨（29）、兰州（30）、武汉（31）、深圳（32）、西安（33）、昆明（34）、太原（35）。其中，有3个东部城市，4个中部城市，3个西部城市。整体看来，东部地区要高于中西部地区。排名上升比较明显的城市有：贵阳（21）、郑州（19）、海口（10）、南昌（9）、大连（13）等城市。排名下降比较明显的城市有长春（-17）、石家庄（-17）、广州（-14）、银川（-14）长沙（-12）、杭州（-10）等城市。①

---

① 括号内的数字代表上升或下降的位次。

2013年中国35个城市生活质量分指数

表4-7 中国35个城市居民人力资本满意度指数

城 市	2013年得分	2013年排序	2012年得分	2012年排序	上升位次
青岛市	62.61	1	62.62	5	4
济南市	61.99	2	62.2	7	5
乌鲁木齐市	61.86	3	61.18	10	7
大连市	61.67	4	59.2	17	13
郑州市	61.54	5	58.45	24	19
合肥市	61.37	6	59.71	13	7
呼和浩特市	60.96	7	61.07	11	4
上海市	60.35	8	58.79	22	14
宁波市	60.14	9	64.19	1	-8
西宁市	60.09	10	58.8	21	11
北京市	59.68	11	59.33	16	5
贵阳市	59.60	12	55.48	33	21
福州市	59.60	13	62.72	4	-9
天津市	59.30	14	61.27	9	-5
南京市	59.29	15	59.36	15	0
杭州市	59.24	16	62.38	6	-10
海口市	59.11	17	58	27	10
厦门市	59.03	18	59.01	19	1
长春市	58.90	19	63.37	2	-17
石家庄市	58.86	20	63.31	3	-17
南宁市	58.73	21	58.18	25	4
银川市	58.52	22	61.98	8	-14
南昌市	58.45	23	56.1	32	9
长沙市	58.20	24	60.38	12	-12
成都市	58.17	25	59.14	18	-7
沈阳市	57.79	26	57.61	28	2
重庆市	57.74	27	58.83	20	-7
广州市	57.59	28	59.43	14	-14
哈尔滨市	57.23	29	56.76	30	1
兰州市	57.20	30	58.52	23	-7
武汉市	57.09	31	58.09	26	-5
深圳市	57.03	32	57.34	29	-3
西安市	56.65	33	56.19	31	-2
昆明市	54.33	34	55.45	34	0
太原市	53.49	35	55.2	35	0
全国平均	58.89		59.42		

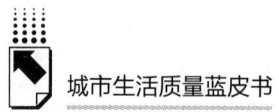

4.3.2 人力资本客观指数（社会经济数据指数）

人力资本客观指数由教育提供指数、教育文化娱乐消费支出比2个二级指标构成。表4-8是2013年35个城市的人力资本客观指数的计算结果。

表4-8 中国35个城市人力资本客观指数

城 市	2013年得分	2013年排序	上升位次	2012年得分	2012年排序
广州市	80.00	1	0	80.01	1
南京市	79.73	2	0	79.52	2
西安市	72.94	3	0	79.42	3
北京市	68.76	4	0	70.96	4
长沙市	66.65	5	6	58.8	11
太原市	64.68	6	-1	69.05	5
上海市	63.03	7	-1	66.15	6
长春市	61.79	8	13	54.72	21
贵阳市	61.65	9	-2	62.79	7
武汉市	60.89	10	3	58.52	13
合肥市	60.28	11	-1	59.72	10
宁波市	59.09	12	0	58.62	12
呼和浩特市	58.83	13	-5	61.75	8
南宁市	58.27	14	-5	60.93	9
银川市	56.57	15	1	57.57	16
福州市	56.38	16	12	51.09	28
昆明市	56.19	17	0	57.2	17
济南市	55.28	18	-3	57.66	15
石家庄市	55.22	19	14	47.11	33
沈阳市	54.67	20	0	55.9	20
兰州市	53.68	21	2	54.33	23
哈尔滨市	52.90	22	3	52.83	25
杭州市	52.89	23	1	53.38	24
大连市	52.62	24	3	52.09	27
南昌市	51.88	25	5	48.30	30

续表

城　　市	2013年得分	2013年排序	上升位次	2012年得分	2012年排序
成都市	51.79	26	3	50.62	29
天津市	51.63	27	-9	56.58	18
深圳市	49.79	28	-6	54.43	22
乌鲁木齐市	49.17	29	-10	56.49	19
重庆市	48.03	30	1	48.28	31
郑州市	48.02	31	1	47.5	32
海口市	46.39	32	-18	58.08	14
青岛市	46.32	33	1	45.56	34
厦门市	43.09	34	-8	52.32	26
西宁市	40.00	35	0	39.99	35
全国平均	57.78			57.66	

表4-8显示，2013年，35个城市人力资本客观指数加权平均值为57.78分，比2012年平均值57.66分有所提升。有27个城市超过50分，比2012年减少了2个。人力资本客观指数排名前10位的城市是：广州（1）、南京（2）、西安（3）、北京（4）、长沙（5）、太原（6）、上海（7）、长春（8）、贵阳（9）、武汉（10）。其中，有4个东部城市，4个中部城市，2个西部城市。排名后10位的城市是：成都（26）、天津（27）、深圳（28）、乌鲁木齐（29）、重庆（30）、郑州（31）、海口（32）、青岛（33）、厦门（34）、西宁（35）。其中，有5个东部城市，1个中部城市，4个西部城市。排名前4位的广州、南京、西安、北京排名与2012年相比没有发生变化。排名上升比较明显的城市有石家庄（14）、长春（13）、福州（12）等城市。排名下降比较明显的城市有海口（-18）、乌鲁木齐（-10）、天津（-9）、深圳（-6）等城市。①

---

① 括号内的数字代表上升或下降的位次。

4.4 社会保障指数

社会保障指数包括主观满意度指数和客观指数（社会经济数据指数）。

4.4.1 主观满意度指数

社会保障主观满意度指数用医疗保障满意度和城市安全满意度来描述。我们通过询问受访者对享有的医疗保障和养老保障的满意程度，以及对城市安全（社会治安）状况的满意程度，并结合答案赋值，分别得到医疗保障满意度指数和城市安全满意度指数。然后将两个指数进行加权平均得到生活保障满意度（主观）指数。表4-9给出了35个城市社会保障主观满意度指数和排序情况。

表4-9显示，2013年，35个城市社会保障主观满意度指数加权平均值为56.64分，比2012年的平均值59.19分有所降低。35个城市的得分均超过了50分，得分超过60分的有5个城市，比2012年少9个。城市社会保障主观满意度指数的下降主要是由于城市安全（社会治安）状况的满意度下降造成的。[1] 城市社会保障主观满意度指数排名前10位的城市是：青岛（1）、厦门（2）、杭州（3）、宁波（4）、银川（5）、济南（6）、西宁（7）、南京（8）、北京（9）、上海（10）。其中，有8个东部城市，2个西部城市。排名后10位的城市是：深圳（26）、广州（27）、南昌（28）、长沙（29）、昆明（30）、海口（31）、武汉（32）、呼和浩特（33）、南宁（34）、贵阳（35）。其中，有3个东部城市，3个中部城市，4个西部城市。整体上看，东部城市的主观满意度要高于中西部城市。排名上升比较明显的城市有哈尔滨（9）、南京（9）、上海（8）、沈阳（7）、青岛（6）等城市。排名下降比较明显的城市有呼和浩特（-19）、重庆（-19）、长春（-9）、武汉（-6）等城市。[2]

---

[1] 下文将进行更为详细的分析。
[2] 括号内的数字代表上升或下降的位次。

2013 年中国 35 个城市生活质量分指数

表 4-9　中国 35 个城市居民社会保障满意度指数

城　市	2013 年得分	2013 年排序	2012 年得分	2012 年排序	上升位次
青岛市	61.87	1	62.26	7	6
厦门市	61.25	2	62.79	4	2
杭州市	60.76	3	64.68	1	-2
宁波市	60.52	4	63.65	2	-2
银川市	60.03	5	62.24	8	3
济南市	59.82	6	62.65	6	0
西宁市	59.31	7	62.04	9	2
南京市	59.22	8	59.17	17	9
北京市	58.94	9	61.27	12	3
上海市	58.04	10	58.71	18	8
合肥市	57.71	11	59.8	15	4
长春市	57.59	12	62.83	3	-9
大连市	57.18	13	61.73	10	-3
成都市	57.05	14	61.33	11	-3
石家庄市	56.64	15	61.24	13	-2
太原市	56.63	16	58.66	19	3
乌鲁木齐市	56.57	17	58.06	22	5
沈阳市	56.40	18	57.04	25	7
西安市	56.27	19	59.65	16	-3
福州市	56.23	20	58.6	20	0
哈尔滨市	55.86	21	56.27	30	9
郑州市	55.74	22	56.67	28	6
兰州市	55.65	23	57.67	23	0
重庆市	55.61	24	62.78	5	-19
天津市	55.14	25	58.57	21	-4
深圳市	55.11	26	57.04	24	-2
广州市	54.70	27	56.81	27	0
南昌市	54.09	28	55.18	33	5
长沙市	54.09	29	56.14	31	2
昆明市	54.09	30	54.65	34	4
海口市	53.86	31	55.75	32	1
武汉市	52.64	32	56.83	26	-6
呼和浩特市	52.63	33	60.18	14	-19
南宁市	52.43	34	56.33	29	-5
贵阳市	51.98	35	52.26	35	0
全国平均	56.64		59.19		

表 4–10 给出了 35 个城市社会保障主观满意度指数中的医疗保障状况满意度的调查结果。

表 4–10 中国 35 个城市医疗状况满意度指数

城　市	2013 年得分	2013 年排序	2013 年上升位次	2012 年得分	2012 年排序	2012 年排序*	2011 年排序	2012 年上升位次
西宁市	61.67	1	2	57.87	3	2	8	6
宁波市	58.96	2	0	58.24	2	—	—	—
兰州市	58.33	3	20	52.27	23	18	1	-17
青岛市	58.19	4	13	53.42	17	—	—	—
北京市	57.29	5	7	55.71	12	10	5	-5
贵阳市	56.64	6	10	53.57	16	14	7	-7
银川市	56.59	7	4	55.73	11	9	3	-6
石家庄市	56.39	8	1	56.55	9	8	11	3
乌鲁木齐市	56.36	9	-5	57.57	4	3	6	3
杭州市	56.11	10	-9	58.37	1	1	4	3
西安市	55.96	11	-3	57.04	8	7	27	20
厦门市	55.83	12	-2	56.4	10	—	—	—
南昌市	55.64	13	15	51.63	28	23	30	7
郑州市	54.82	14	8	52.38	22	17	12	-5
重庆市	54.79	15	0	53.74	15	13	17	4
南京市	54.61	16	16	49.74	32	27	20	-7
呼和浩特市	54.53	17	-12	57.5	5	4	9	5
昆明市	54.42	18	9	51.76	27	22	29	7
合肥市	54.42	19	-6	55.58	13	11	16	5
成都市	54.40	20	-6	55.26	14	12	21	9
沈阳市	54.37	21	10	50	31	26	28	2
济南市	54.24	22	4	51.96	26	21	10	-11
太原市	54.05	23	-16	57.18	7	6	15	9
福州市	53.75	24	6	51.3	30	25	14	-11
海口市	53.11	25	9	49.5	34	29	2	-27
长春市	52.90	26	-20	57.22	6	5	13	8
哈尔滨市	52.47	27	6	49.52	33	28	18	-10
长沙市	52.45	28	-3	52.05	25	20	26	6
广州市	52.37	29	0	51.38	29	24	22	-2

042

续表

城 市	2013年得分	2013年排序	2013年上升位次	2012年得分	2012年排序	2012年排序*	2011年排序	2012年上升位次
大连市	52.13	30	-12	53.37	18	—	—	
南宁市	52.11	31	-10	52.47	21	16	23	7
上海市	51.96	32	3	48.93	35	30	24	-6
天津市	51.64	33	-9	52.06	24	19	19	0
深圳市	51.23	34	-15	52.98	19	—	—	
武汉市	50.45	35	-15	52.52	20	15	25	10
全国平均		54.34			53.61		52.75	

* 未包含5个计划单列城市的排序。

表4-10显示，2013年，35个城市的医疗保障满意度指数加权平均值为54.34分，比2012年有所提高，但提高的幅度不大。得分超过60分的城市有1个（西宁），2012年没有得分超过60分的城市。所有城市的得分均超过了50分，2012年则有4个城市的得分没有超过50分。医疗保障满意度指数排名前10位的城市是：西宁（1）、宁波（2）、兰州（3）、青岛（4）、北京（5）、贵阳（6）、银川（7）、石家庄（8）、乌鲁木齐（9）、杭州（10）。其中，有5个东部城市，5个西部城市。排名后10位的城市是：长春（26）、哈尔滨（27）、长沙（28）、广州（29）、大连（30）、南宁（31）、上海（32）、天津（33）、深圳（34）、武汉（35）。其中，有5个东部城市，4个中部城市，1个西部城市。与2012年相比，上升幅度较为明显的城市有兰州（20）、南京（16）、南昌（15）、青岛（13）、贵阳（10）、昆明（9）、郑州（8）、北京（7）等城市。下降幅度较为明显的城市有长春（-20）、深圳（-15）、武汉（-15）、大连（-12）、南宁（-10）、天津（-9）等城市。①

表4-11给出了社会保障主观满意度指数中的城市安全（社会治安）状况满意度的调查结果。

---

① 括号内的数字代表上升或下降的位次。

表 4－11　中国 35 个城市安全（社会治安）状况满意度指数

城　市	2013 年得分	2013 年排序	上升位次	2012 年得分	2012 年排序
厦门市	66.67	1	5	69.19	6
青岛市	65.55	2	1	71.11	3
杭州市	65.42	3	1	70.99	4
济南市	65.41	4	－3	73.34	1
上海市	64.12	5	5	68.48	10
南京市	63.83	6	3	68.59	9
银川市	63.46	7	1	68.75	8
长春市	62.29	8	3	68.45	11
大连市	62.22	9	－4	70.09	5
宁波市	62.08	10	－3	69.05	7
合肥市	61.00	11	8	64.03	19
北京市	60.58	12	1	66.82	13
成都市	59.69	13	－1	67.4	12
哈尔滨市	59.25	14	7	63.03	21
太原市	59.22	15	16	60.15	31
深圳市	58.98	16	11	61.11	27
福州市	58.71	17	－1	65.9	16
天津市	58.64	18	－1	65.08	17
沈阳市	58.43	19	－1	64.09	18
广州市	57.02	20	4	62.25	24
西宁市	56.94	21	－7	66.2	14
石家庄市	56.89	22	－7	65.93	15
乌鲁木齐市	56.78	23	10	58.55	33
郑州市	56.66	24	4	60.95	28
西安市	56.58	25	－2	62.26	23
重庆市	56.43	26	－24	71.83	2
长沙市	55.73	27	2	60.23	29
武汉市	54.83	28	－2	61.13	26
海口市	54.61	29	－4	62	25
昆明市	53.75	30	4	57.53	34
兰州市	52.97	31	－11	63.07	20
南宁市	52.75	32	－2	60.19	30
南昌市	52.55	33	－1	58.74	32
呼和浩特市	50.73	34	－12	62.86	22
贵阳市	47.32	35	0	50.95	35
全国平均	58.93			64.58	

表4-11显示,2013年,35个城市安全(社会治安)状况满意度指数加权平均值为58.93分,低于2012年的平均值64.58分。得分超过60分的城市有12个,而2012年得分超过60分的城市有31个。城市安全(社会治安)状况满意度指数下降是造成社会保障主观满意度指数下降的主要原因。城市安全(社会治安)状况满意度指数排名前10位的城市是:厦门(1)、青岛(2)、杭州(3)、济南(4)、上海(5)、南京(6)、银川(7)、长春(8)、大连(9)、宁波(10)。其中,有8个东部城市,1个中部城市,1个西部城市。排名后10位的城市是:重庆(26)、长沙(27)、武汉(28)、海口(29)、昆明(30)、兰州(31)、南宁(32)、南昌(33)、呼和浩特(34)、贵阳(35)。其中,有1个东部城市,3个中部城市,6个西部城市。排名上升幅度明显的城市有太原(16)、深圳(11)、合肥(8)、厦门(5)、上海(5)、乌鲁木齐(10)等城市。排名下降幅度明显的城市有重庆(-24)、兰州(-11)、呼和浩特(-12)、西宁(-7)、石家庄(-7)等城市。①

4.4.2 社会保障客观指数（社会经济数据指数）

我们用社会保障覆盖率、基本医疗保险覆盖率及失业保险覆盖率3个二级指标来度量社会保障客观指数。表4-12是社会保障客观指数的计算结果。

表4-12显示,2013年,35个城市社会保障客观指数加权平均值为55.26分,高于2012年的50.85分。超过50分的城市有18个,比2012年多4个,所有城市的得分均超过了40分。社会保障客观指数排名前10位的城市是:深圳(1)、北京(2)、厦门(3)、宁波(4)、上海(5)、广州(6)、杭州(7)、天津(8)、沈阳(9)、长春(10)。排名后10位的城市是:重庆(26)、福州(27)、海口(28)、合肥(29)、南昌(30)、石家庄

---

① 括号内的数字代表上升或下降的位次。

表4-12 中国35个城市社会保障客观指数

城　市	2013年得分	2013年排序	上升位次	2012年得分	2012年排序
深圳市	80.00	1	0	80.01	1
北京市	77.24	2	0	71.82	2
厦门市	74.37	3	0	71.43	3
宁波市	72.36	4	4	56.19	8
上海市	67.23	5	-1	68.68	4
广州市	66.71	6	-1	60.11	5
杭州市	63.84	7	0	58.36	7
天津市	63.13	8	-2	59.89	6
沈阳市	62.01	9	3	55.2	12
长春市	59.84	10	7	48.23	17
大连市	59.82	11	-2	55.67	9
南京市	58.11	12	-2	55.65	10
乌鲁木齐市	52.63	13	0	51.44	13
青岛市	52.34	14	2	48.63	16
西安市	52.15	15	-4	55.62	11
银川市	51.93	16	2	47.15	18
成都市	50.84	17	5	45	22
武汉市	50.48	18	-3	49.51	15
太原市	49.08	19	-5	50.61	14
济南市	47.36	20	0	46.08	20
呼和浩特市	46.91	21	0	45.68	21
南宁市	46.09	22	12	40.85	34
长沙市	45.97	23	4	43.07	27
兰州市	45.14	24	-5	46.35	19
贵阳市	44.95	25	-1	44.14	24
重庆市	44.57	26	6	41.48	32
福州市	44.06	27	4	42.17	31
海口市	43.91	28	2	42.54	30
合肥市	43.72	29	-6	44.71	23
南昌市	43.05	30	-5	43.46	25
石家庄市	41.77	31	2	40.86	33
哈尔滨市	41.73	32	-6	43.21	26
昆明市	41.21	33	-4	42.85	29
郑州市	40.98	34	-6	42.99	28
西宁市	40.00	35	0	39.98	35
全国平均	55.26			50.85	

(31)、哈尔滨(32)、昆明(33)、郑州(34)、西宁(35)。通过排名比较发现,东部城市的这些指标均明显高于中西部城市。具体表现为:社会保障客观指数排名前10位的城市中,有9个为东部城市,1个为中部城市;排名后10位的城市中,有3个东部城市,3个西部城市,4个中部城市。排名上升幅度较明显的城市有南宁(12)、长春(7)、重庆(6)、成都(5)等城市。排名下降幅度较明显的城市有合肥(-6)、哈尔滨(-6)、郑州(-6)、南昌(-5)等城市。①

4.5 生活感受指数

生活感受指数也分为主观满意度指数和客观指数(社会经济数据指数)。

4.5.1 主观满意度指数

生活感受主观满意度指数包括生活节奏满意度指数和生活便利满意度指数。我们通过询问受访者对所在城市生活节奏的满意程度,以及对城市生活便利的满意程度,并结合答案赋值,分别得到生活节奏满意度指数和生活便利满意度指数。然后将两个指数加权平均得到生活感受主观满意度指数。

表4-13给出了35个城市生活感受主观满意度指数的调查结果,包括得分和排序情况。

表4-13显示,2013年,35个城市生活感受主观满意度指数加权平均值为55.07分,比2012年的平均值55.63分有所降低,35个城市的得分位于50~60分区间,均处于满意区间,整体上保持了比较稳定的态势。城市生活感受主观满意度指数排名前10位的城市是:银川(1)、西宁(2)、南京(3)、杭州(4)、天津(5)、厦门(6)、重庆(7)、宁波(8)、

---

① 括号内的数字代表上升或下降的位次。

表4-13 中国35个城市居民生活感受满意度指数

城 市	2013年得分	2013年排序	2012年得分	2012年排序	上升位次
银川市	58.24	1	59.9	1	0
西宁市	57.76	2	57.41	7	5
南京市	57.54	3	58.08	5	2
杭州市	57.05	4	58.25	3	-1
天津市	56.75	5	56.63	13	8
厦门市	56.67	6	59.01	2	-4
重庆市	56.66	7	56.18	16	9
宁波市	56.56	8	55.34	19	11
青岛市	56.20	9	56.96	11	2
福州市	56.20	10	56.72	12	2
长春市	56.14	11	58.22	4	-7
济南市	56.13	12	57.23	8	-4
上海市	56.10	13	56.58	14	1
郑州市	56.09	14	54.17	25	11
成都市	56.06	15	57.86	6	-9
西安市	55.96	16	55.46	18	2
海口市	55.63	17	55.75	17	0
太原市	54.75	18	53.84	28	10
石家庄市	54.43	19	57.11	9	-10
大连市	54.35	20	55.06	22	2
沈阳市	54.21	21	55.33	20	-1
合肥市	54.09	22	55.31	21	-1
哈尔滨市	53.95	23	53.62	31	8
长沙市	53.94	24	57.02	10	-14
北京市	53.87	25	53.3	32	7
南昌市	53.84	26	53.86	27	1
武汉市	53.29	27	54.31	24	-3
贵阳市	53.18	28	53.81	29	1
呼和浩特市	53.07	29	52.68	34	5
深圳市	53.07	30	54.02	26	-4
广州市	52.99	31	53.67	30	-1
南宁市	52.96	32	54.86	23	-9
兰州市	52.47	33	50	35	2
昆明市	52.40	34	53.13	33	-1
乌鲁木齐市	50.85	35	56.25	15	-20
全国平均	55.07		55.63		

青岛（9）、福州（10）。其中，有7个东部城市，3个西部城市。排名后10位的城市是：南昌（26）、武汉（27）、贵阳（28）、呼和浩特（29）、深圳（30）、广州（31）、南宁（32）、兰州（33）、昆明（34）、乌鲁木齐（35）。其中，有2个东部城市，2个中部城市，6个西部城市。排名上升幅度较明显的城市有宁波（11）、太原（10）、重庆（9）、哈尔滨（8）、北京（7）等城市。排名下降幅度较明显的城市有乌鲁木齐（-20）、长沙（-14）、石家庄（-10）、成都（-9）等城市。① 35个城市生活感受主观满意度指数的得分和排名的变化可以从生活节奏满意度指数和生活便利满意度指数的调查结果得到进一步解释。表4-14给出了35个城市生活节奏满意度的调查结果及排序情况。

表4-14显示，2013年，35个城市生活节奏满意度指数加权平均值为42.97分，与前两次调查结果基本维持在同一个水平上。35个城市的主观满意度指数均低于50分，说明居民普遍感到生活节奏过快。城市生活节奏满意度指数排名前10位的城市是：长春（1）、西宁（2）、海口（3）、成都（4）、兰州（5）、郑州（6）、贵阳（7）、杭州（8）、太原（9）、银川（10）。其中，有2个东部城市，3个中部城市，5个西部城市。排名后10位的城市中，有7个东部城市，2个中部城市，1个西部城市。排名后10位的城市是：大连（26）、长沙（27）、哈尔滨（28）、沈阳（29）、乌鲁木齐（30）、北京（31）、青岛（32）、上海（33）、广州（34）、深圳（35）。排名上升比较明显的城市有兰州（20）、郑州（12）、济南（8）、天津（8）、呼和浩特（11）等城市。排名下降比较明显的城市有长沙（-21）、乌鲁木齐（-20）、厦门（-15）、石家庄（-11）、南昌（-9）、银川（-9）、南宁（-8）、武汉（-7）等城市。② 调查结果显示，居民普遍感受到生活节奏过快，并且东部城市的生活节奏明显快于中西部地区。

---

① 括号内的数字代表上升或下降的位次。
② 括号内的数字代表上升或下降的位次。

表4-14　中国35个城市生活节奏满意度指数

城　市	2013年得分	2013年排序	2013年上升位次	2012年得分	2012年排序	2012年排序*	2011年排序	2012年上升位次
长春市	49.88	1	4	45.72	5	5	19	14
西宁市	47.95	2	2	47.22	4	4	2	-2
海口市	47.25	3	0	47.5	3	3	21	18
成都市	47.22	4	-2	48.39	2	2	22	20
兰州市	46.47	5	20	41.48	25	24	29	5
郑州市	46.27	6	12	42.98	18	17	13	-4
贵阳市	45.90	7	0	45.48	7	7	10	3
杭州市	45.83	8	0	44.93	8	8	4	-4
太原市	45.11	9	6	43.32	15	14	11	-3
银川市	45.05	10	-9	50	1	1	1	0
济南市	45.02	11	8	42.92	19	18	5	-13
天津市	44.95	12	8	42.7	20	19	7	-12
昆明市	44.90	13	3	43.27	16	15	8	-7
福州市	44.90	14	7	42.49	21	20	20	0
呼和浩特市	44.74	15	11	41.43	26	25	17	-8
南京市	44.62	16	1	43.21	17	16	3	-13
西安市	44.32	17	7	42.23	24	23	16	-7
合肥市	44.27	18	5	42.27	23	22	15	-7
南宁市	44.23	19	-8	44.44	11	10	25	15
重庆市	44.01	20	2	42.34	22	21	18	-3
武汉市	43.69	21	-7	43.49	14	13	14	1
南昌市	43.62	22	-9	43.9	13	12	23	11
石家庄市	43.11	23	-11	44.35	12	11	12	1
厦门市	43.06	24	-15	44.77	9	—	—	—
宁波市	42.99	25	3	40.54	28	—	—	—
大连市	42.87	26	5	39.57	31	—	—	—
长沙市	42.81	27	-21	45.61	6	6	6	0
哈尔滨市	42.54	28	2	39.96	30	27	26	-1
沈阳市	41.81	29	-2	40.86	27	26	9	-17
乌鲁木齐市	41.81	30	-20	44.74	10	9	27	18
北京市	39.32	31	2	37.11	33	29	30	1
青岛市	39.22	32	-3	40.09	29	—	—	—
上海市	38.20	33	1	37.05	34	30	24	-6
广州市	36.67	34	-2	38.12	32	28	28	0
深圳市	34.93	35	0	35.81	35	—	—	—
全国平均	42.97			42.87			42.67	

*未包含5个计划单列城市的排序。

2013 年中国 35 个城市生活质量分指数

表 4-15 给出了 35 个城市生活便利满意度的调查结果及排序情况。

表 4-15　中国 35 个城市生活便利满意度指数

城　市	2013 年得分	2013 年排序	2013 年上升位次	2012 年得分	2012 年排序	2012 年排序*	2011 年排序	2012 年上升位次
上海市	73.993	1	0	76.12	1	1	9	8
青岛市	73.179	2	0	73.82	2	—	—	—
银川市	71.429	3	13	69.79	16	11	5	-6
深圳市	71.205	4	1	72.22	5	—	—	—
南京市	70.461	5	-1	72.95	4	2	10	8
厦门市	70.278	6	-3	73.26	3	—	—	—
宁波市	70.139	7	5	70.14	12	—	—	—
重庆市	69.313	8	5	70.01	13	8	2	-6
广州市	69.307	9	9	69.23	18	13	20	7
天津市	68.551	10	0	70.56	10	7	15	8
北京市	68.419	11	6	69.5	17	12	16	4
杭州市	68.264	12	-6	71.58	6	3	3	0
西安市	67.590	13	6	68.69	19	14	22	8
西宁市	67.565	14	9	67.59	23	18	19	1
福州市	67.493	15	-7	70.95	8	5	13	8
济南市	67.251	16	-9	71.54	7	4	1	-3
沈阳市	66.604	17	-2	69.8	15	10	8	-2
郑州市	65.907	18	8	65.36	26	21	14	-7
大连市	65.833	19	-8	70.55	11	—	—	—
石家庄市	65.751	20	-6	69.86	14	9	21	12
哈尔滨市	65.359	21	4	67.28	25	20	17	-3
长沙市	65.068	22	-2	68.42	20	15	23	8
成都市	64.901	23	1	67.32	24	19	6	-13
太原市	64.385	24	5	64.36	29	24	26	2
南昌市	64.059	25	7	63.82	32	27	27	0
海口市	64.011	26	4	64	30	25	12	-13
合肥市	63.910	27	-6	68.35	21	16	7	-9
武汉市	62.887	28	0	65.13	28	23	30	7
长春市	62.392	29	-20	70.72	9	6	11	5
南宁市	61.690	30	-3	65.28	27	22	29	7
呼和浩特市	61.404	31	0	63.93	31	26	28	2
贵阳市	60.452	32	2	62.14	34	29	24	-5
昆明市	59.904	33	0	62.98	33	28	25	-3
乌鲁木齐市	59.887	34	-12	67.76	22	17	18	1
兰州市	58.475	35	0	58.52	35	30	4	-26
全国平均		67.18		68.39			56.24	

*未包含 5 个计划单列城市的排序。

表4-15显示,2013年,35个城市生活便利满意度指数加权平均值为67.81分,整体上仍旧保持了较高水平,但比2012年的平均值68.39分有所降低。城市生活便利满意度指数排名前10位的城市是:上海(1)、青岛(2)、银川(3)、深圳(4)、南京(5)、厦门(6)、宁波(7)、重庆(8)、广州(9)、天津(10)。其中,有8个东部城市,2个西部城市。排名后10位的城市是:海口(26)、合肥(27)、武汉(28)、长春(29)、南宁(30)、呼和浩特(31)、贵阳(32)、昆明(33)、乌鲁木齐(34)、兰州(35)。其中,有1个东部城市,3个中部城市,6个西部城市。排名上升比较明显的城市有银川(13)、广州(9)、西宁(9)、郑州(8)、南昌(7)、北京(6)、西安(6)等城市。排名下降比较明显的城市有长春(-20)、乌鲁木齐(-12)、大连(-8)、合肥(-6)、杭州(-6)等城市。① 上海、青岛、天津、武汉、呼和浩特、兰州、昆明等城市的排名没有发生变化。调查结果表明,政府在基础设施方面的投资,大大提高了居民生活的便利性,东部城市基础设施较中西部地区更为完善,生活便利满意度指数整体上高于中西部地区。

4.5.2 生活感受客观指数(社会经济数据指数)

在生活感受客观指数中,包括了生活便利指数、生态环境指数和收入差距感受指数3个一级指标,3个一级指标中又包含了交通提供能力、万人影剧院数、医疗提供能力、人均绿地面积、空气质量和基尼系数等6个二级指标。表4-16给出了35个城市生活感受客观指数的计算结果。

表4-16显示,2013年,35个城市生活感受客观指数的加权平均值为53.67分,高于2012年的51.89分。超过50分的城市有22个,比2012年多5个。城市生活感受客观指数排名前10名的城市是:北京(1)、

---

① 括号内的数字代表上升或下降的位次。

2013年中国35个城市生活质量分指数

表4-16　中国35个城市生活感受客观指数

城　市	2013年得分	2013年排序	上升位次	2012年得分	2012年排序
北京市	80.00	1	0	80.01	1
深圳市	65.12	2	0	71.86	2
广州市	64.16	3	4	58.88	7
沈阳市	62.56	4	1	62.9	5
武汉市	60.15	5	-2	64.52	3
南京市	59.70	6	2	58.24	8
呼和浩特市	58.74	7	6	54.5	13
杭州市	58.41	8	-4	64.43	4
海口市	57.80	9	3	55.45	12
昆明市	57.57	10	0	55.61	10
太原市	57.34	11	10	48.1	21
哈尔滨市	56.98	12	8	48.25	20
青岛市	55.68	13	6	48.97	19
银川市	54.74	14	0	52.58	14
上海市	54.71	15	-6	56.45	9
合肥市	54.46	16	15	42.91	31
西安市	54.32	17	-6	55.46	11
乌鲁木齐市	54.20	18	5	46.58	23
长春市	53.70	19	-3	51.25	16
厦门市	52.07	20	-14	58.95	6
兰州市	51.76	21	-4	50.77	17
石家庄市	51.39	22	0	46.63	22
宁波市	48.24	23	1	46.35	24
大连市	47.37	24	-6	49.07	18
天津市	47.28	25	0	46.2	25
长沙市	46.47	26	2	45.23	28
福州市	45.93	27	-12	51.84	15
西宁市	45.51	28	-1	45.6	27
贵阳市	44.89	29	3	41.91	32
南昌市	44.81	30	0	43.4	30
济南市	44.71	31	-5	45.72	26
南宁市	43.97	32	-3	44.47	29
成都市	43.35	33	1	41.3	34
重庆市	43.18	34	1	40.02	35
郑州市	40.00	35	-2	41.65	33
全国平均		53.67			51.89

深圳（2）、广州（3）、沈阳（4）、武汉（5）、南京（6）、呼和浩特（7）、杭州（8）、海口（9）、昆明（10）。其中，有7个东部城市，1个中部城市，2个西部城市。排名后10位的城市是：长沙（26）、福州（27）、西宁（28）、贵阳（29）、南昌（30）、济南（31）、南宁（32）、成都（33）、重庆（34）、郑州（35）。其中，2个东部城市，3个中部城市，5个西部城市。排名上升较明显的城市有合肥（15）、太原（10）、哈尔滨（8）、青岛（6）等城市。排名下降较明显的城市有厦门（-14）、福州（-12）、上海（-6）、西安（-6）等城市。[①] 北京、深圳、昆明、银川、石家庄、天津、南昌等城市的排名没有发生变化。

4.6 中国城市生活质量一级指标雷达图

下图给出了35个城市主客观指数的一级指标雷达图。根据雷达图可以看出一个非常明显的特征，即高生活成本是拉低城市生活质量主客观指数的一个非常重要的因素。

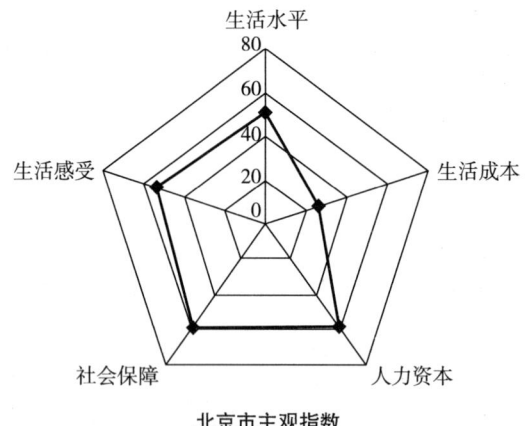

北京市主观指数

---

① 括号内的数字代表上升或下降的位次。

2013年中国35个城市生活质量分指数

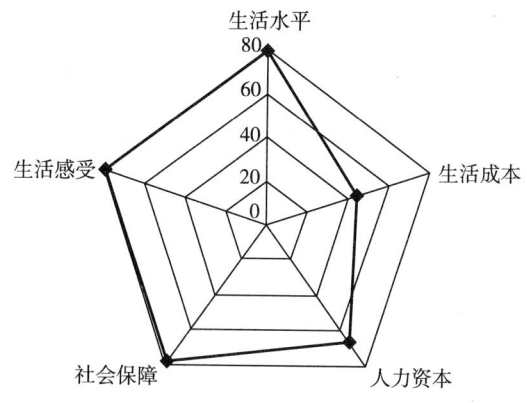

北京市客观指数

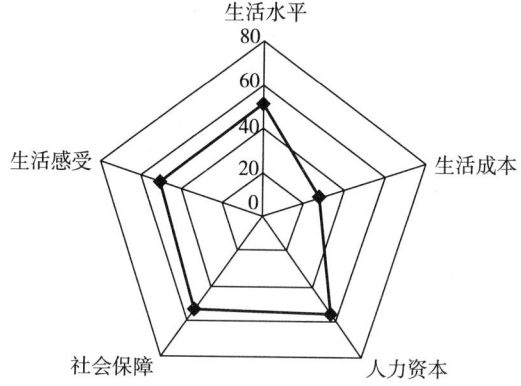

广州市主观指数

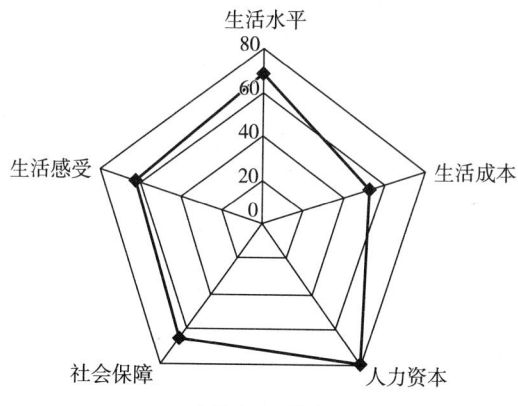

广州市客观指数

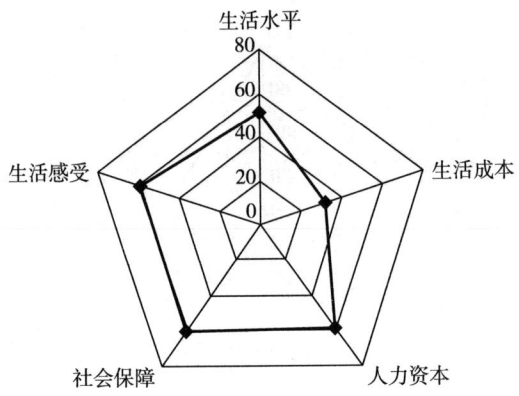

南京市主观指数

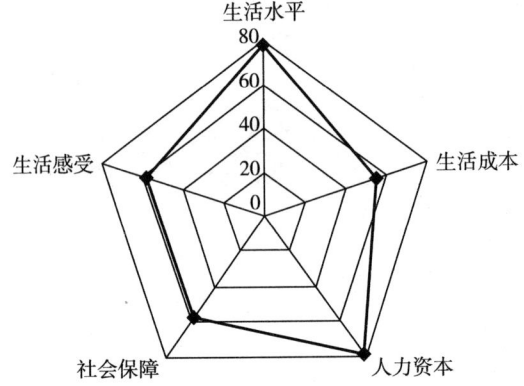

南京市客观指数

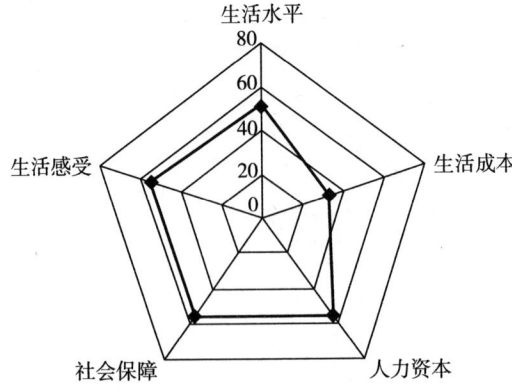

西安市主观指数

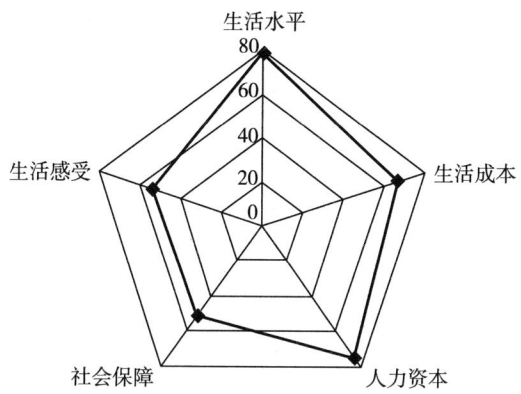

西安市客观指数

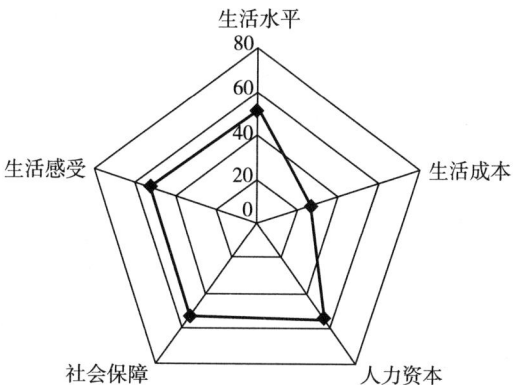

深圳市主观指数

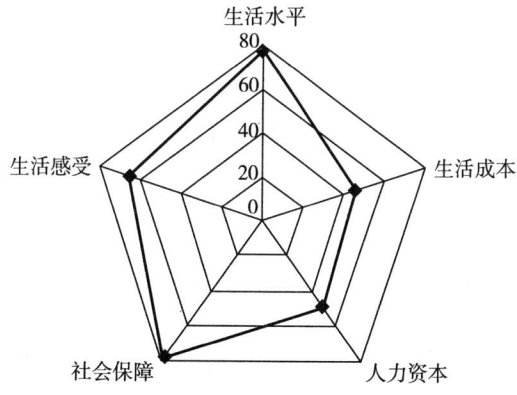

深圳市客观指数

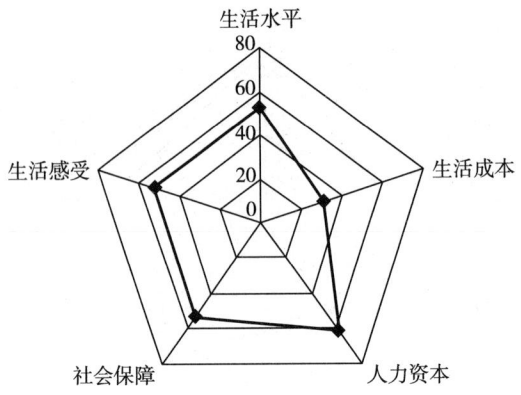

呼和浩特市主观指数

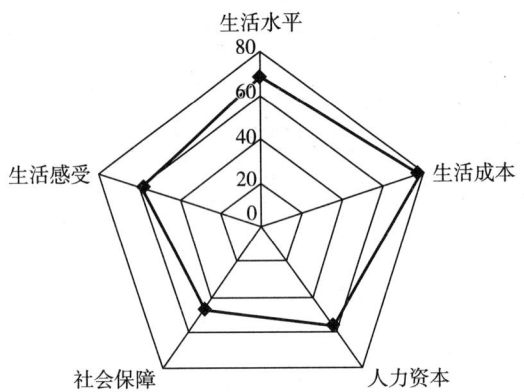

呼和浩特市客观指数

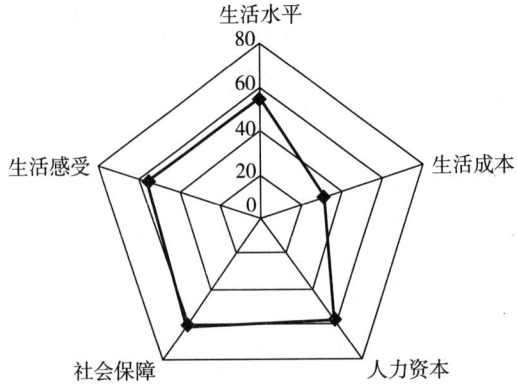

厦门市主观指数

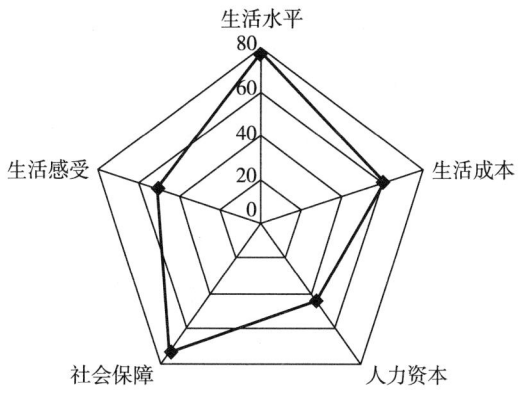

厦门市客观指数

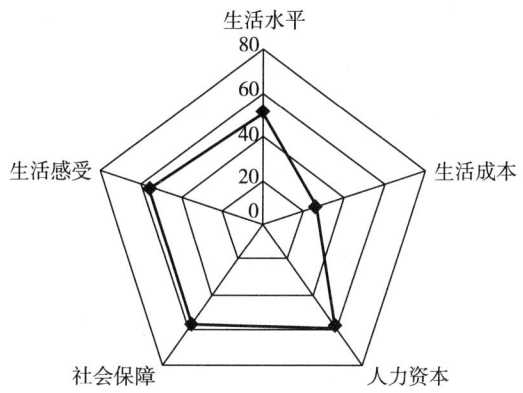

上海市主观指数

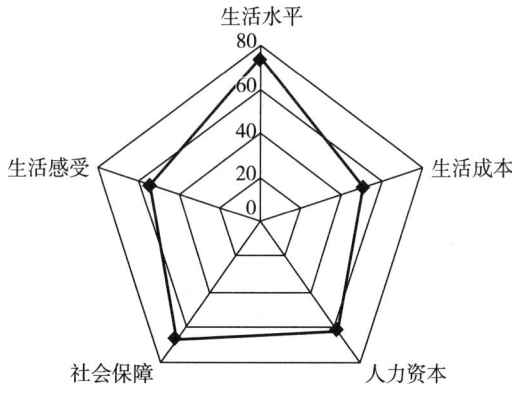

上海市客观指数

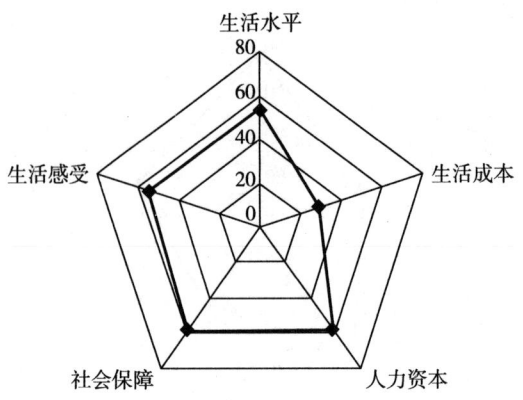

宁波市主观指数

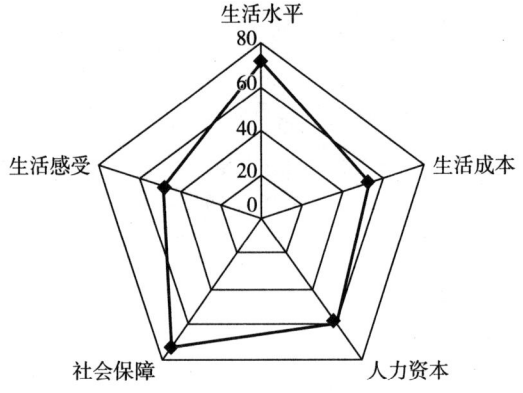

宁波市客观指数

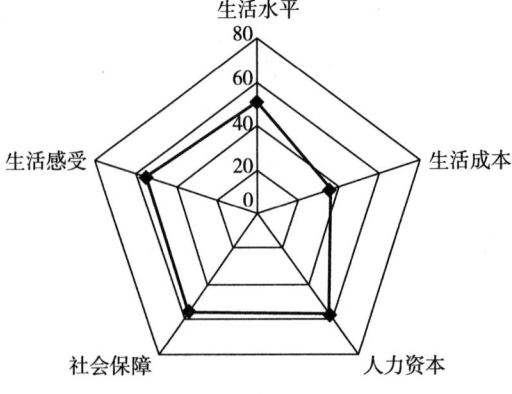

沈阳市主观指数

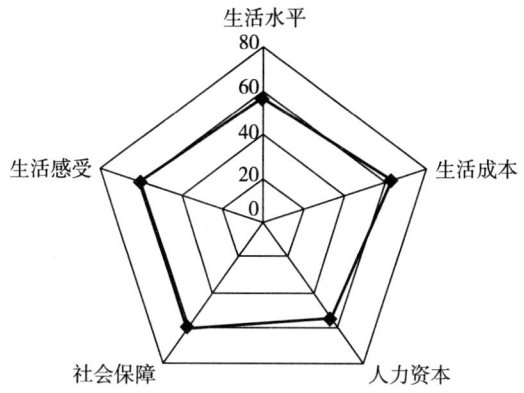

沈阳市客观指数

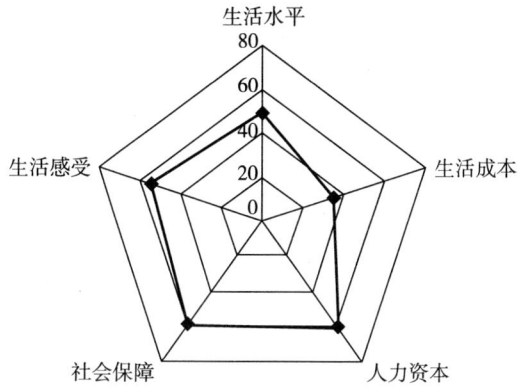

长春市主观指数

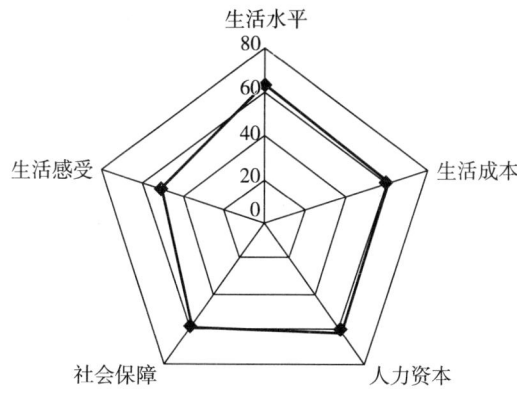

长春市客观指数

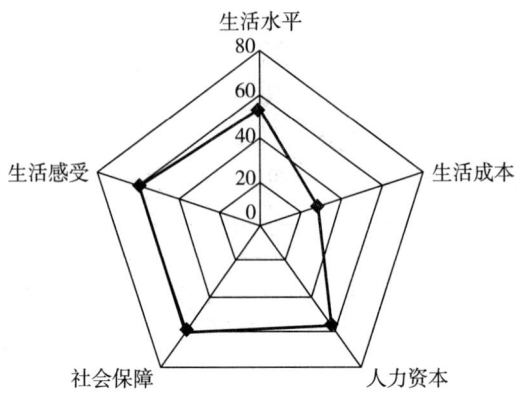

杭州市主观指数

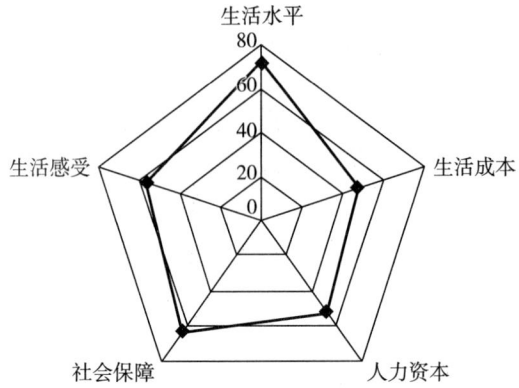

杭州市客观指数

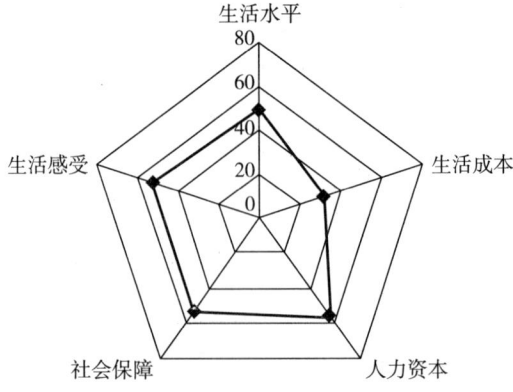

武汉市主观指数

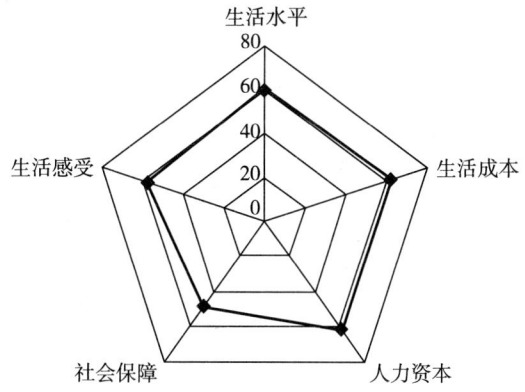

武汉市客观指数

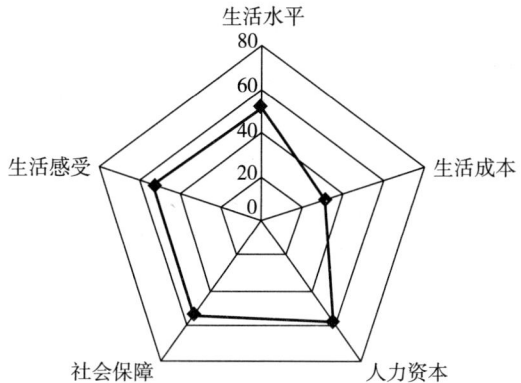

长沙市主观指数

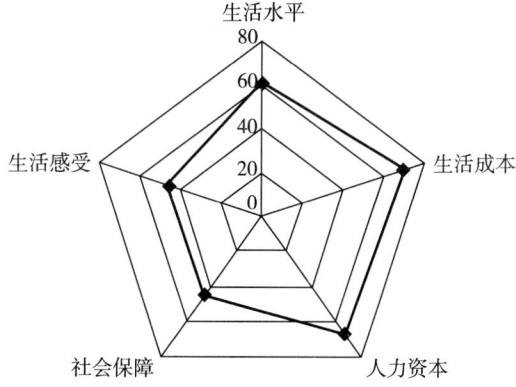

长沙市客观指数

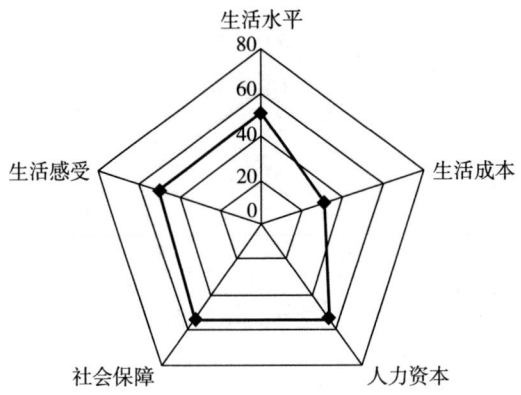

昆明市主观指数

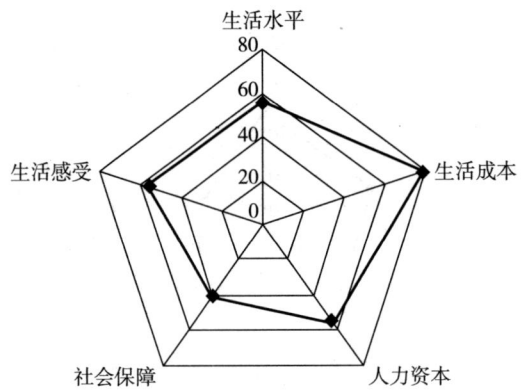

昆明市客观指数

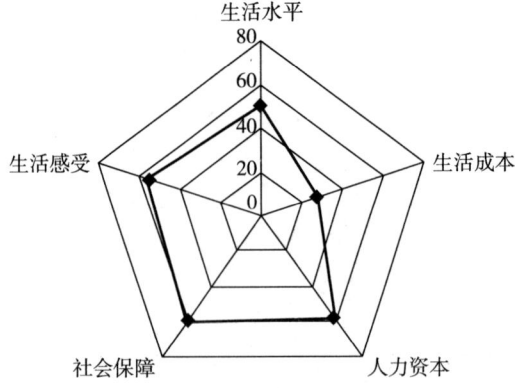

银川市主观指数

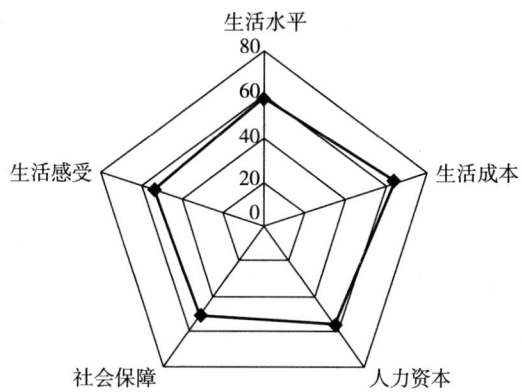
银川市客观指数

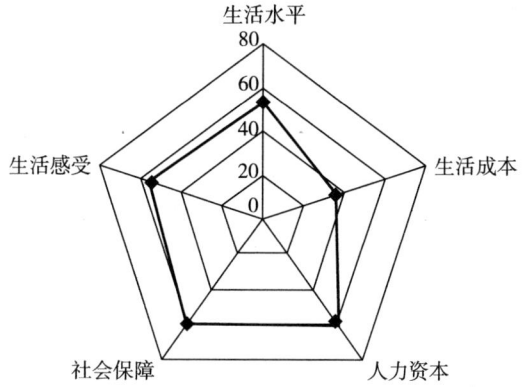
济南市主观指数

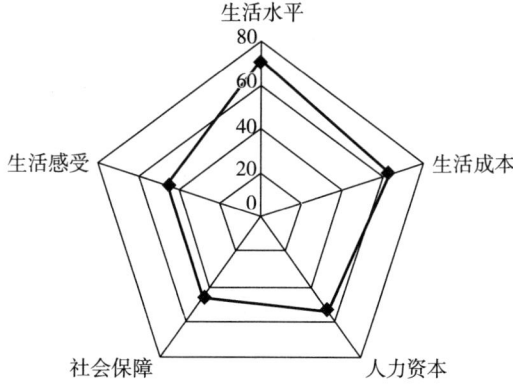
济南市客观指数

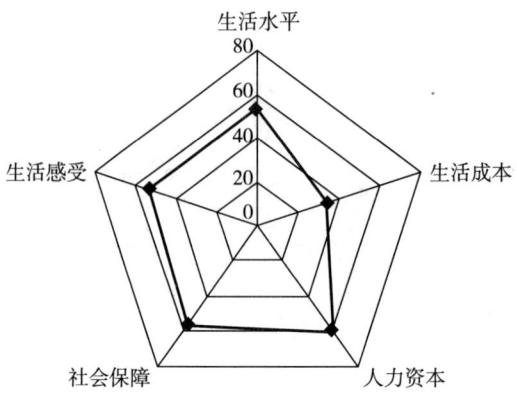

合肥市主观指数

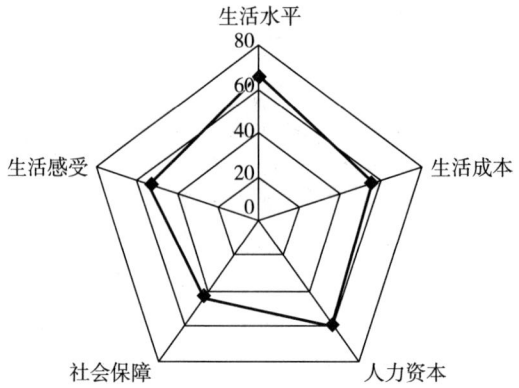

合肥市客观指数

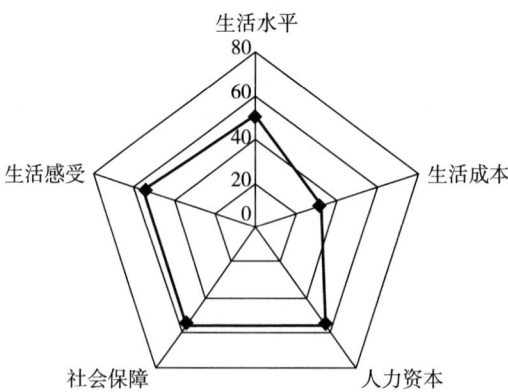

成都市主观指数

2013 年中国 35 个城市生活质量分指数

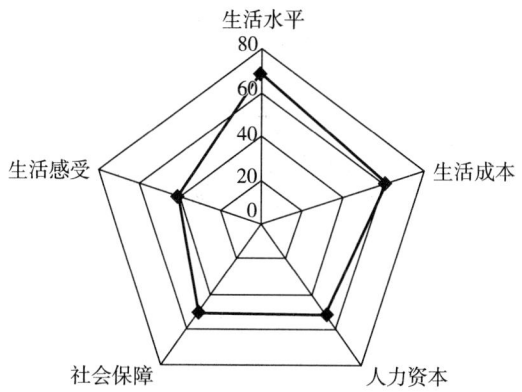

成都市客观指数

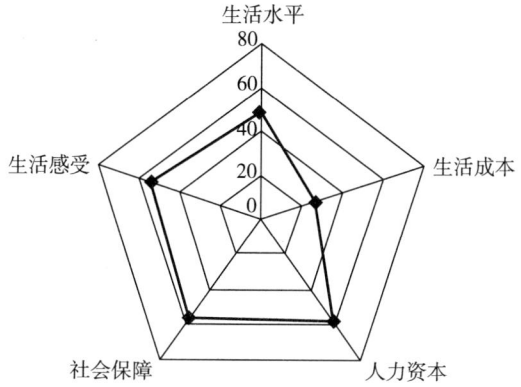

大连市主观指数

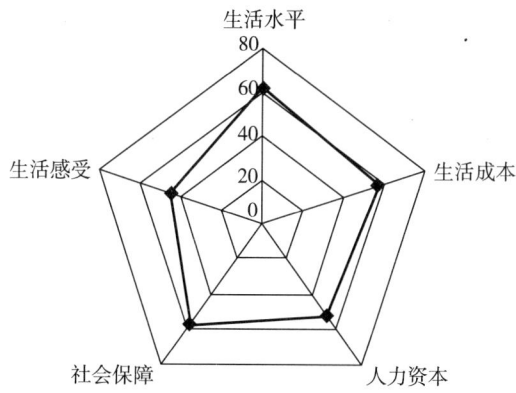

大连市客观指数

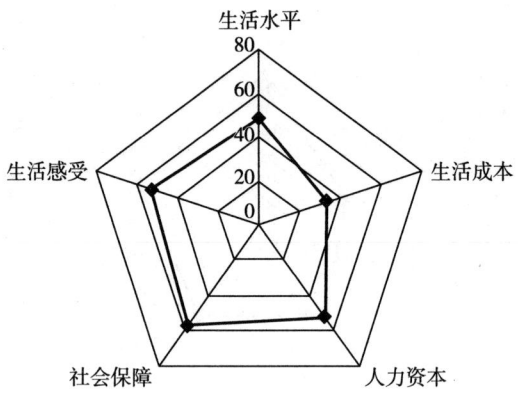

太原市主观指数

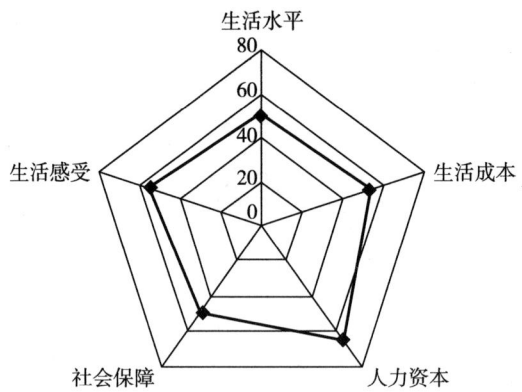

太原市客观指数

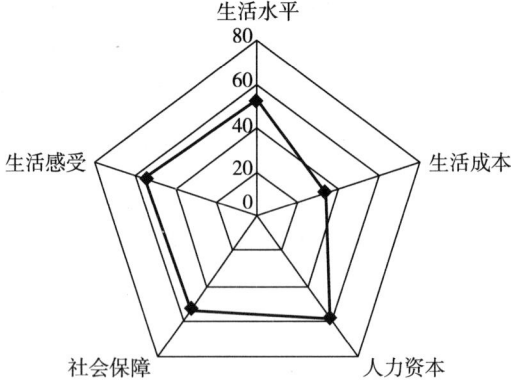

天津市主观指数

2013年中国35个城市生活质量分指数

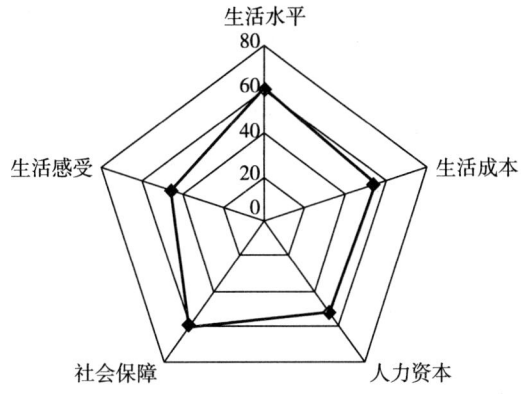

天津市客观指数

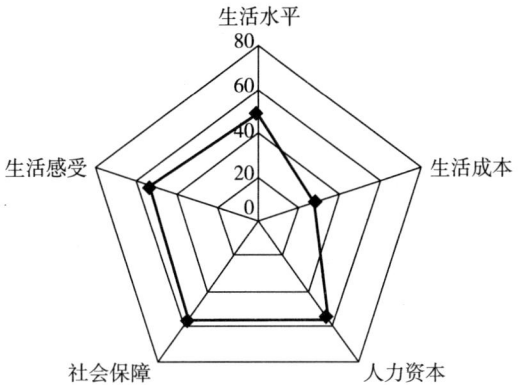

兰州市主观指数

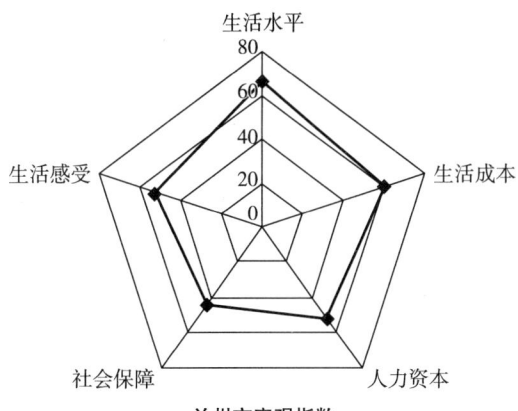

兰州市客观指数

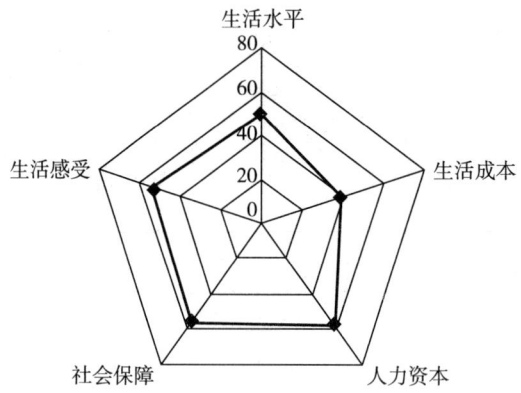

石家庄市主观指数

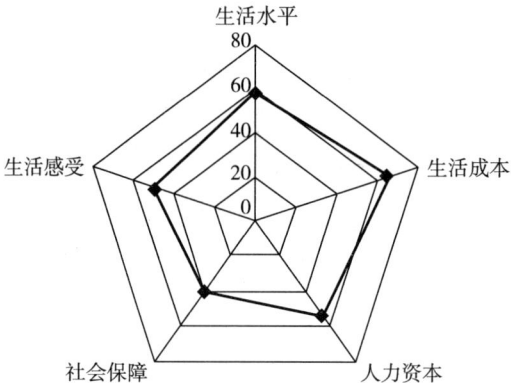

石家庄市客观指数

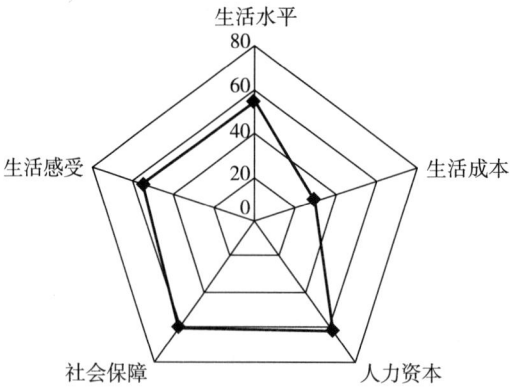

青岛市主观指数

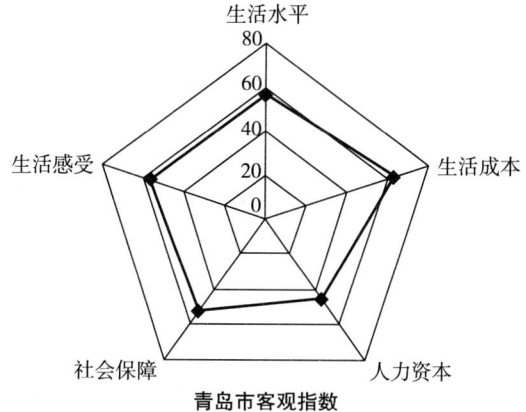
青岛市客观指数

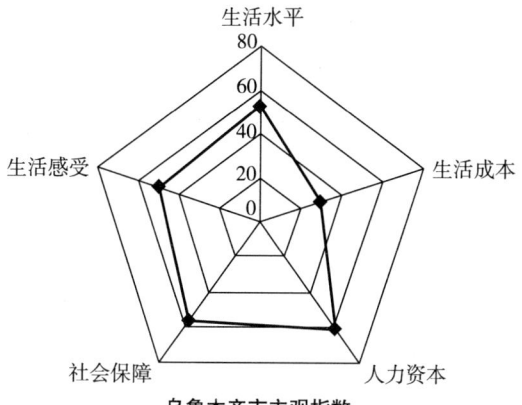
乌鲁木齐市主观指数

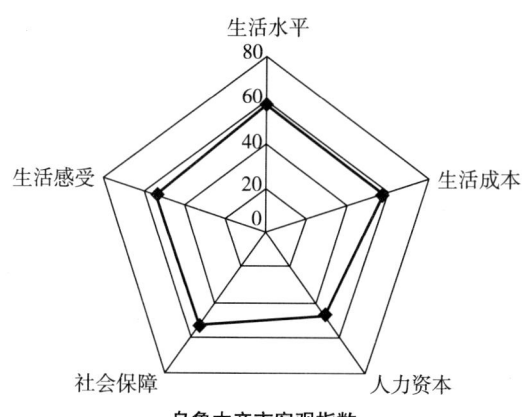
乌鲁木齐市客观指数

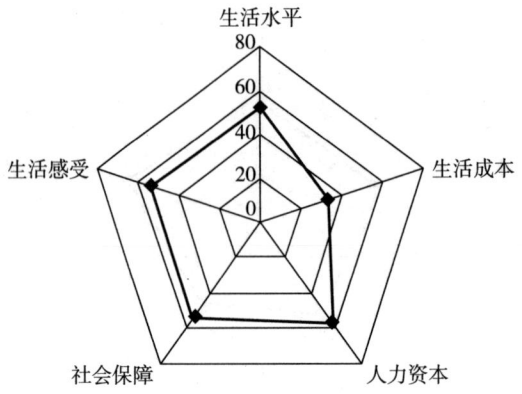

南昌市主观指数

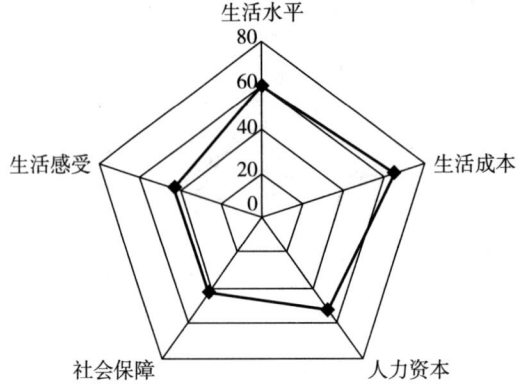

南昌市客观指数

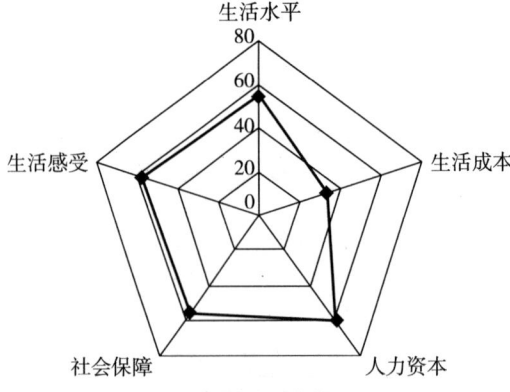

福州市主观指数

2013年中国35个城市生活质量分指数

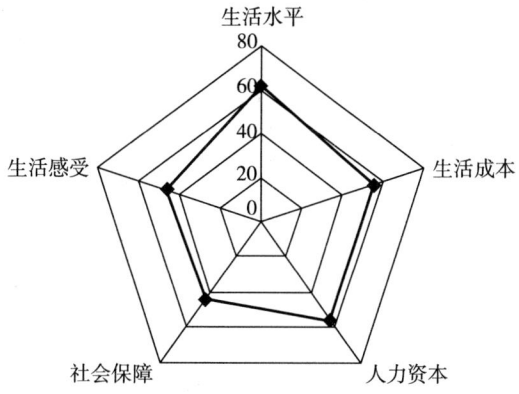

福州市客观指数

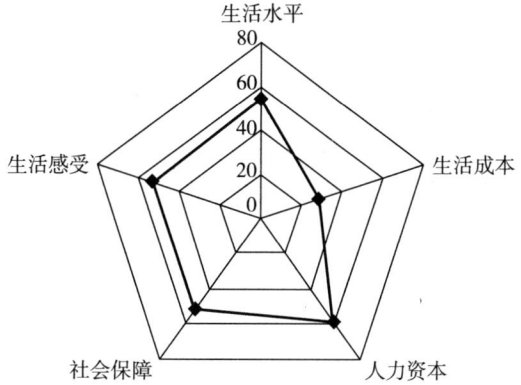

贵阳市主观指数

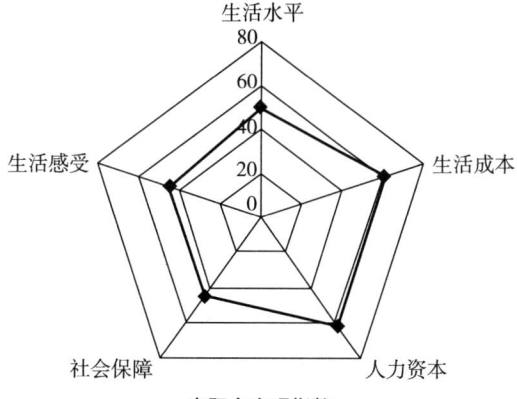

贵阳市客观指数

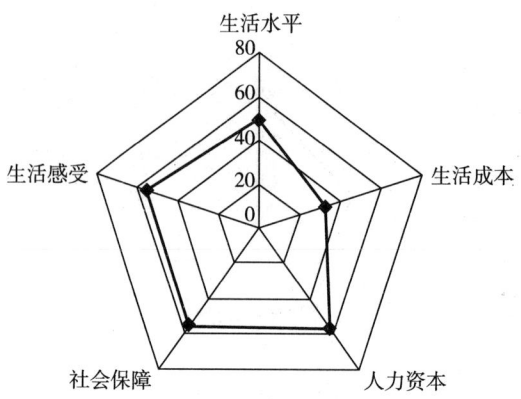

哈尔滨市主观指数

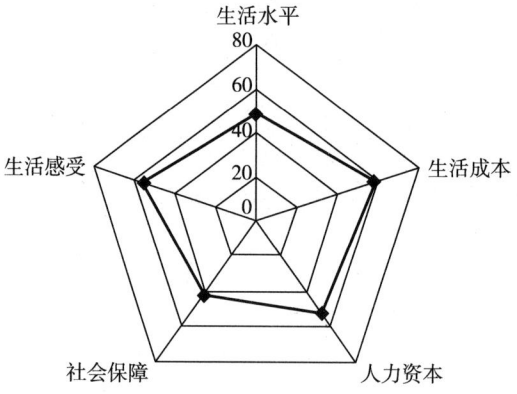

哈尔滨市客观指数

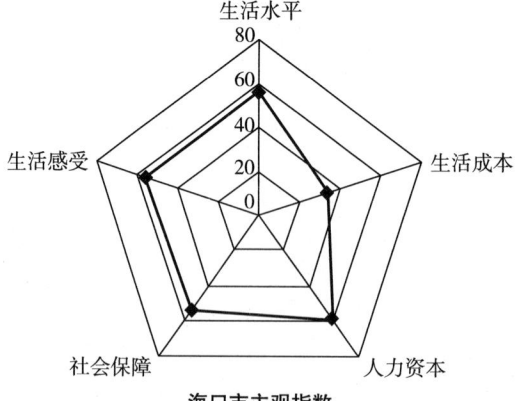

海口市主观指数

2013 年中国 35 个城市生活质量分指数

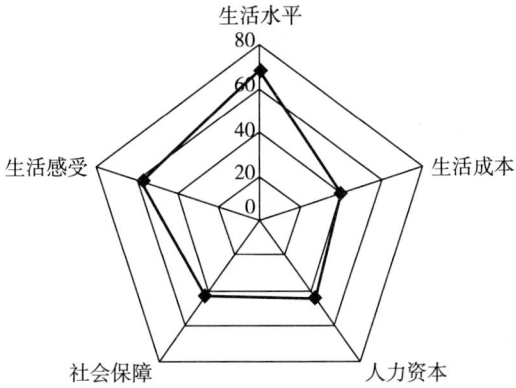

海口市客观指数

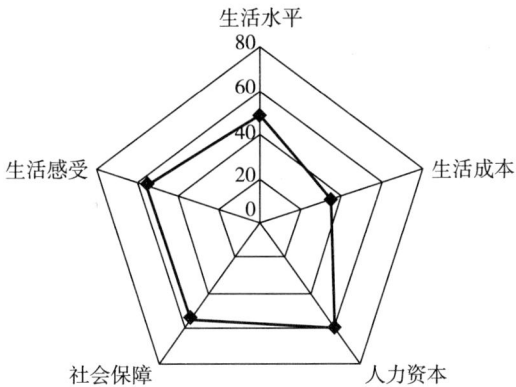

郑州市主观指数

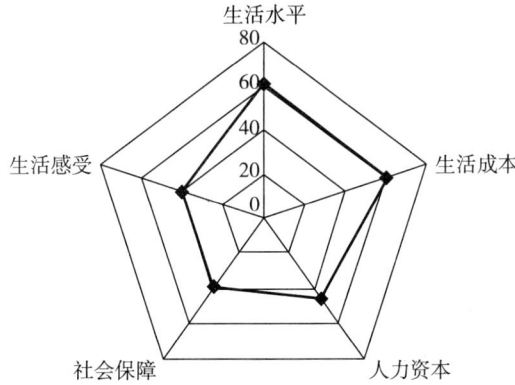

郑州市客观指数

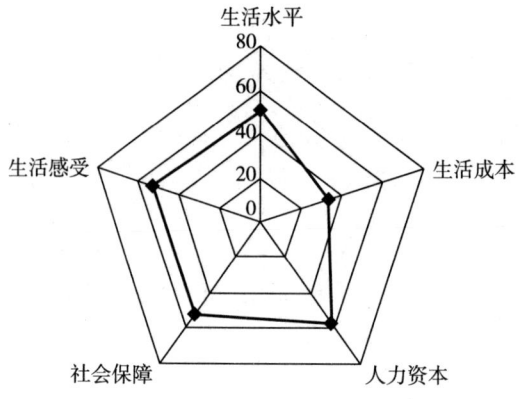

南宁市主观指数

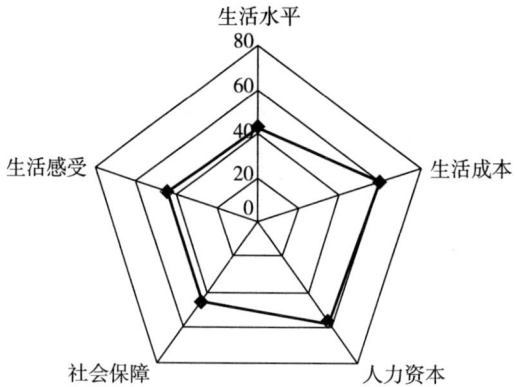

南宁市客观指数

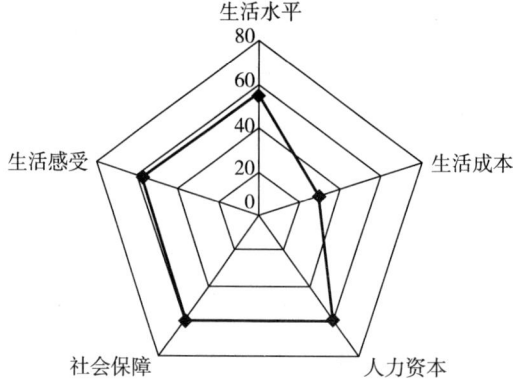

西宁市主观指数

2013年中国35个城市生活质量分指数

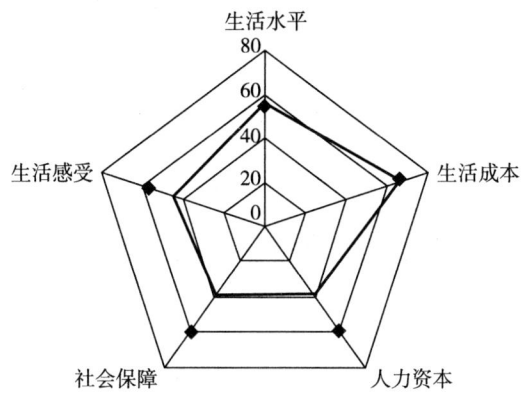
西宁市客观指数

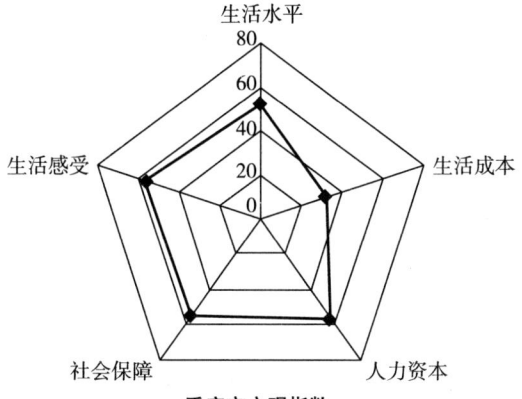
重庆市主观指数

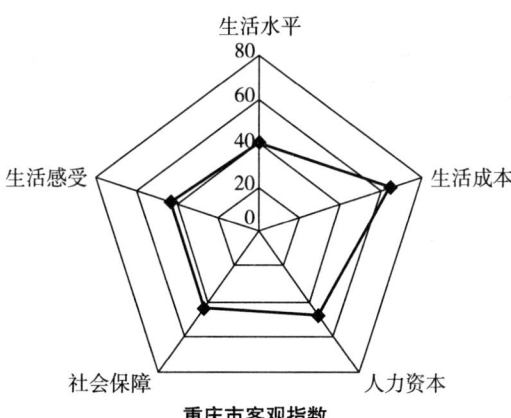
重庆市客观指数

结论与对策篇

B.5
结论和启示

通过本次调查,可以得出以下几点结论和启示。

5.1 城市生活质量整体态势平稳

2013 年的调查结果显示,城市生活质量主观满意度指数得分为 50.87 分,基本与 2012 年持平,维持在满意区间,但满意程度较低。城市生活质量客观指数为 57.75 分,比 2012 年的 54.56 分有所提高。在描述 35 个城市生活质量主观满意度指数的 5 个分指数中,加权平均值从高到低依次分别为:人力资本(58.89,59.42)、社会保障(56.64,59.19)、生活感受(55.07,55.63)、生活水平(52.51,51.28)、生活成本(31.22,28.91)[①]。这与 2012 年的排序相同。但与 2012 年相比,生活水平、生活成本满意度指数有所上升,而人力

---

① 括号内前面的值是 2013 年全国平均值,后面的值是 2012 年全国平均值。

结论和启示

资本、社会保障、生活感受满意度指数有所下降，总体上生活质量主观满意度指数基本没有发生变化。从生活质量客观指数的5个分指数来看，2013年，35个城市的加权平均值从高到低依次为：生活水平（63.39，56.28）、生活成本（58.67，56.10）、人力资本（57.78，57.66）、社会保障（55.26，50.85）、生活感受（53.67，51.89）。[①] 与2012年相比，虽然生活质量5个客观分指数均有了不同程度的提升，但排序发生了变化。总体上看，与2012年相比，城市生活质量主客观指数保持了平稳的态势。

5.2 两个"反差"依然存在

2011年和2012年的调查均得出了我国经济发展过程中存在"两大反差"的结论。2013年"两大反差"是否依然存在，是我们关注的焦点。改革开放以来，我国年平均经济增长率接近10%，实现了高速增长。近年来，尽管经济增长率有所降低，2012年经济增长率降为7.8%，2013年第一季度经济增长率为7.7%，低于预期水平，但整体看，我国经济增长率依旧保持了较高的水平。但高水平的经济增长并没有带来城市生活质量的大幅度上升，城市居民的主观满意度指数尽管进入了满意区间，但依旧维持在一个较低的水平，生活质量客观指数也没有能够达到60分。这表明，快速的经济增长没有能够带来人们生活质量的大幅度提高，第一个反差仍然存在。

此外，城市生活质量主观满意度指数（50.87）低于生活质量客观指数（57.75），并且这种主客观的差距还有所扩大。这种现象在大城市更为显著。如北京、广州、深圳、上海的客观指数排名分别为第1、第2、第5、第8，但主观满意度指数的排名却分别为第24、第31、第34、第20。进一步的分析表明，全国35个城市中，有31个城市的主观指数低于客观指数，比2012年增加了6个。说明第二个反差不仅依然存在，还有扩大的趋势。

---

① 括号内前面的值是2013年全国平均值，后面的值是2012年全国平均值。

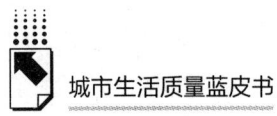

5.3 居高不下的生活成本仍然是影响生活质量满意度提高的主要因素

2013年城市生活质量主观满意度5个分指数中，尽管生活成本主观满意度指数较2012年有所提高，但仍然是5个分指数中最低的（31.22），说明过高的生活成本仍然是拖累生活质量满意度提高的主要因素。具体到城市而言，这表现得更为明显：生活成本主观满意度指数的排名靠后的城市，生活质量主观满意度指数的排名也靠后。例如，乌鲁木齐（28，21）、广州（29，31）、兰州（30，35）、银川（31，18）、大连（32，26）、深圳（33，34）、北京（34，24）、上海（35，20）。生活成本主观满意度指数的排名靠前的城市，生活质量主观满意度指数的排名也靠前。例如，石家庄（1，8）、济南（3，1）、长春（4，4）、郑州（5，15）、合肥（6，5）、海口（8，11）。① 在被调查的城市中，北京、上海、深圳、广州等大城市的生活成本主观满意度仍旧偏低。

从客观指数来看，2013年，35个城市生活成本客观指数加权平均值为58.67分，高于2012年的56.10分，这说明城市生活成本有所下降，但仍旧偏高。衡量生活成本客观指数的3个二级指标是房屋销售价格指数、通货膨胀率以及房价收入比。我们认为，生活成本指数的微降可能主要是经济增长速度下降导致的通货膨胀率下降的结果。2013年全年居民消费价格指数（CPI）比2012年上涨了2.6%，增速呈下降趋势，这在一定程度上降低了人们的通货膨胀预期。尽管如此，我国目前仍旧面临着货币存量偏大、食品价格上涨和输入性通货膨胀等多方面的压力，物价形势比较严峻，政府在未来仍旧需要实行稳健的货币政策，兼顾经济增长和物价稳定的双重目标。

---

① 括号前面的值是生活成本主观满意度指数，后面的值是生活质量主观满意度指数。

结论和启示

5.4 房价上涨预期趋强

2013 年对房价上涨预期的主观满意度调查结果显示，全国 35 个城市房价预期指数加权平均值为 64.65 分，比 2012 年高 9.66 分，这表明居民对房价上涨的预期进一步趋强。2012 年全国主要城市的实际房价普遍上升，与 2012 年 3~4 月间我们对房价预期的调查结果相一致。这印证了经济学的一个基本原理：实际通货膨胀是通货膨胀预期的函数。

2013 年对房价上涨预期的调查结果是否会导致该年度房价的进一步上涨。这不仅引起了人们的担忧，而且构成了政府对房地产价格宏观调控的严峻挑战。值得思考的是，过去几年，在严厉的宏观调控、行政控制、政策打压的大环境中，我国的房地产价格普遍上涨，35 个城市的居民对房价仍然存在普遍的上涨预期，这表明我们对房地产价格的一系列调控政策实际上未能奏效。事实表明，如果不推进制度变革和经济转型，从根本上减少地方政府对"土地财政"的依赖，所有调控房地产的政策都有可能失灵。

房价的高低直接影响着城市居民对生活质量的主观感受。城市居民购买住房的成本与生活质量存在显著的相关关系，同时，过高的房价也不利于城市化的进一步发展，对经济的健康发展也会产生负面影响。因此，推进制度改革和经济转型，在市场机制作用的基础上构建合理的房地产价格形成机制，是我们当前面临的一项艰巨任务。

5.5 食品安全形势严峻

尽管我们没有把食品安全问题最终纳入生活质量指标体系中，但食品安全直接关系到居民的生活感受。因此，居民对食品安全的满意度能直接影响居民对生活质量的满意度。我国 35 个城市食品安全满意度指数加权平均值仅为 41.67 分，处于不满意区间，这与我国当前的食品安全形势一致。

我们认为，城市居民对食品安全满意度不高，与近几年我国食品安全问题频出有关。例如近年不断曝出的毒奶粉、地沟油、死猪肉、混合羊肉等事件，使消费者对食品安全的信心急剧下降。食品不安全已成为不争的事实。与此同时，消费者在食品安全的维权方面，面临着举证难、投诉难、索赔难等诸多问题。食品安全问题的不断出现，暴露出我国食品安全监管体系不健全等诸多弊端。如何提高居民对食品安全的满意度，为消费者营造放心的消费环境，是摆在政府面前的一个巨大挑战。

5.6 加快经济转型，实现生活质量的整体提高

根据调查结果，生活质量整体水平偏低，房价上涨预期进一步趋强，食品安全问题频出，空气质量和社会治安状况堪忧，都要求中国经济必须加快转型和进一步推进体制改革。体制改革是经济转型的前提。经济转型不仅要体现在转变增长方式上，更要体现在人们生活质量的提高上；不仅要使人们的实际收入实现可持续增长，也要让人们享受到较高的社会保障水平和优美的生活环境，要让人们能够呼吸上清洁空气、喝上洁净水、吃上安全食品。我们的城市必须成为人们能够过上有尊严、健康、安全、幸福、充满希望、享受美满生活的地方。①

为了实现经济转型，打造中国经济升级版，各级政府要增强紧迫感，更要主动地采取措施，解决面临的突出问题，这需要政府政策在以下几方面做出调整。第一，应当改变对传统经济增长方式的过度依赖，从要素驱动、投资驱动向创新驱动、消费驱动过渡；从过度依赖人口红利、土地红利，转向依靠改革来形成制度红利。第二，以经济转型升级为主线，以提高居民生活品质为目标，加大投资、统筹发展、加强生态环境建设。第三，继续深入推进民生工程，完善社会保障制度建设。

---

① 《伊斯坦布尔人居宣言》，1996年6月14日。

专题研究篇

B.6
中国与国际房地产价格动态比较*

根据国家统计局公布的全国平均商品房销售价格计算，2013年9月份商品房销售价格累计平均值同比上涨9%，其中现房价格同比大涨12%，期房价格同比上涨8%。但是各城市价格涨幅差异巨大，与上年同月相比，70个大中城市中，新建商品住宅（不含保障性住房）价格下降的城市有1个，上涨的城市有69个。9月份同比价格变动中，北京涨幅最高，为20.6%，温州涨幅最低，为1.8%。房价上涨受到各方面的关注，我们通过构建宏观土地价格模型和住房使用者成本模型以计算均衡房价水平，同时参考房价收入比、月供收入比、家庭负债率和房屋存量等指标，从历史的动态对中国与美国、德国、韩国、日本、新加坡等国家和地区进行比

---

* 作者为：张平，中国社会科学院经济研究所副所长、研究员；吴伟，中航证券金融研究所，研究员；汪红驹，中国社会科学院经济研究所，研究员。

较分析，探讨一国经济在不同经济发展阶段中房地产价格的演进过程，从而理解中国房地产所处的发展阶段，找到中国房地产未来发展的战略。

6.1 房地产价格波动方向与GDP及货币供应同步

6.1.1 国际房价与GDP及货币供应量同步

通过国际比较来看我国房地产业的发展趋势可以发现，我国房地产价格与GDP波动一致，房地产价格的不确定性来自三个方面——经济下滑、国内购房需求放缓及货币条件过于严厉，而且我国房地产价格只有在这三个因素的同时作用下才会发生极大的调整，具体而言可归纳为以下几个方面。

1) 经济增长速度与房价走势基本一致，也就是说经济增长决定了房价的涨幅。我们比较了美国、日本、韩国、中国香港和泰国的房价与GDP的走势，得出的基本结论是房价与GDP基本同步，但波动大于GDP（见图6-1）。

2) 国内购房需求放缓依赖很多长期因素，短期因素更明显依赖于货币条件，即货币供应量。在货币供应量不出现大幅度增加或减少的情况下，房价暴涨暴跌的空间有限。货币供给量基本上是房价的先行指标（见图6-2）。

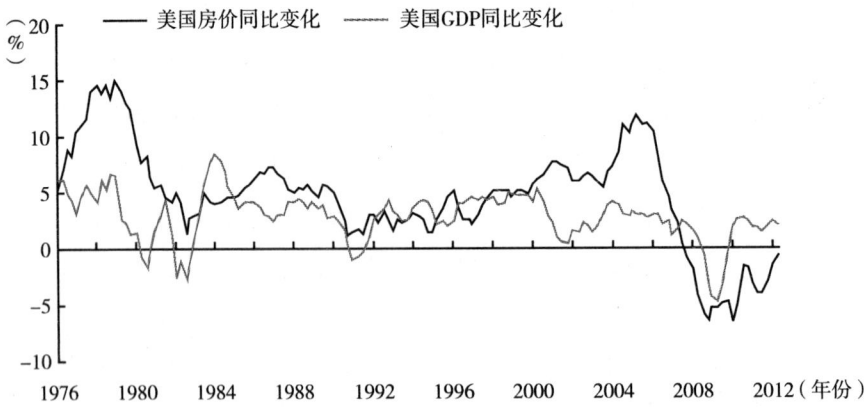

中国与国际房地产价格动态比较

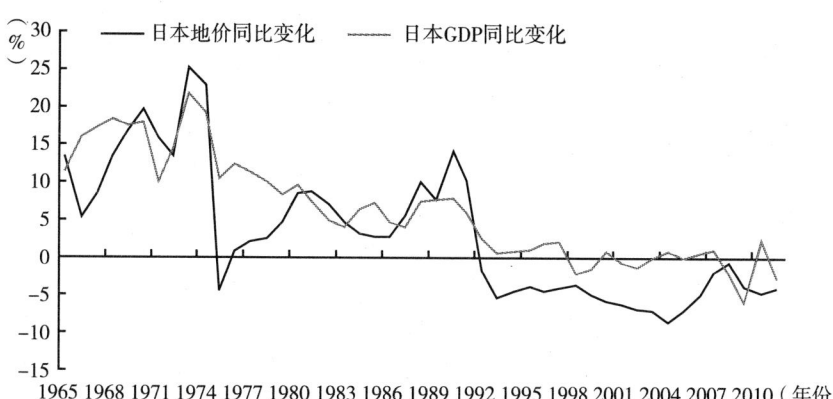

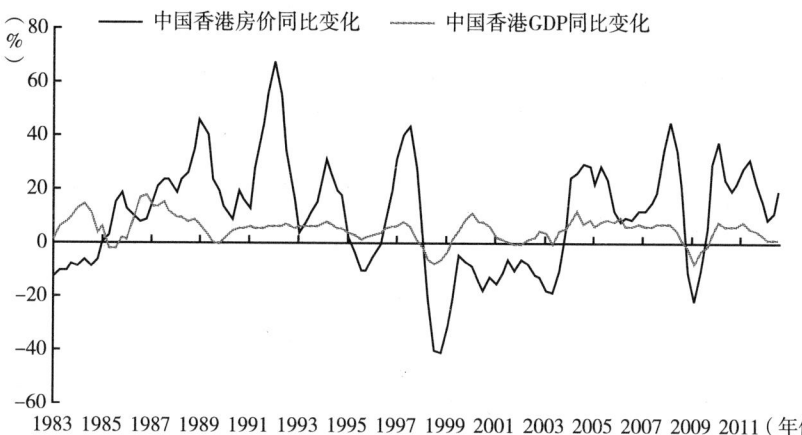

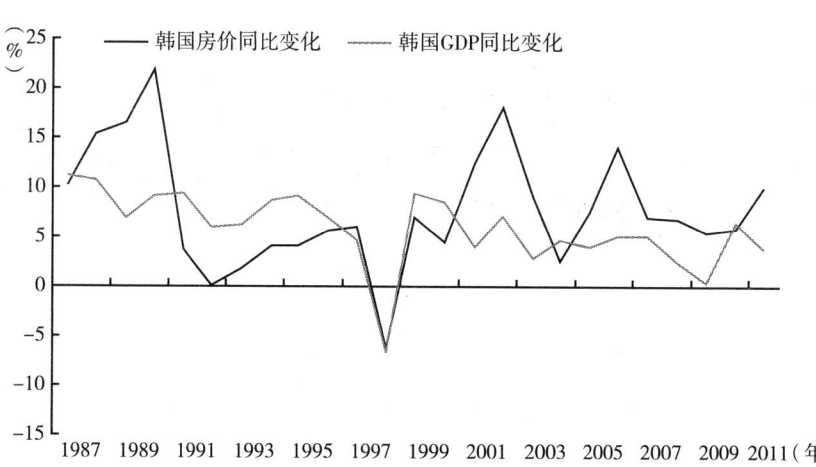

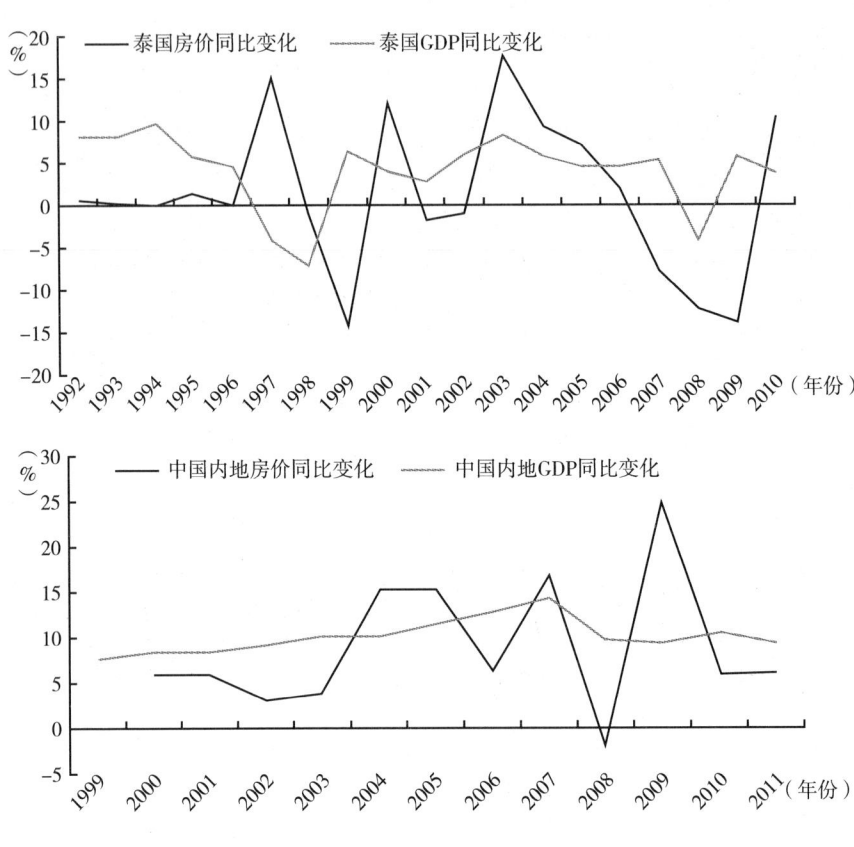

图 6-1 房价与 GDP 同比变化

资料来源：CEIC，WIND，中航证券金融研究所。

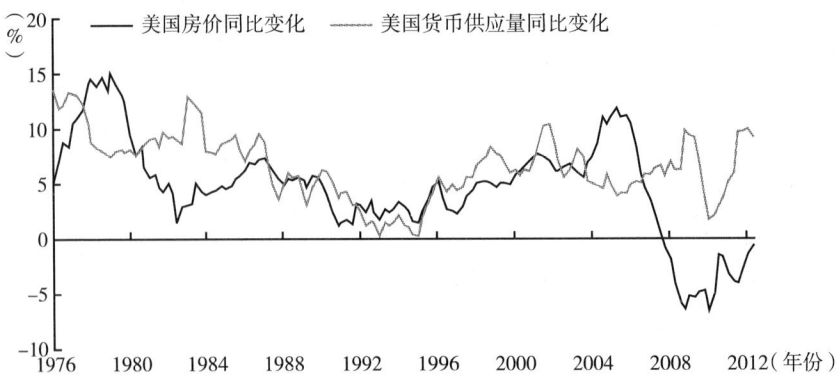

中国与国际房地产价格动态比较

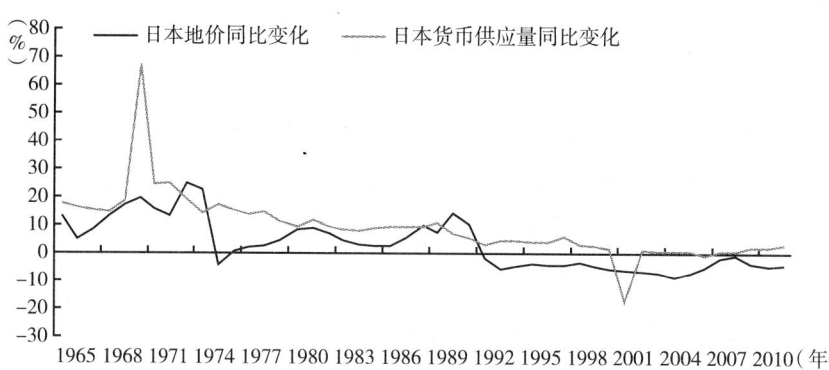

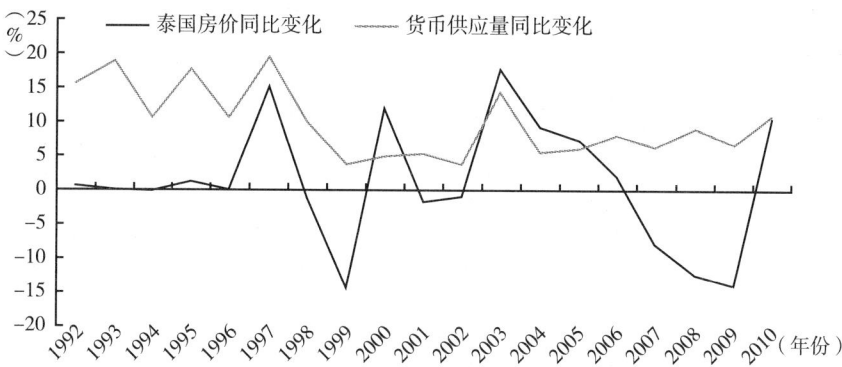

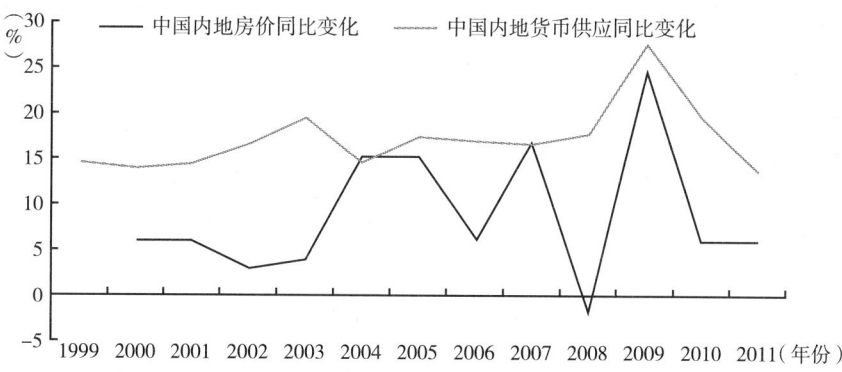

图 6-2 房价与货币供应比较

资料来源：CEIC，WIND，中航证券金融研究所。

6.1.2 中国房地产发展的三个阶段

中国房地产市场的快速发展、居民收入的快速增长、城市化率的快速提升、人民币升值和住房制度改革是推动房地产市场快速发展的重要因素。中国房地产市场发展共经历了三个阶段。第一，调整阶段（1999～2005）。1998年之前中国均采用计划划拨用地，土地要素价格被长期压低，1999～2005年房地产市场处于逐步调整阶段，中国居民对房屋价值的认识不断加深。第二，要素重估阶段（2005～2007）。该阶段以经济高速增长和被人为压低的汇率、土地等价格得到修复为特征，2005年中国启动汇率改革，全球资金流入套利，股权、债权、房产、收藏品等各类资产进入重新估值阶段，70个大中城市新建住宅销售价格指数同期上涨幅度达到25%，北京、深圳、上海和杭州等一线城市住宅价格上涨幅度更大，居民对未来房价的预期发生改变，压抑已久的土地价格得到修正。第三，资产估值阶段（2007年至今）。随着中国经济从高速增长进入平稳增长阶段，人民币升值压力下降，要素价格重估结束，汇率对资产价格的影响逐步减弱。根据艾森格林（2011）的研究，2007年是中国经济增长速度的分界线，一方面，中国汇率调整后相同生产率的劳动力成本与美国趋近，另一方面，中国的潜在增长率已到极限。根据世界银行的研究，预计中国长期经济增速将回落至5%，经济增速放缓和2008年针对金融危机采取的一系列政策导致的资产价格和通胀双升使中国房地产市场迅速进入估值阶段。

6.1.3 中国房地产价格与GDP和货币供应量同步

从宏观角度看，一国的不动产价值是未来国内生产总值（GDP）按预期收益率折现后的净现值。假设未来长期GDP增速和资本成本不变，则短期内不动产的均衡价格取决于初始国内生产总值，其间不动产价格增速应与GDP增速一致。过去13年，中国全国范围住宅销售价格指数增速远低于GDP增速，以1997年为定基100计算，2012年6月份，房价指数

为199，而名义GDP指数为508，按美元计算的名义GDP指数为641，单季度住房销售指数同比增速仅在2010年6月份高于名义GDP增速，2005年以来全国房价的快速上涨仅仅是经济快速增长的一个结果，并没有透支未来的经济增长（见图6-3）。

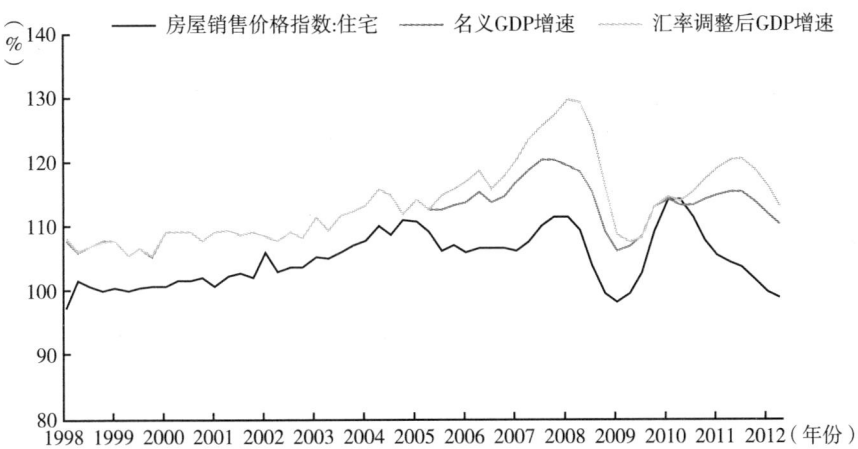

图6-3　中国GDP与房价增速*比较

注：*图中各指标均为本年/上年×100后的比值，单位为%。
数据来源：WIND。

根据Shiller在Long-Term Perspectives on the Current Boom in Home Prices中的研究结果，长期来看，房价本质是一个货币现象，货币供给量是影响房价表现的主要因素之一。我们对1999年以来中国M2与实际房价进行单变量回归分析发现，M2对中国房地产价格有显著影响，能解释大部分的房价变化。2007年和2009年实际房价相对货币供应量决定的均衡房价有一定偏离，但受到2008年经济危机和2010年以来调控政策的影响，实际房价偏离度回落，目前低于货币供应量决定的均衡房价（见图6-4）。

因此全国范围内，中国房地产价格与GDP增长和货币供应数量同步，并没有过多地透支未来。

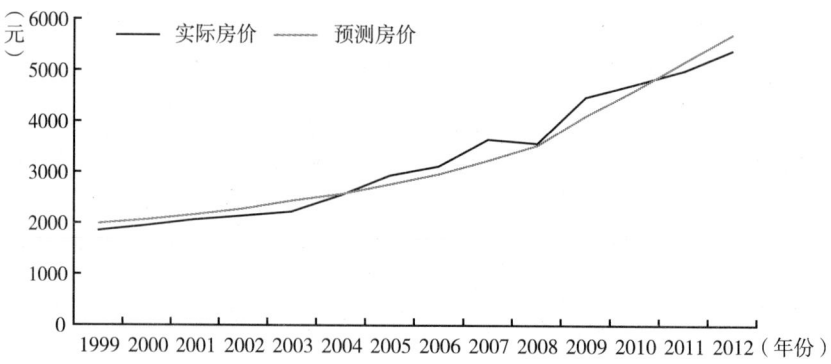

图6-4 中国住房实际价格与货币供给量单方程预测结果

数据来源：WIND，中航证券金融研究所。

6.2 度量房地产价格波动：离均衡值模型

房地产价格波动方向与一国GDP增长和货币供应量同步，与经济可能过热或下滑、货币供应过多或紧缩一样，房地产价格波动可能过高（泡沫）、合理或偏低。衡量房地产价格水平有较多方法，如相对房价收入比、房价租金比等衡量方法。住房使用者成本模型能够反映利率变化以及不同地区房价增长速度对当地房屋价格的影响，因此该模型对未来房价变动有更好的预测作用。Himmelberg et al.（2005）基于该模型对过去25年美国46个大都市区的房价进行分析发现，20世纪80年代房价偏离度较高的城市随后均出现了房价的大幅调整。住房使用者成本模型主要基于资产定价模型的无套利假设，在信贷市场和租赁市场较为完善的地区，同一时期房屋租赁成本应等于房屋持有成本，假如住房持有成本过高，则住房使用者可以转向租赁市场，反之亦然，最终住房使用者的行为将对住房租赁市场和住房买卖市场的供需造成影响，从而影响最终的房屋价格和租赁价格，直至住房持有成本和租赁成本两者趋于一致。

房屋持有成本主要受无风险利率、按揭贷款利率、房屋折旧、税收、

预期房价升值率和风险溢价的影响,而租赁成本主要为房屋租金。模型用数学公式展示如下:

$$r_t = u_t \times P_t$$
$$u_t = r_{ft} + r_{mt} + d_t - \overline{P}_{t-1}/P_t + r_p$$

其中 r_t 为单位租金,u_t 为使用成本率,P_t 为房屋单位价格,r_{ft} 为无风险利率,r_{mt} 为按揭利率,d_t 为房屋折旧率,$\overline{P}_{t-1}/P_t$ 为房价预期升值率,r_p 为持有房屋的其他风险。

我们构建了住房使用者成本模型来衡量中国内地住房价格水平。2012年7月中国内地住宅实际销售价格偏离度为39%,美国(1990)、德国(1995)、中国香港(1997)、日本(1990)和韩国(1991)在各国房地产泡沫破灭前夕房价偏离度最高分别达到73%、131%、152%、488%和876%,与之相比中国内地房价偏离度较低(见表6.1)。另外,目前中国内地按揭贷款利率较高,同2008年相比高出47%,也远高于美国、日本、中国香港等国家和地区。如果重新实行按揭利率85折优惠政策,则房价偏离度将下降至11%。因此,我们认为目前中国内地房价仍较合理,对未来的透支并不太大(见图6-5)。

表6-1 各地实际房价偏离度比较

单位:%

国家和地区	2011年	最大值	最小值	平均值	中值	标准差
美 国	-14	73(1990)	-70(2003)	8	9	38
德 国	-78	131(1995)	-78(2011)	2	-7	56
中国香港	-103	152(1997)	-106(2004)	-2	8	80
日 本	-72	488(1990)	-86(1998)	27	-43	158
韩 国	-18	876(1991)	-48(2003)	284	238	289
新 加 坡	-11	21(2006)	-20(2008)	-1	-5	13
中国内地	48	63(2007)	-41(2003)	8	4	31

数据来源:CEIC,中航证券金融研究所。

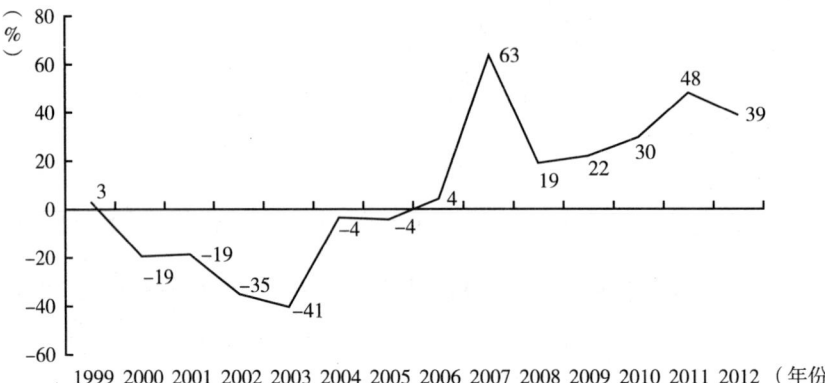

图 6-5 中国内地住宅销售价格偏离度

数据来源：中航证券金融研究所，WIND，国家统计局，Google。

6.3 中国房地产价格波动趋势的多维度因素比较

6.3.1 从 GDP 变化看中国房价

GDP 增速决定了未来长期房价的上涨预期。世界银行预计中国经济增速将逐步下滑，2011～2015 年下降至 8.9%，2016～2020 年为 7.0%，2021～2025 年为 5.9%，2026～2030 年为 5.0%，中国全国平均房价预期增速也随着下降。假设房价升值率等于 GDP 增速，根据前述偏离度的计算方法就可以计算出房价偏离度。比如，假设 2012 年房价预期增速下降至 7.0%，则房价偏离度将上升至 67%，接近美国泡沫高峰期水平，但仍然与韩国、日本、中国香港和德国的泡沫高峰期偏离度相差较远。如果 GDP 增速仍维持 8%～9% 的增速，则房价偏离度将下降至 14%。鉴于我国各区域经济增速和城市化阶段均不同，因此不同区域房地产市场表现差异将较大，区域市场仍存在大量投资机会（见表 6-2）。

表6-2 GDP增速与房价偏离度敏感性分析

单位：%

预期房价升值率 （GDP增速）	2012年房价偏离度	预期房价升值率 （GDP增速）	2012年房价偏离度
8.9	14	5.9	97
8.0	39	5.0	122
7.0	67		

数据来源：中航证券金融研究所。

6.3.2 房价与信贷关系

房地产泡沫往往与信贷的过度发展有关，中国家庭房地产杠杆率水平仍较低，数据较为理想。2011年中国内地按揭贷款余额占国民可支配收入的比例为43%，而美国、德国、韩国、日本、新加坡、中国香港按揭贷款余额占国民可支配收入的比例则分别达到84%、101%、92%、103%、32%和46%。然而，我们需要警惕的是，中国按揭贷款余额2009年开始快速增长，按揭贷款余额占国民可支配收入的比例从30%上升至43%，这说明近3年房地产热潮的背后有信贷的大规模扩张，同时也说明，只要有机会中国居民可以快速地提高家庭负债率水平，从而进一步支撑房地产市场的发展（见图6-6）。

房屋存量价值可以作为评估房地产泡沫的一种方法，但由于房屋本身折旧、位置、各国住房相关税收、金融体系均有较大差异，因此各国之间的可比性相对较小。我们估算中国住房存量价值约为44.9万亿元，占2011年GDP比重为95%，而美国、德国、日本和英国2006年住房存量价值占GDP比重分别达到160%、250%、200%和350%，这说明中国住宅价值仍有较大上升空间。然而，中国1998年以来累计住宅竣工面积为55.8亿平方米，约6000万套，加上1999年之前的城镇住房存量约9000万套，目前中国城镇住房总存量达到1.5亿套，相对于2011年约2.2亿户城镇居民，该数量较高，这说明弥补历史欠账的住宅建设活动已接近尾声。

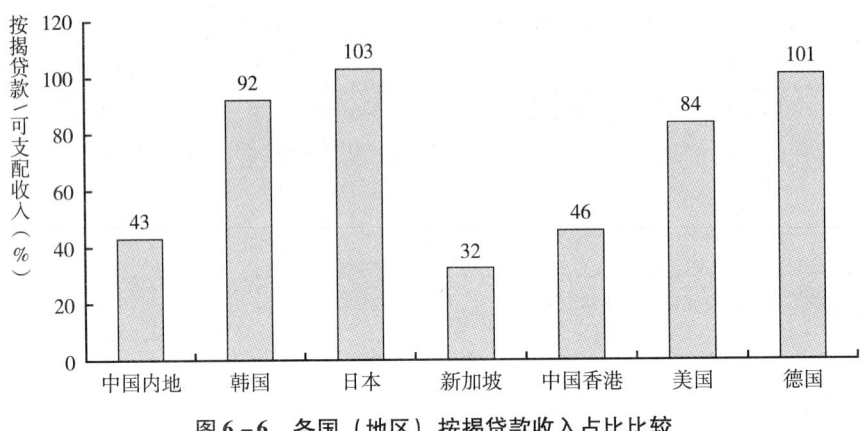

图6-6 各国（地区）按揭贷款收入占比比较

数据来源：WIND，中航证券金融研究所。

6.3.3 从房价收入比、月供收入比看中国城市的房地产价格水平

房价与衍生出的房价收入比、月供收入比是衡量房地产泡沫的一种方式，2011年中国内地整体房价收入比为7.4，同美国、英国和德国等发达国家相比，中国房价收入比偏高，但同中国香港、韩国、日本相比，中国内地目前房价收入比仍处于较为合理水平，且与三个国家（地区）泡沫高峰期超过20的房价收入比差距较大（见表6-3）。由于中国与东亚地区文化较相近，我们认为韩国和日本等对于中国有更大参考意义。中国居民收入增长速度相对较快，同时，计算中国房价收入比使用的是平均家庭收入，而中国购买住房的仍然只是城市中的中高收入群体。按照排名前20%的群体收入计算的房价收入比在4~5之间，与国际4~6正常水平较为接近，因此全国性房价泡沫存在的可能性较小。但北京、上海和杭州等一线城市房价收入比同全球国际大都市相比较高，目前东京、伦敦、纽约、悉尼、巴黎地区，单套住宅总价大多在300万~400万人民币，北京、上海绝对房价已经实现与国际接轨，仅低于新加坡和香港，可见一线城市房价有泡沫化倾向（见图6-7~图6-12）。

表6-3 房价收入比比较

国家和地区	房价收入比 2011年	泡沫高峰期	高峰期时间
中国内地	7.40	—	—
美国	3.10	5.0	2006
德国	5.21	7.0	1994
英国	5.00	6.0	2007
中国香港	12.60	22.3	1997
韩国	11.65	25.0	1991
日本	18.89	39.5	1991
新加坡	5.80	6.0	较为平稳

数据来源：CEIC，WIND，中航证券金融研究所。

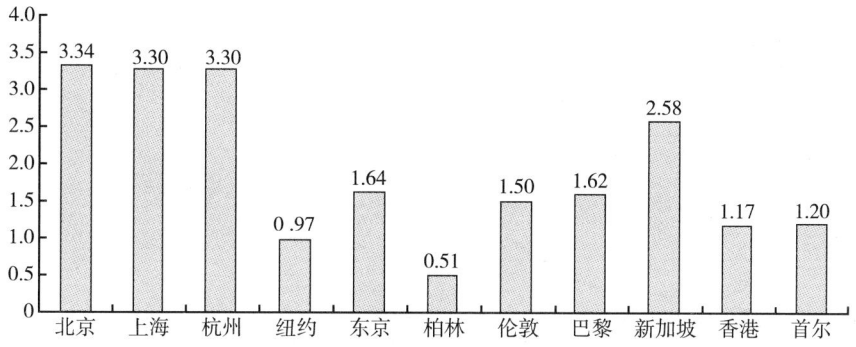

图6-7 2012年6月国际大都市房价收入比比较

数据来源：www.numbeo.com。

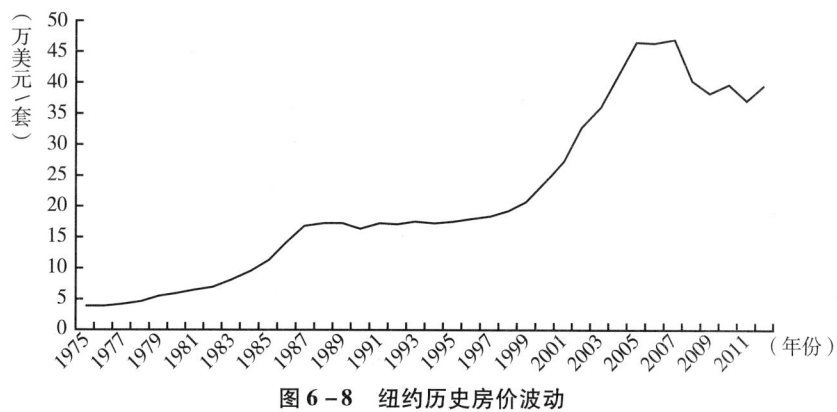

图6-8 纽约历史房价波动

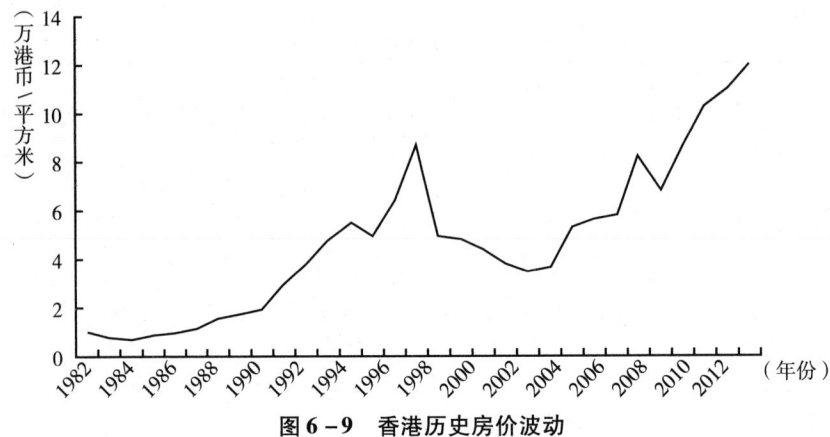

图 6-9　香港历史房价波动

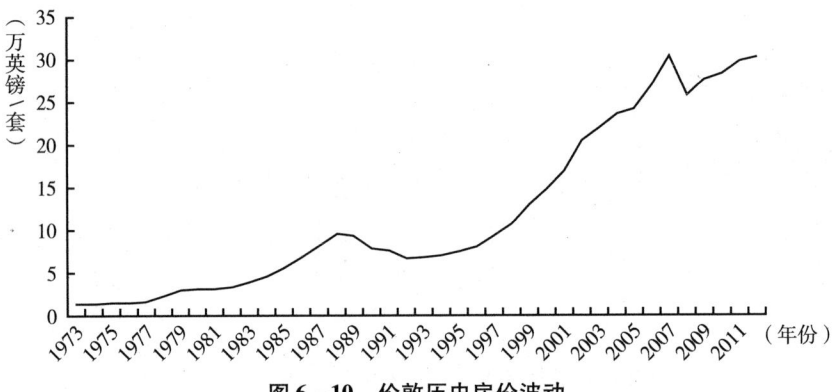

图 6-10　伦敦历史房价波动

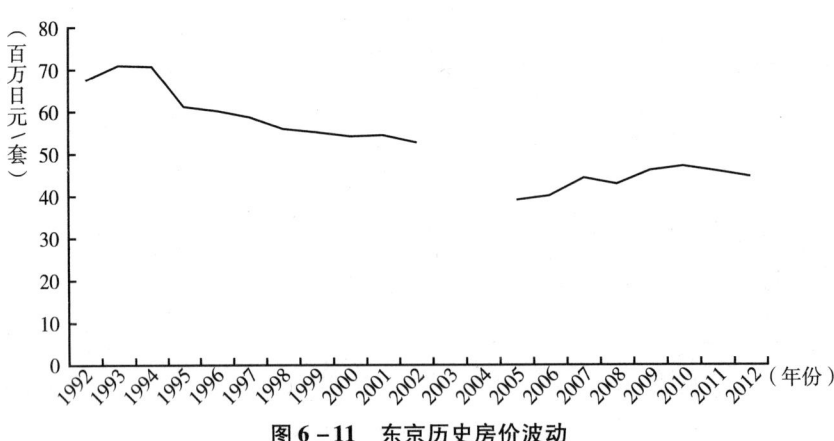

图 6-11　东京历史房价波动

中国与国际房地产价格动态比较

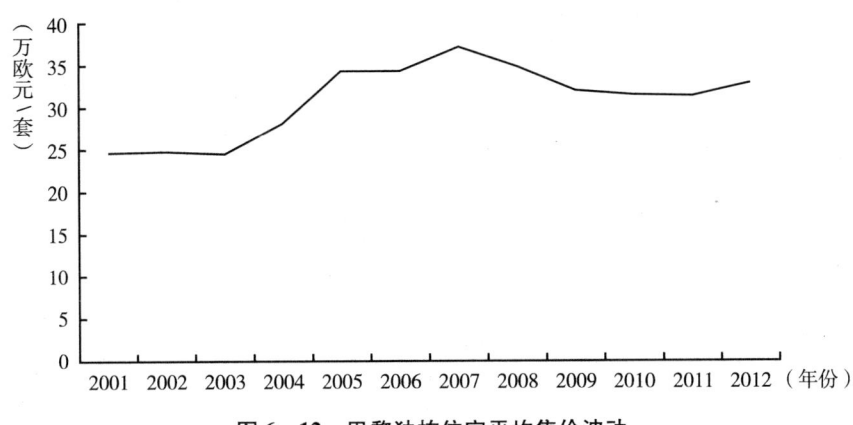

图6-12 巴黎独栋住宅平均售价波动

上述五组数据来源：CEIC，FHFA，日本不动产研究所，香港差饷署。

通过比较月供收入比的数据我们得到同样的结论，即中国内地并没有出现房地产泡沫，但部分区域特别是一线城市的房价有泡沫化倾向。2012年6月，我国一线城市加权平均的月供收入比为1.1，平均房价较刚性需求可支撑的房价上限高出29%，考虑收入上涨和利率下调的预期后，平均房价仍高出20%；二线城市加权平均的月供收入比为0.51，平均房价较刚性需求可支撑的房价上限高出9%，考虑预期因素后，平均房价高出4%；三四线城市房价基本处于刚性需求可承受范围内（见图6-13）。

6.3.4 警惕不利因素

从更长期的角度看，我们必须警惕房地产业可能面临的种种不利因素，抓住机遇实现转型。

（1）人口红利减弱。OECD国家经验显示，人口抚养比与房价负相关，人口抚养比例增加一个百分点，房屋价格会降低3～4个百分点，两者关系在中国则不显著，但随着资产估值时代的来临，基本面因素对中国房价的影响将更加显著。预计中国人口抚养比在2013年达到最低值38.3%，随后开始上升，联合国（2009）预测中国人口抚养比在2020年

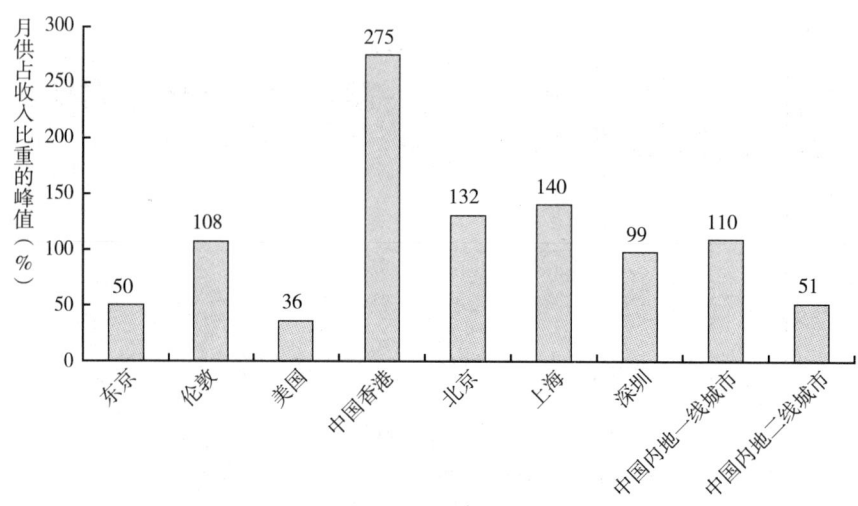

图6-13 全球主要地区月供占收入比重的比较

数据来源：贝塔工作室，中航证券金融研究所。

注：国外为月供占收入比重的历史峰值，中国为2012年6月份数值。

将上升至40.3%，假设其他因素不变，预计房屋价格将降低6~8个百分点。人口红利减弱对应着居民收入的快速增长，该因素将对冲人口红利对房地产市场的负面影响。同时，随着人口老龄化，居民对于养老住宅的需求也将随着上升，部分细分市场将迎来发展机会。

（2）人民币升值结束，房地产市场进入资产估值阶段。在全球资本可以自由流动的背景下，汇率变动对短期住房价格有较大影响，根据有些学者计算（张平，2007），如果汇率年升值1%，则短期住房估值将会推动价格上涨10%，但是其波动具有很强的不确定性，因为汇率的核心作用是影响货币供给。

（3）制度的变化。在中国仍需谈到政策对房地产市场的影响，1998年房改直接开启了中国房地产市场的黄金十年。未来十年，不动产税开征、3600万套保障性住房逐渐推出都将对中国房地产市场的发展造成较大的影响。不动产税将增加用户的使用成本，理论上将降低均衡房价，假设不动产税为1%，预计全国均衡房价将下降16.7%，但如果第一套房不

征税,则不动产税可能使均衡房价大幅度下降。

(4)保障性住房直接增加住房存量。3600万套保障性住房(占城镇人口5.2%)竣工后,预计全国城镇住房存量将达到1.86亿,占城镇居民总户数的85%,保障性住房将分流大量刚性需求用户,为房地产价格制造下行压力,韩国1988年汉城奥运会后推出200万套保障房(占人口比例4.7%),1992年交付,当年房价下降6.4%,至1995年,房价累计下降14.6%,但当时韩国房地产市场泡沫化严重,房价下跌受多重因素影响。

我们认为未来十年对房地产市场的主要影响因素有10个(见表6-4),总体看来房地产市场的发展仍有很大的空间,但必须抓住机遇实施转型,才能在未来房地产转变阶段中生存、发展和壮大。

表6-4 未来十年房地产市场主要影响因素

有利因素	不利因素
城市化进程进入第二阶段	GDP潜在增速下滑
居民收入快速增长	人口红利减退
第三产业快速发展	保障房和房产税等制度性变化
居民杠杆率有提升空间	人民币升值预期减弱

资料来源:中航证券金融研究所。

6.4 资产估值阶段的城市化与房地产市场细分化

麦肯锡全球研究院于2008年发布了题为《欢迎中国十亿城市大军》的报告,认为到2025年将有大约10亿中国人居住在城市,中国将出现221座百万人口以上的城市(目前欧洲只有35座类似规模的城市),其中包括15个平均人口超过2500万人口规模的超级城市,或11个超过6000万人口的城市圈。世界银行《2009年世界发展报告:重塑世界经济地理》

认为，促进长期经济增长最有效的政策是那些有利于地理集中和经济一体化的政策，指出城市化是规模收益递增的重要道路，未来城市圈的集中一体化和功能性发展是城市化的重要战略。

中国2012年人均GDP达到6100美元，城市化超过52%，按国际城市规律来看，城市化率处于30%～70%是快速城市化快速增长期。其中城市化率处于50%以下是加速增长期，其模式是遍地开花式的城市化发展。城市化率处于50%以上增速将逐步放缓，城市化发展趋向于都市圈集中发展，各国放缓点是有差异的。依据国际经验，我国数据模拟的中国城市化增长趋缓的转折点为56%，约在2017年前后。从房地产发展的规律看，都市圈房地产价格平稳趋高，持有物业显著提升。在美国的GDP构成中，住宅开发（Home Building）是归入建筑业的，持有物业（Real Estate）归入金融服务业，在2011年以现价计算的美国GDP中，建筑业的贡献仅为3.5%，而持有物业及相关租赁业务的GDP贡献为12.6%。在中国的GDP构成中，房地产业主要就是住宅开发产业，占GDP的5.6%。从开发投资角度看，2011年住宅开发投资4.4万亿元，但办公楼的开发投资额仅为2559亿元，商业营业用房的开发投资额为7424亿元，两者加起来仅占住宅开发投资额的22.5%。中国进入城市化放缓转折点后，持有物业比重将明显上升，到2025年前后，中国人均GDP将超过13000美元，城市化率将超过65%，届时中国的城市化将主要受持有物业驱动。

1994～2011年，中国城市人口复合年均增长率为4.2%。2011年，中国城市化率已经超过50%，城镇人口达到6.9亿人。麦肯锡全球研究院预测，2025年中国城市人口将增加到9.26亿，2011～2025年复合年均增长率将为2.1%，城市化速度将逐步放缓，但不同类型城市城市化速度将不一致。其中，巨型城市和中型城市（人口150万～500万）将在未来20年里增长更快，2005～2011年预计复合年均增长率分别达到6.9%和3.4%。深圳、广州、天津、武汉、成都和重庆将继北京和上海之后跻身人口超过千万的巨型城市（见图6-14）。

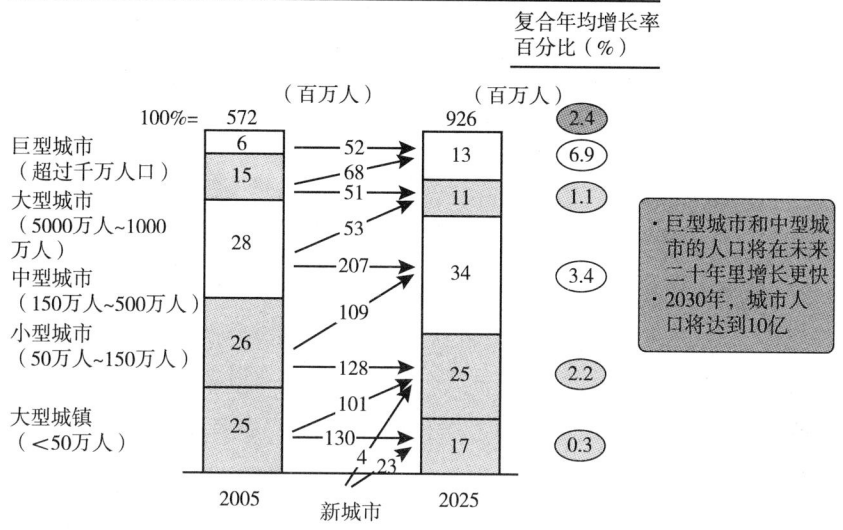

图6-14 中国城市化发展预测

资料来源：麦肯锡全球研究院。

随着城市化进入大都市化阶段，大多数新建城市将位于现有城市周边，其相应经济圈也将形成，"十二五"规划中提出的"两横三纵"城市化战略格局，将随着各经济区经济快速增长，在传统的珠三角、长三角和京津冀经济区布局之外，地产开发商将有越来越丰富的布局选择。我们更新了区域选择模型，从城市化率、抚养比、贷款增速、贷存比以及月供收入比五个维度对各区域房地产潜力进行评估。从城市化潜力和人口红利的角度看，河南、四川、新疆、青海、河北、陕西、湖南、山西、湖北区域较有潜力。从金融资源的角度看，宁夏、青海、贵州、重庆、海南、广西、福建、安徽、内蒙古、浙江、江苏的金融资源较为丰富。同2009年的研究结果相比，天津、湖北未入围，而浙江、江苏、重庆、安徽、广西、内蒙古、宁夏的金融资源仍丰富，福建、贵州、青海、海南为新进入区域。从月供收入比角度看，成都、哈尔滨、海口、杭州、合肥、呼和浩

特、济南、南京、沈阳、石家庄、太原、银川、郑州、重庆的市场仍较健康。同2009年结果一样，三个指标的指向并不完全一致，但中西部的四川区域（成都）同时符合三个标准，而湖北（武汉）由于金融资源缺少和月供收入比过高而没有达到上述标准。

在资产估值阶段，不仅区域市场将进一步细分，而且不同产品类别的市场细分也将加速。与要素重估阶段不同，多重因素将影响房地产市场的表现，且各因素相互作用，导致不同类别的产品市场在不同区域和不同时期差异较大。2010年住宅市场调控使得住宅销售大幅下降，但写字楼、商业物业等不受调控影响的产品反而销售大增。人口老龄化导致人口红利减退后，经济增速出现下滑，但居民对于医疗、交通配套齐全的"一屋三代"产品的需求反而上升。因此GDP潜在增速下滑、人口红利减退等各种不利因素虽然对整体住宅市场会有一定的冲击，但对部分细分市场产品需求反而有促进作用，未来市场产品细分化将加速，企业需要多样化发展以应对市场波动。

综上，未来市场受不同因素影响，市场产品细分化加速，企业需关注客户，关注细分市场需求，以抓住机会，同时规避风险。从大类上分，持有商业物业是企业战略必然的选择，以对冲频繁的住宅市场调控政策对企业现金流的影响。这种持有模式要求企业有更长期的资金来源，要使持有物业的比例达到50%，就必须借助金融模式创新，国际经验要求净租金回报率达到5%以上，例如美国近10年间权益型基金REITs分红形成的回报率约6.1%，2001年以来全球REITs的合理回报率在6.4%左右。在住宅产品方面，企业需要根据住宅市场客户的需求重新定义产品线，以打造自身的品牌和形成核心竞争优势。

B.7 参考文献

中文部分

[1] 杜丽虹：《2009年度地产上市公司综合实力排名报告》，贝塔策略工作室，2010。

[2] 杜丽虹：《租售并举转型之路》，贝塔策略工作室，2010。

[3] 杜敏杰、刘霞辉：《人民币升值预期与房地产价格变动》，《世界经济》2007年第1期。

[4] 国家发展和改革委员会：《中华人民共和国国民经济和社会发展第十二个五年规划纲要》，人民出版社，2011。

[5] 徐建炜、徐奇渊、何帆：《房价上涨背后的人口结构因素》，《世界经济》2012年第1期。

[6] 张连城等：《经济发展中的两个反差——中国30个城市生活质量调查报告》，《经济学动态》2011年第7期。

[7] 张连城：《高生活成本拖累城市生活质量满意度提高——中国35个城市生活质量调查报告》，《经济学动态》2012年第7期。

[8] 张平、王宏淼：《"双膨胀"的挑战与宏观政策选择》，《经济学动态》2007年第12期。

[9] 中国经济实验研究院城市生活质量研究中心：《中国城市生活质量报告（2012）》，社会科学文献出版社，2013。

英文部分

[1] Eichengreen B., Park, D., Shin K. 2011. "When Fast Growing Economies Slow Down: International Evidence and Implications for

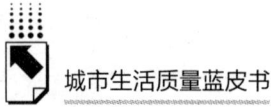

China." *NBER Working Paper*, No. 16919.

[2] Himmelberg C., Mayer, C., Sinai T. 2005. "Assessing High House Prices: Bubbles, Fundamentals and Misperceptions." *NBER Working Paper*, No. 11643.

[3] Hirata, H., Kose, M. A., Otrok, C., Terrones, M. E. 2012. "Global House Price Fluctuations: Synchronization and Determinants." *NBER Working Paper*, No. 18362.

[4] Shiller, R. 2006. "Long-Term Perspectives on the Current Boom in Home Prices." *The Economists' Voice* 3 (4): 1–11.

[5] The World Bank. 2012. *China 2030, Building a Modern, Harmonious, and Creative High-Income Society*. http://www.worldbank.org/en/news/feature/2012/02/27/china-2030-executive-summary.

[6] Woetzel, J., Devan, J., Jordan, L., Negri, S., Farrel D. 2008. *Preparing for China's Urban Billion*. McKinsey Global Institute Publish.

"十二五"国家重点图书出版规划项目
皮书系列

权威·前沿·原创

广视角·多方位·多品种

城市生活质量蓝皮书

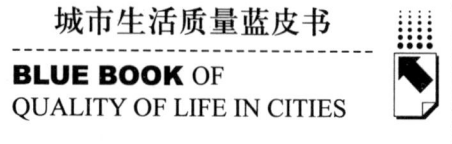

BLUE BOOK OF
QUALITY OF LIFE IN CITIES

REPORT ON THE QUALITY OF
LIFE IN CHINESE CITIES
(2013)

Quality of Life: Stable Indexes
versus Severe Challenges

National Institute for Economic Experimentation

社会科学文献出版社
SOCIAL SCIENCES ACADEMIC PRESS (CHINA)

National Institute for Economic Experimentation

Authors of the main report   Zhang Liancheng, Zhao Jiazhang, Zhang Ziran

Authors of the subject report   Zhang Ping, Wu Wei, Wang Hongju

Final Editors   Zhang Liancheng, Zhang Ping, Yang Chunxue

Researchers attended in this study   Zhang Ping, Zhang Liancheng, Yang Chunxue, Ji Hong, Liu Xiahui, Lang Lihua, Xu Xue, Wang Cheng, Zhang Xiaojing, Tian Xinmin, Yuan Fuhua, Zhang Ziran, Zhao Jiazhang, Wang Yin, Ma Li

National Institute for Economic Experimentation (NIEE)

Since the reform and opening up, especially after the establishment of socialist market economic system, China's economic development has entered a new stage. China has become the world's second largest economy; its per capita income has reached the level of middle-income countries. Meanwhile, China's reform is changing from the "shallow water area" into "deep water area", the reform will face more difficult and complex situation, the "practice trial and error" of China reform must change from "feeling the stones" policy toward the "experimental trial and error" by the use of modern means of simulation and evaluation. On the other hand, from the perspective of academic development, current scientific research is directing to cooperative study and cross-disciplinary collaborative research. This situation requires China's universities, research institutions to break the disciplinary boundaries and sectoral boundaries, integrating all available resources, cooperate and innovate together, so as to face new challenges in China's society. In this context, after a long term investigation, demonstration and carefully prepared, Capital University of Economics and Business (CUEB) and Institute of Economics of Chinese Academy of Social Sciences (CASS) decide to set up the "National Institute for Economic Experimentation" jointly.

Early in the year of 2006, CUEB has set up "Research Center of China Economic Growth and Business Cycle" together with Institute of Economics of CASS. Since 2007, this Center has successfully held six sessions of "Forum on China Economic Growth and Business Cycle" with Hong Kong Economic Herald. This Forum has become an important platform for academic exchanges for well-known economists whose research field focus on macroeconomics. In 2010, CUEB established "Research Center of the Quality of Life in Chinese Cities" together with Institute of Economics of CASS. After months of research on the city's life quality index, the center firstly released life quality index of 30 capital cities in China in the fifth session of the "Forum on China

Economic Growth and Business Cycle" in 2011, which caused a great response, and attracted the attention of international counterparts including the World Bank and other international bodies. NIEE is based on the above research institute.

Currently, the Institute has set up "Research Center of China Economic Growth and Business Cycle " "Research Center of the Quality of Life in Chinese Cities ""Research Center of Quantitative Economics " and "WTO Research Center", and the Economic Operation and International Trade Laboratory, Economic Warning Laboratories, Economic Data Processing and Computer Simulation Lab and Digital Investigations Center.

After integration of the original institutions and laboratories, NIEE proposed the following institutions:

1. Experts Committee of National Institute for Economic Experimentation
2. Research Center of China Economic Growth and Business Cycle
3. Research Center of the Quality of Life in Chinese Cities
4. Research Center of Quantitative Economics
5. Post-doctoral Stations
6. Forum on China Economic Growth and Business Cycle
7. Research Center for Beijing Economic Transition and Development
8. Economic Operation and Warning Laboratories, Computer Simulation Laboratories

The recent tasks of NIEE are as follows:

Firstly, we will continue the research on the economic growth and business cycle of China, and we will try our best to make the forum better and better, and to make it an international forum.

Secondly, we will expand research on Quality-of-life Indexes, gradually extended from the capital cities to medium-sized cities, from domestic to international cities, while normalizing the release of the indexes. In addition, quality of life is only part of economic growth quality, so after the Institute was founded, the quality of the whole economic growth will gradually be incorporated into the institute's research horizon and strive for a group of high-quality scientific research.

Thirdly, the institute will continue to expand the scope of research on economic experiments, carry out experiments for economic reform, policies effect and economic growth pressure, and provide quantitative decision support for China's reform, government agencies and relevant departments, as well as the whole society.

Fourth, we will establish a graduates guidance team with international features, closely cooperate with foreign universities, co-direct master and doctoral students, and enroll post doctors for the benefits of talent construction for Capital University of Economics and Business.

Finally, NIEE have a close working relationship with more than 20 universities abroad, after the Institute was founded, it will carry out extensive international cooperation and academic exchanges, joint research, collaborative innovation, which further international character of the institute.

The purpose of National Institute for Economic Experimentation (NIEE) is: Promote economic experimentation research, prosper science and economic, push forward China's economic system reform, improve the quality of economic growth, and promote economic development. The objective of NIEE is: Through our unremitting efforts, NIEE will become an internationally first class research institute in this field in the future.

Abstract

In 2011 and 2012, the Quality of Urban Life Research Centre under National Institute for Economic Experimentation (NIEE) released the Quality-of-life Index of Chinese Cities (QLICC) [①]. From March to May 2013, a follow-up survey was conducted in 35 cities around China, in order to further the study on Chinese economic growth and residents' quality of life (QOL). Related subjective satisfaction index and objective economy index were thus obtained through statistical analysis.

The survey once again adopted the standard CATI (Computer Assisted Telephone Interview) method. The first 3 or 4 digits of telephone numbers were fixed to ensure widespread spatial distribution, while the last 4 digits were chosen randomly. For the survey, 298,590 calls were made to 257,150 landline telephone numbers and 41,440 mobile phone numbers. 12,759 effective random samples were obtained. The standard error of overall subjective index was reduced from 0.24 last year to 0.19 this year, which improved the creditability of the entire report. Besides the survey for QLICC, two special surveys were conducted about urban house price expectation and satisfaction with food safety. The latter is newly added in order to gain further insights into the QOL of city dwellers.

As is shown by the survey, the average(subjective) satisfaction indexes for 35 Chinese cities is 50.87 (about the same as last year, which was 50.88) - slightly better than the cutoff for satisfaction, which is 50 . Twenty-six cities score over 50 in the satisfaction index, 3 more than in 2012. Among the five sub-indexes satisfaction with living standard and living costs has both improved compared to those of 2012, while satisfaction with human capital, social security and

---

① The English translation for "中国城市生活质量指数" was "Chinese City Life Quality Index" (CCLQI) in 2012 and has been franslated into "Quality of Life Index of Chinese Cities" (QLICC)since 2013.

Blue Book of Quality of Life in Cities

living experience has dropped slightly. Despite this improvement, high living costs remain the most important element which pulls down the satisfaction level with QOL among city dwellers.

The survey also shows that compared to the figures for 2012, the overall level of QLICC has remained stable, with its objective indexes somewhat improved and its satisfaction indexes roughly unchanged. The thorough implementation of life-improving projects by the central government counts for much in the improvement of objective indexes. At the same time, we are still facing severe challenges, such as high living costs, widespread expectations for house price appreciation and worries about food safety, public order and air quality. During the period of transition and upgrade, the government needs to take effective measures to change people's expectations about long-term rises in home prices, strengthen the supervision on food safety, and increase investments in life-improving projects, in order to achieve actual improvement in residents' QOL and their satisfaction with it.

Keywords: Quality of Urban Life, Subjective Satisfaction Index, Objective Index, Food Safety, House Price Expectation

CONTENTS

₿ I General Report

₿.1 2013 : Improving the Quality of Urban Life Faces Severe Challenges / 001

₿ II Overall Report

₿.2 Introduction to the 2013 Survey on the Quality-of-life Index
of Chinese Cities / 007

₿ III Observation Report

₿.3 The 2013 Quality-of-Life Indexes for 35 Chinese Cities / 010

₿.4 Sub-Indexes of Quality of Life for the 35 Chinese Cities in 2013 / 023

₿ IV Conclusions and Policy Suggestions

₿.5 Conclusions and Lessons / 082

₿ V Subject Report

₿.6 Dynamic Comparison of Real Estate Prices in China and
Other Countries / 088

General Report

B.1
2013: Improving the Quality of Urban Life Faces Severe Challenges

1.1 Introduction

In 2011, for the first time, the Quality of Urban Life Research Centre under NIEE released the general quality-of-life index (QLI) and the related sub-indexes of 30 Chinese cities during the 5th Forum on China's Economic Growth and Business Cycle. A comprehensive analysis of the results showed that there existed "Two Contrasts" attendant to China's rapid economic growth: the contrast between rapid economic growth and residents' quality of life (QOL) improvement, and the contrast between residents' objective QOL and their subjective feelings. The 2011 survey provided important lessons for understanding and grasping the overall picture of QOL in Chinese cities.

In 2012, in order for the survey results to reflect the QOL of city dwellers more objectively, more comprehensively and more accurately, the research group increased

Blue Book of Quality of Life in Cities

the number of sample cities, and made some improvements and partial adjustments to the Quality-of-life Index of Chinese Cities (QLICC) System. First, the number of surveyed cities was increased. Second, permanent urban resident population was used in the calculations. Third, the number of survey samples for questions about subjective feelings was also increased. Fourth, the accuracy of survey results was further improved. With a confidence level of 95%, the absolute estimation error of subjective indexes decreased from ±0.27 to ±0.24. Fifth, a special survey on house price expectations was conducted. Main findings of the survey were as follows. Compared with the figures for 2011, the overall subjective satisfaction level rose while the "Two Contrasts" still existed. High living costs were a drag on people's satisfaction level with QOL in the cities. Widespread expectations for rising home prices became a potential problem which might result in even higher urban living costs. The excessive size of a city might hinder improvements in QOL. The objective indexes of QLICC in the eastern regions were generally higher than those of the central or the western regions. Given all this, the government should take effective measures to curb rising living costs, stabilize house prices and prices in general, manage expectations for inflation, and control the size of large cities. These were the keys to improving QOL. The survey did bring us some lessons. For example, the thorough implementation of life-improving projects by the central government helped to improve residents' QOL, but given high living costs, QOL further improvement world not be possible unless fast rise in home prices are curbed effectively, consumer prices were stabilized and expectations for inflation are well managed. As for regional governments, they should pay attention not only to economic growth, but also to increasing investments toward and innovations in the institutional arrangements life-improving projects and of social security, so as to make city dwellers more satisfied with their QOL as their lives actually improve.

From March to May 2013, the Centre launched the third annual QOL survey in 35 Chinese cities after its index releases in 2011 and 2012. Related subjective satisfaction indexes and objective economy indexes were thus obtained through

2013: Improving the Quality of Urban Life Faces Severe
Challenges

statistical analysis and calculation, and would be released during the 7th Forum on China's Economic Growth and Business Cycle this year. This report presents the results of this survey.

1.2 Survey Results and Main Findings

As is shown by the survey, the QOL satisfaction indexes of 35 Chinese cities average 50.87 (about the same with the average of 50.88 last year) - a squeak up to the satisfaction level, since 50 is the critical point between satisfaction and dissatisfaction. 26 cities score over 50 in satisfaction index, 3 more than in 2012. The five sub-indexes of satisfaction index average respectively: human capital (58.89), social security (56.64), living experience (55.07), living standard (52.51) and living costs (31.22). Compared with 2012, the satisfaction with living standard and living costs has improved, while that of human capital, social security and living experience has dropped slightly. Despite its improvement, high living costs remains the most important element which pulls down the satisfaction with QOL among city dwellers.

Cities ranked top 10 in the list of QOL satisfaction (subjective) index are: Jinan (1), Qingdao (2), Xiamen (3), Changchun (4), Hefei (5), Xining (6), Ningbo (7), Shijiazhuang (8), Fuzhou (9) and Hangzhou(10), including 7 eastern cities, 2 central cities and 1 western city. The bottom 10 cities are: Dalian (26), Taiyuan (27), Nanning (28), Harbin (29), Guiyang (30), Guangzhou (31), Wuhan (32), Kunming (33), Shenzhen (34) and Lanzhou (35), including 3 eastern cities, 3 central cities and 4 western cities.

The special survey on house price expectations shows that the average for house price expectation indexes of 35 cities is 64.65 (17.6% higher than in 2012), which indicates not only widespread expectations for rising home prices, but also a bigger expected increase than that of 2012. Cities ranked top 10 in the list of house price expectation index are: Guangzhou (68.64), Xining (68.33), Urumqi (67.37), Nanchang (66.73), Zhengzhou (66.60), Hefei (66.07), Shanghai (65.97), Shenzhen

003

Blue Book of Quality of Life in Cities

(65.96), Yinchuan (65.93) and Nanjing (65.92). In addition, the 10 cities for which the biggest annual increases are expected are: Qingdao (37.9%), Hangzhou (33.2%), Jinan (31.4%), Beijing (26.3%), Changchun (24.4%), Hefei (23.7%), Shanghai (23.7%), Ningbo (22.6%), Changsha (22.1%) and Fuzhou (22%).[①]

The survey on the satisfaction with food safety shows that the average for satisfaction indexes of food safety is 41.67, which is below the satisfaction level. Among the 35 cities, only Xiamen scores over 50. Generally speaking, city dwellers have low satisfaction level with food safety. In other words, except for Xiamen, residents in the other 34 cities are not satisfied with food safety. Cities that ranked top 10 in the list of food safety satisfaction index are: Xiamen (53.06), Xining (49.44), Haikou (46.98), Chongqing (45.67), Yinchuan (45.05), Guiyang (44.49), Chengdu (44.39), Ningbo (44.03), Beijing (43.55) and Shenzhen (43.25). The bottom 10 cities are: Wuhan (36.47), Taiyuan (36.87), Changsha (36.90), Zhengzhou (37.08), Shenyang (38.49), Shijiazhuang (38.51), Lanzhou (38.84), Shanghai (39.12), Fuzhou (39.24) and Harbin (39.24). In addition, classified gender, male interviewees are more satisfied with food safety (43.61) than females (39.46). Classified by age, interviewees from 20 to 30 years old are the most satisfied with food safety (43.68), while the ones from 41 to 60 years old are the least satisfied (39.56).

The average for objective indexes (social and economic data index) is 57.75 - better than the 2012 average of 54.56. Thirty-three cities score 50 or more, 2 more than in 2012. The averages of the five sub-indexes are, respectively, living standard (63.39), living costs (58.67), human capital (57.78), social security (55.26) and living experience (53.67). Compared to 2012, all of them represent improvements. Cities ranked top 10 in the list of objective index are: Beijing (69.80), Guangzhou (66.85), Nanjing (66.65), Xi'an (64.65), Shenzhen (63.93), Hohhot (62.22), Xiamen (61.89), Shanghai (61.78), Ningbo (61.47) and Shenyang (59.99). The bottom 10 cities are: Chongqing (47.83), Xining (49.29), Nanning (50.00), Zhengzhou (50.54), Haikou (51.50), Harbin (51.86), Guiyang (52.45), Fuzhou (52.66), Nanchang (53.03) and

---

① The percentages in the brackets are obtained by: subtracting the score of 2012 from the score of 2013, then dividing the difference by the score of 2012.

Urumqi (54.59). Eastern regions generally have higher objective indexes than the central or the western regions.

Findings of the survey show that, compared with the results of 2012, the overall level of QLICC remains stable, with its objective indexes somewhat improved and its satisfaction indexes roughly unchanged. The "Two Contrasts" still exist in the development of Chinese economy. High living costs remain the most important element that affects QOL satisfaction level. Expectations for rising home prices are strong. House prices tend to perk further up. The problem of food safety is serious. At present, to improve the quality of urban life, we are facing five severe challenges, such as high living costs, widespread expectations for rising home prices, and worries about food safety, public order and air quality. Given all this, we will have to accelerate economic transition, upgrade the Chinese economy, and promote the reform of the economic system. To achieve these goals, it will be necessary for the government to make the following adjustments. First, we should not be over-dependent on the traditional model of economic growth, and should transition from being driven by production factors and investment to being driven by innovations and consumption, from being over-dependent on population dividend and land dividend to generating institutional dividend through reform. Second, we should plan well, carry out economic transformation and upgrade, raise residents' QOL, increase investments, and improve the ecological environment. Third, we should continue implementing life-improving projects and better the social security system.

1.3　Report Outline

The second part of the book is an explanation of the adopted methods, the sampling choices, and the set-up and adjustments to the QLICC system in the 2013 survey.

The third part is an introduction of and related explanations about the general information and the ranking system of the survey, including the satisfaction indexes and the objective indexes (social and economic data indexes) of the 35 cities. Besides, there are also the results of house price indexes and food safety satisfaction

 Blue Book of Quality of Life in Cities

indexes – the two special surveys. For the convenience of analyzing QOL changes dynamically, the general index and ranking of each city are also listed in this part, and compared with the overall indexes of 2011 and 2012.

The fourth part is the survey results of all the sub-indexes of QLICC, from which changes in both satisfaction indexes and objective indexes can be seen clearly. In this part, we provide the sub-indexes and their respective rankings of each city, along with the radar charts for primary indicators and the results of the dynamic comparison.

The fifth part is about main findings and lessons from the survey.

Last, we Conducted a Special research on the "comparison of real estate prices in China and other countries", which is presented in the sixth part.

Overall Report

B.2

Introduction to the 2013 Survey on the Quality-of-life Index of Chinese Cities

To ensure the continuity and the comparability of survey results, the 2013 survey retained the whole set of adopted method, sample choosing and index system set-up used last year, while making slight adjustments and improvements.

2.1 Introduction to the Survey and the Related Adjustments

There are still 35 city samples in the 2013 survey, including 30 provincial capitals and 5 municipalities separately listed on the State plan. To obtain their satisfaction indexes, again we adopted the standard CATI (Computer Assisted Telephone Interview) method for the survey and the stratified two-stage random sampling method for the drawing of fixed telephone numbers. In stage one, stratified sampling was performed according to the distribution of surveyed cities. In stage two, the same sampling method was again adopted based on telephone numbers within the administrative division of each city to ensure widespread spatial distribution, while the last 4 digits

007

 Blue Book of Quality of Life in Cities

of telephone numbers were chosen through random digit dialing to guarantee the randomness of sample choosing. Besides, a survey on mobile phone users was newly added this year, in which extensiveness of spatial distribution and randomness of samples choosing were stressed as well. For the survey, 298,590 calls were made to 257,150 fixed telephone numbers and 41,440 mobile phone numbers. 12,759 effective random samples were obtained. The standard error of overall subjective indexes was reduced to 0.19, which enhanced the creditability of the survey.

As for objective indexes, the biggest difference is that the permanent resident population of the cities was used in calculating certain per capita objective indexes this year, while the population of the municipal district had been used in some cities last year. Result of the 6th national census served as the criterion of permanent resident population. Using permanent resident population made the evaluation of QOL more accurate, but it may lead to technical changes in the objective indexes of some cities.

2.2 Set–up of Subjective and Objective Index Systems and Special Surveys

In 2013, the QLICC System still consists of two parts: the subjective satisfaction index system and the objective index (social and economic data index) system, same as the structure of 2012. The subjective index system is made up of the following 5 sub-indexes: living standard, living costs, human capital, social security and living experience. Among them, the satisfaction index of living standard was again divided into income status and income expectation, weighting 50% each. In the same way, the satisfaction index of social security was divided into health care and safety condition, and the satisfaction index of living experience was divided into pace of life and living convenience. Thus, we obtained 8 subjective questions for the satisfaction survey, and each question was provided with 5 different choices of "very satisfied", "satisfied", "average", "not satisfied" and "very dissatisfied". Then we asked the interviewees to answer these questions, and assigned different values to their answers, which in turn generated the satisfaction indexes. The abovementioned

Introduction to the 2013 Survey on the Quality-of-life Index of Chinese Cities

8 sub-indexes concerned not only people's income status and living costs, but also the livability of their cities and the pressures of life. In view of the present stage of economic development, we believe the sub-indexes can generally reflect residents' subjective feelings toward the QOL in their cities. [1]

Besides the special survey on house price expectation, a new survey on food safety was also added to the telephone survey. House price expectation indexes were obtained by asking interviewees the subjective question of whether the house prices in their cities would rise or fall (in the coming 1-2 years), requiring them to choose from the 5 options of "surge", "rise", "even", "fall" and "crash", and then assigning different values to their answers. Similarly, the satisfaction indexes of food safety were obtained by asking interviewees whether they were satisfied with the food safety in their cities, requiring them to choose from the 5 options of "very satisfied", "satisfied", "average", "not satisfied" and "very dissatisfied", and then assigning different values to their answers. Results of the two special surveys were not calculated in the QLICC system, but they might serve as references for resident' satisfaction with QOL.

The objective index system of QLICC consists of the following 5 objective sub-indexes: living standard, living costs, human capital, social security and living experience. The 5 sub-indexes are in turn made up of 8 primary indicators and 20 secondary indicators. On the basis of these 20 economic indicators, we obtained the 8 primary indicators of QOL with the weighted average normalization method. Then we averaged the primary indicators to generate the 5 objective sub-indexes. At last, we applied the efficacy coefficient method to make adjustments, so that the sub-indexes might be connected with the satisfaction indexes. [2] It should be noted that, the objective data of the 20 secondary indicators were chosen from official documents, and the results of calculation reflected the economic conditions of 2012.

---

[1] For specifics of the index system, please refer to: Zhang, Liancheng et al., "High Living Costs Encumbering Improvement in Satisfaction with the Urban Quality of Life——Report on Life Quality of 35 Chinese Cities (2012)", *Economic Perspectives*, Vol. 7, 2012. See also the Blue Book of *Report on Chinese City Life Quality (2012)*, Social Sciences Academic Press (China), February 2013.

[2] The 5 municipalities separately listed on the State plan are not included. The method of calculating the average value for the 35 Chinese cities is to calculate the weighted average of the sub-indexes based on the distribution of the samples. This calculating method is also applied to the averaging of sub-indexes for the subjective satisfaction, as well as to theaverage values in the special survey.

009

Observation Report

B.3

The 2013 Quality-of-Life Indexes for 35 Chinese Cities

Table 3.1 and Table 3.2 list QLI (including subjective satisfaction index and objective index) and ranking information of the 35 surveyed provincial capitals and municipalities directly under the Central Government or separately listed on the State plan.

3.1 2013 Subjective Satisfaction Index of QLICC

Survey result and ranking of satisfaction indexes in 2013 are shown as below in Table 3.1:

As it is shown in Table 3.1, the weighted average of satisfaction indexes is 50.87 (about the same with the weighted average of 50.88 last year) - a squeak up to the satisfaction level, since 50 is the critical point between satisfaction and dissatisfaction. 26 cities score over 50 on satisfaction index, 3 cities more than in 2012. 4 out of the 5 municipalities separately listed on the State plan score over 50,

The 2013 Quality-of-Life Indexes for 35 Chinese Cities

Table 3.1   Subjective Satisfaction Index of the 35 Chinese Cities

City	Score in 2013	Ranking in 2013	Places risen in 2013	Score in 2012	Ranking in 2012	Ranking in 2012[1]	Ranking in 2011	Places risen in 2012
Jinan	53.68	1	3	53.78	4	4	4	0
Qingdao	53.05	2	6	52.31	8	—	—	—
Xiamen	53.00	3	6	52.30	9	—	—	—
Changchun	52.34	4	-3	54.51	1	1	10	9
Hefei	52.34	5	0	53.20	5	5	6	1
Xining	52.21	6	8	51.57	14	11	9	-2
Ningbo	52.17	7	0	52.51	7	—	—	—
Shijiazhuang	52.17	8	-5	53.86	3	3	21	18
Fuzhou	52.06	9	-3	52.60	6	6	11	5
Hangzhou	52.05	10	-8	54.04	2	2	3	1
Haikou	51.80	11	12	50.05	23	19	1	-18
Nanjing	51.70	12	4	50.75	16	13	16	3
Chengdu	51.40	13	-1	52.13	12	9	7	-2
Tianjin	51.35	14	-1	52.07	13	10	17	7
Zhengzhou	51.28	15	0	50.76	15	12	19	7
Shenyang	51.25	16	10	49.73	26	22	18	-4
Xi'an	51.16	17	0	50.40	17	14	14	0
Yinchuan	51.07	18	-8	52.29	10	7	5	-2
Chongqing	51.01	19	-8	52.28	11	8	8	0
Shanghai	50.53	20	0	50.24	20	16	23	7
Urumqi	50.38	21	0	50.23	21	17	13	-4
Hohhot	50.37	22	0	50.14	22	18	29	11
Nanchang	50.35	23	10	48.41	33	28	28	0
Beijing	50.16	24	4	49.47	28	24	20	-4
Changsha	50.15	25	-6	50.29	19	15	24	9
Dalian	50.10	26	-8	50.37	18	—	—	—
Taiyuan	49.90	27	2	49.38	29	25	27	2

Blue Book of Quality of Life in Cities

Continued table

City	Score in 2013	Ranking in 2013	Places risen in 2013	Score in 2012	Ranking in 2012	Ranking in 2012¹	Ranking in 2011	Places risen in 2012
Nanning	49.81	28	-1	49.60	27	23	22	-1
Harbin	49.79	29	2	48.78	31	26	12	-14
Guiyang	49.58	30	5	47.33	35	30	15	-15
Guangzhou	49.21	31	-6	49.74	25	21	25	4
Wuhan	49.07	32	-8	49.95	24	20	30	10
Kunming	48.73	33	-1	48.72	32	27	26	-1
Shenzhen	48.68	34	-4	49.16	30	—	—	—
Lanzhou	48.57	35	-1	47.95	34	29	2	-27
National average	50.87①			50.88			49.71	

① National average value is obtained by calculating the weighted averages of sub-indexes of the 35 cities, according to the distribution of the survey samples. The same method was adopted for all the national average values of subjective satisfaction sub-indexes below and the ones in the special surveys.

similar to the result of 2012. Shenzhen scores less than 50 and the ranking drops by 4 places to No.34. Among the provincial capitals and the municipalities directly under the Central Government, 22 score over 50, while in 2011 there were only 11. It means the satisfaction index remains roughly the same as that of 2012 and is better than that of 2011.

The averages of the 5 sub-indexes are respectively: human capital (58.89), social security (56.64), living experience (55.07), living standard (52.51) and living costs (31.22). Compared to 2012, the satisfaction with living standard and living costs has somewhat improved, while that of human capital, social security and living experience has dropped slightly. ①

Cities ranked top 10 in the list of QOL (subjective) satisfaction index are: Jinan (1), Qingdao (2), Xiamen (3), Changchun (4), Hefei (5), Xining (6), Ningbo

---

① Sub-indexes will be analyzed detailedly in the following paragraphs.

The 2013 Quality-of-Life Indexes for 35 Chinese Cities

(7), Shijiazhuang (8), Fuzhou (9) and Hangzhou (10). The bottom 10 cities are: Dalian (26), Taiyuan (27), Nanning (28), Harbin (29), Guiyang (30), Guangzhou (31), Wuhan (32), Kunming (33), Shenzhen (34) and Lanzhou (35). Their regional distribution is roughly the same as in 2012. Among the top 10 cities, there are 7 eastern cities, 2 central city and 1 western city. As for the bottom 10 cities, there are 3 eastern cities, 3 central cities and 4 western cities. The top 10 cities are all medium-sized cities, including no megacity like Beijing, Shanghai or Guangzhou. This indicates the size of a city may bring negative influence on the QOL satisfaction of its residents - same as the conclusion of 2012.

Viewed by ranking alone, Jinan, Hefei and Changchun have already ranked among the top 5 continuously for two years, while Lanzhou, Shenzhen and Kunming have stayed among the bottom 5 during the same period. Cities such as Haikou (12), Shenyang (10), Nanchang (10) and Xining (8) have climbed up the ranking remarkably,[1] especially Haikou which has shot up from No.23 last year to No.11 this year. This can be explained by analyzing its sub-indexes. In 2013, its satisfaction index of living costs has changed dramatically from No.29 last year to No.8, and its house price expectation index ranks No.33. Low HPA expectation might have somehow affected its living cost index. Moreover, its satisfaction index of food safety ranks No.3 nationwide, which also must have helped to improve the satisfaction index.

The satisfaction index of Shenyang has also experienced a great rise of 10 places - from No.26 in 2012 to No.16 in 2013. Viewed by sub-indexes, the rise in ranking should be attributed mostly to improvements in the satisfaction indexes of social security (7), living standard (7) and living costs (5).[2] Shenyang also has a low HPA expectation which ranks No.30. As for its satisfaction index of food safety, the ranking is comparatively low at No.31.

Nanchang is also among the cities with the greatest rise - from No.33 last year to No.23 this year. Credit should be given to its remarkable improvements in the

---

① Numbers in brackets stand for the places risen.
② Numbers in brackets stand for the places risen.

Blue Book of Quality of Life in Cities

satisfaction indexes of living standard (9), human capital (9) and social security (5).[①] Indexes of living costs and living experience have only gone up a little. The former is pulled down mainly by strong HPA expectation which has risen 10 places compared to that of 2012.

Xining has experienced a similar rise in satisfaction index - from No.14 last year to No.6 this year. Possible explanation can be found in satisfaction sub-indexes as well, since its human capital satisfaction index and living standard satisfaction index have risen 11 and 8 places respectively.

Besides, Qingdao and Xiamen, two municipalities separately listed on the State plan, have also risen 6 places. In the case of Qingdao, it is because of the great improvements in the satisfaction indexes of living standard (8), human capital (4) and social security (6).[②] As for Xiamen, the improvement is in the living standard (10) satisfaction index.

Cities whose rankings have dropped significantly are Hangzhou (-8), Yinchuan (-8), Chongqing (-8), Dalian (-8), Wuhan (-8), Changsha (-6) and Guangzhou (-6).[③] As to other cities, the rankings remain roughly unchanged.

Hangzhou has dropped from No.2 in 2012 to No.10 in 2013, due to dramatic decline in the satisfaction indexes of living standard (-9), living costs (-8) and human capital (-10). Rankings of its social security and living experience indexes have dropped slightly also, while the income expectation index has dropped drastically by 21 places, from No.2 in 2012 to No.23 in 2013. Ranking of the living cost index may have fallen because of the rise in house price expectation index.

The ranking of Yinchuan has dropped 8 places, from No.10 last year to No.18 this year, due to significant drops in human capital and living costs indexes by 14 and 9 places respectively. The living standard index has also dropped slightly. Drop in the living costs index may have happened mainly because of its strong HPA

---

① Numbers in brackets stand for the places risen.
② Numbers in brackets stand for the places risen.
③ Numbers in brackets stand for the places dropped.

014

The 2013 Quality-of-Life Indexes for 35 Chinese Cities

expectation which has risen 8 places.

The ranking of Chongqing has dropped 8 places, from No. 11 in 2012 to No.19 in 2013, mainly due to drops in the social security (-19) and the living standard (-15) indexes. The living costs (-4) and the human capital (-7) indexes have also somewhat fallen[1] . Only the ranking of living experience has experienced a small rise.

The ranking of Dalian has dropped 8 places, from No.18 last year to No.26 this year, mainly due to drops in the living standard (-10), the living experience (-8) and the social security (-3) indexes. However, its living costs (1) and human capital (7) indexes have somewhat risen.[2]

The ranking of Wuhan has dropped 8 places, from No.24 last year to No.32 this year, due to drops in all the 5 sub-indexes of living standard (-5), living costs (-5), human capital (-5), social security (-6) and living experience (-3).[3]

The ranking of Changsha has dropped 6 places, from No.19 last year to No.25 this year, mainly due to drops in the living experience (-14) and the human capital (-12) indexes.[4]

The ranking of Guangzhou has dropped 6 places, from No.25 last year to No.31 this year, mainly due to dramatic drops in the human capital (-14) and the living costs (-9) indexes. The other sub-indexes remain roughly unchanged.

3.2   2013 Objective Index (Social and Economic Data Index) of QLICC

The objective indexes of QLICC were obtained in the same way as 2012. First, we calculated the 20 objective economic secondary indicators of the 35 cities. Then, we got the 8 primary indicators of QOL with the weighted average normalization method. At last, we averaged the primary indicators to generate the 5 objective sub-indexes, which in turn were averaged to obtain the general objective index (social

---

① Numbers in brackets stand for the places dropped.
② Numbers in brackets stand for the places risen.
③ Numbers in brackets stand for the places dropped.
④ Numbers in brackets stand for the places dropped.

Blue Book of Quality of Life in Cities

and economic data index) of each city.[①] The results of general objective indexes are shown in Table 3.2.

Table 3.2 Objective Indexes and Rankings of the 35 Chinese Cities

City	Score in 2013	Ranking in 2013	Places risen	Score in 2012	Ranking in 2012
Beijing	69.80	1	0	68.72	1
Guangzhou	66.85	2	0	64.87	2
Nanjing	66.65	3	2	62.38	5
Xi'an	64.65	4	2	61.59	6
Shenzhen	63.93	5	-2	64.24	3
Hohhot	62.22	6	1	59.55	7
Xiamen	61.89	7	2	58.86	9
Shanghai	61.78	8	-4	62.72	4
Ningbo	61.47	9	3	55.21	12
Shenyang	59.99	10	1	56.59	11
Changchun	59.64	11	8	52.29	19
Hangzhou	59.54	12	-4	59.09	8
Wuhan	58.93	13	-3	56.61	10
Changsha	58.36	14	2	53.53	16
Kunming	58.05	15	-1	54.08	14
Yinchuan	57.68	16	2	52.45	18
Jinan	56.84	17	0	53.22	17
Hefei	56.73	18	8	50.92	26
Chengdu	55.96	19	5	51.15	24
Dalian	55.64	20	1	52.00	21
Taiyuan	55.45	21	-1	52.15	20
Tianjin	55.42	22	-9	54.30	13
Lanzhou	55.22	23	8	50.08	31
Shijiazhuang	54.78	24	4	50.49	28
Qingdao	54.76	25	-10	54.05	15
Urumqi	54.59	26	6	49.73	32
Nanchang	53.03	27	7	49.03	34
Fuzhou	52.66	28	-6	51.37	22

---

① For specifics of index design, see "High Living Costs Encumbering Improvement in Satisfaction with the Urban Quality of Life", *Economic Perspectives*, Vol. 7, 2012. Or the Blue Book of *Report on Chinese City Life Quality (2012)*, Social Sciences Academic Press (China), February 2013.

The 2013 Quality-of-Life Indexes for 35 Chinese Cities

Continued table

City	Score in 2013	Ranking in 2013	Places risen	Score in 2012	Ranking in 2012
Guiyang	52.45	29	-4	50.98	25
Harbin	51.86	30	-1	50.44	29
Haikou	51.50	31	-8	51.17	23
Zhengzhou	50.54	32	-2	50.26	30
Nanning	50.00	33	-6	50.69	27
Xining	49.29	34	1	45.21	35
Chongqing	47.83	35	-2	49.40	33
National average	57.75[①]			54.56	

① National average value of objective index was obtained by calculating the weighted averages according to the population proportions of the 35 cities in the 6th national census. The same method was adopted for all the national average values of the following 5 objective sub-indexes.

As it is shown in Table 3.2, the weighted average of the objective indexes is 57.75, better than the national average of 54.56 in 2012. 33 cities score over 50, including 23 cities over 55 and 9 cities over 60. Averages of the 5 sub-indexes are respectively: living standard (63.39), living costs (58.67), human capital (57.78), social security (55.26) and living experience (53.67) - all improved compared to those of 2012. Cities ranked top 10 in the list of objective index are: Beijing (1), Guangzhou (2), Nanjing (3), Xi'an (4), Shenzhen (5), Hohhot (6), Xiamen (7), Shanghai (8), Ningbo (9) and Shenyang (10). The bottom 10 cities are: Urumqi (26), Nanchang (27), Fuzhou (28), Guiyang (29), Harbin (30), Haikou (31), Zhengzhou (32), Nanning (33), Xining (34) and Chongqing (35). Objective indexes of the eastern regions are generally higher than those of the central or the western regions. Among the top 10 cities, there are 8 eastern cities and 2 western cities. As for the bottom 10, there are 2 eastern cities, 3 central cities and 5 western cities.

Cities with an obvious rise in the ranking are: Changchun (8), Hefei (8), Lanzhou (8), Nanchang (7), Urumqi (6) and Chengdu (5).[①] Cities with an obvious drop are: Qingdao (-10), Tianjin (-9), Haikou (-8) and Nanning (-6).[②] Beijing, Guangzhou,

---

① Numbers in brackets stand for the places risen.
② Numbers in brackets stand for the places dropped.

Blue Book of Quality of Life in Cities

Nanjing and Shenzhen have already ranked among the top 5 continuously for two years, while Xining and Chongqing have stayed among the bottom 5 during the same period.

The ranking of Changchun has risen 8 places, from No.19 in 2012 to No.11 in 2013, because of its rises in the human capital (13), the social security (7) and the living standard (4) indexes,[1] while the rankings of the living experience (-3) and the living costs (0) indexes remain roughly unchanged.[2]

The ranking of Hefei has risen 8 places, from No.26 in 2012 to No.18 in 2013, mainly because of its rise in the living experience index by 15 places, from No.31 last year to No.16 this year. Rankings of the other 2 indexes have both dropped: social security (-6) and human capital (-1).

The ranking of Lanzhou has risen 8 places, from No.31 in 2012 to No.23 in 2013, mainly because of great rise in the living standard index by 17 places. Its ranking of the social security index has dropped 5 places, while the rest 3 sub-indexes have remained roughly unchanged.

The ranking of Nanchang has risen 7 places, from No.34 in 2012 to No.27 in 2013, mainly because of dramatic rise in the living standard index by 10 places. Rankings of the other sub-indexes remain roughly unchanged.

The ranking of Qingdao has dropped drastically by 10 places, mainly due to a big drop in the living standard index by 20 places, from No.8 in 2012 to No.28 in 2013. Rankings of the other sub-indexes remain roughly unchanged.

The ranking of Tianjin has dropped 9 places, from No.13 last year to No.22 this year, mainly due to drops in the living standard (-10) and the human capital (-9) indexes. The living costs and the social security indexes have only dropped slightly, while the living experience index has remained the same.

The ranking of Haikou has dropped 8 places, from No.23 last year to No.31 this year, mainly due to a dramatic drop in the human capital index (-18). The other sub-indexes are roughly unchanged. Living standard has dropped 2 places, while

---

[1] Numbers in brackets stand for the places risen.
[2] Numbers in brackets stand for the places dropped.

018

The 2013 Quality-of-Life Indexes for 35 Chinese Cities

social security has risen 2 places. Living costs and living experience have remained the same.

The ranking of Nanning has dropped 6 places, from No.27 last year to No.33 this year, mainly due to a dramatic drop in the living standard index (-12). Human capital and living experience have fallen slightly by 5 and 3 places respectively, while social security has risen 12 places, and living costs 1 place.

3.3 Special Surveys

3.3.1 Survey of House Price Expectation

Table 3.3 shows the result of the 2013 special survey on house price expectation. The indexes were obtained by asking interviewees the question of whether house prices in their cities would rise or fall in the coming 1 or 2 years, and assigning different values to their answers.

Table 3.3 House Price Expectation Indexes of the 35 Cities[①]

City	Score in 2013	Ranking in 2013	Score in 2012	Ranking in 2012	Places risen in
Guangzhou	68.64	1	58.55	7	6
Xining	68.33	2	63.89	2	0
Urumqi	67.37	3	55.26	15	12
Nanchang	66.73	4	55.28	14	10
Zhengzhou	66.60	5	55.24	16	11
Hefei	66.07	6	53.42	25	19
Shanghai	65.97	7	53.35	26	19
Shenzhen	65.96	8	56.55	9	1
Yinchuan	65.93	9	55.21	17	8
Nanjing	65.92	10	54.36	22	12
Beijing	65.71	11	52.04	28	17
Jinan	65.68	12	50.00	33	21
Wuhan	65.40	13	54.41	21	8
Kunming	65.38	14	55.77	13	-1

019

Blue Book of Quality of Life in Cities

Continued table

City	Score in 2013	Ranking in 2013	Score in 2012	Ranking in 2012	Places risen in
Shijiazhuang	65.19	15	54.13	23	8
Xiamen	65.14	16	59.59	5	-11
Qingdao	64.57	17	46.82	35	18
Taiyuan	64.53	18	57.18	8	-10
Chongqing	64.46	19	55.84	12	-7
Fuzhou	64.45	20	52.75	27	7
Lanzhou	63.98	21	59.94	4	-17
Changchun	63.70	22	51.20	30	8
Nanning	63.66	23	58.80	6	-17
Xi'an	63.64	24	55.10	18	-6
Changsha	63.39	25	51.90	29	4
Tianjin	63.18	26	53.65	24	-2
Chengdu	63.06	27	54.53	20	-7
Guiyang	62.99	28	60.48	3	-25
Hangzhou	62.85	29	47.17	34	5
Shenyang	62.43	30	56.35	10	-20
Ningbo	62.15	31	50.68	31	0
Dalian	62.13	32	54.91	19	-13
Haikou	61.26	33	64.00	1	-32
Hohhot	61.26	34	56.07	11	-23
Harbin	60.99	35	50.39	32	-3
National average	64.65		National average	54.99	

① The higher the index is, the greater the HPA in expectation is, and vice versa.

As it is shown in Table 3.3, the weighted average of house price expectation indexes is 64.65 - an increase by 9.66 (17.6%) compared to the 2012 average of 54.99. The surveyed 35 cities all score over 60 in house price expectation index, which means all their residents have an expectation of HPA. Except for Haikou, all the other 34 cities are expected to have a bigger increase in HPA than that of 2012. The top 10 cities expected to have the quickest HPA are: Qingdao (37.9%), Hangzhou (33.2%), Jinan (31.4%), Beijing (26.3%), Changchun (24.4%), Hefei (23.7%), Shanghai (23.7%), Ningbo (22.6%), Changsha (22.1%) and Fuzhou

The 2013 Quality-of-Life Indexes for 35 Chinese Cities

(22%). Cities expected to have a slower HPA are: Haikou (-4.3 %), Guiyang (4.2%), Lanzhou (6.7%), Xining (6.9%), Dalian (7.2%), Nanning (8.3%), Hohhot (9.3%) and Xiamen (9.3%). The HPA rates of the other 17 cities are likely to be between 10.8% and 21.9%. [1]

Viewed by ranking, cities with the biggest rises are: Jinan (21), Shanghai (19), Hefei (19), Qingdao (18), Beijing (17), Urumqi (12) and Nanjing (12). [2] Interestingly, Haikou ranked No.1 in house price expectation last year, but drops to No.33 this year. However, Qingdao and Hangzhou where house prices were expected to fall and Jinan where house prices were expected to be even last year, all have the greatest HPA expectation this year.

3.3.2 Survey of Food Safety Satisfaction

Food safety is essential to the survival and health of residents. Thus, people's satisfaction with this issue is a key factor in assessing the life-improving projects carried out by the Government. In view of the serious food safety problems occurred in the past two years, a survey of food safety satisfaction was added to the report. We interviewed the residents through telephone about their satisfaction with the food safety situation in their cities, and then assigned different values to their answers. [3] Table 3.4 shows the results of the survey.

As it is shown in Table 3.4, the weighted average of food safety satisfaction indexes is 41.67, which is below the satisfaction level, since 50 is the critical point between satisfaction and dissatisfaction. Only 1 city, Xiamen, scores over 50. In general, city dwellers are not satisfied with food safety. Cities ranked top 10 in the list of food safety index are: Xiamen (1), Xining (2), Haikou (3), Chongqing (4), Yinchuan (5), Guiyang (6), Chengdu (7), Ningbo (8), Beijing (9) and Shenzhen (10). The bottom 10 cities are: Harbin (26), Fuzhou (27), Shanghai (28), Lanzhou (29), Shijiazhuang (30), Shenyang (31), Zhengzhou (32), Changsha (33), Taiyuan (34) and

---

[1] The percentages in the brackets are obtained by: subtracting the score of 2012 from the score of 2013, then dividing the difference by the score of 2012.

[2] Numbers in brackets stand for the places risen.

[3] The same method of assignment was used here and for the subjective satisfaction indexes.

Blue Book of Quality of Life in Cities

Table 3.4 Satisfaction Indexes of Food Safety

City	Score	Ranking in 2013	City	Score	Ranking in 2013
Xiamen	53.06	1	Jinan	40.77	19
Xining	49.44	2	Hohhot	40.50	20
Haikou	46.98	3	Hangzhou	40.35	21
Chongqing	45.67	4	Guangzhou	40.28	22
Yinchuan	45.05	5	Nanjing	40.01	23
Guiyang	44.49	6	Xi'an	39.40	24
Chengdu	44.39	7	Tianjin	39.35	25
Ningbo	44.03	8	Harbin	39.24	26
Beijing	43.55	9	Fuzhou	39.24	27
Shenzhen	43.25	10	Shanghai	39.12	28
Urumqi	43.08	11	Lanzhou	38.84	29
Hefei	42.86	12	Shijiazhuang	38.51	30
Kunming	42.69	13	Shenyang	38.49	31
Qingdao	42.51	14	Zhengzhou	37.08	32
Changchun	42.16	15	Changsha	36.90	33
Nanning	42.11	16	Taiyuan	36.87	34
Nanchang	41.00	17	Wuhan	36.47	35
Dalian	40.83	18	National average		41.67

Wuhan (35). Among the top 10 cities, there are 5 eastern cities and 5 western cities; while among the bottom 10 cities, there are 4 eastern cities, 5 central cities and 1 western city. It is noteworthy that up to 12 cities score below 40. Besides, viewed by gender, male interviewees are more satisfied with food safety (43.61) than females (39.46). By age, interviewees from 20 to 30 have the highest food safety satisfaction (43.68) while the ones from 41 to 60 have the lowest satisfaction (39.56).

B.4

Sub-Indexes of Quality of Life for the 35 Chinese Cities in 2013

Changes and rankings of satisfaction indexes and objective indexes could all be explained by analyzing sub-indexes. Same as last year, the sub-indexes under the QLI general indexes include: living standard, living costs, human capital, social security and living experience. Each sub-index is in turn made up of a subjective satisfaction index and an objective index (social and economic data index).

4.1　Living Standard Index

Living standard index consists of a satisfaction index and an objective index (social and economic data index). The former was obtained through telephone survey by assigning values to survey answers, and the latter by calculating social and economic indexes of the 35 cities.

4.1.1　Subjective Satisfaction Index of Living Standard

Table 4.1 lists the satisfaction indexes of living standard in the 35 cities, along with their respective rankings and changes in places.

As it is shown in Table 4.1, the weighted average of living standard (subjective) satisfaction indexes is 52.51 - slightly higher than the national average of 51.28 in 2012. 32 out of the 35 cities score over 50, up to the satisfaction level. Cities ranked top 10 in the list of living standard index are: Haikou (1), Qingdao (2), Xiamen (3), Xining (4), Fuzhou (5), Ningbo (6), Hohhot (7), Jinan (8), Hefei (9) and Hangzhou (10), including 7 eastern cities, 1 central city and 1 western city. Except

023

Blue Book of Quality of Life in Cities

for Hangzhou, Hefei and Fuzhou, rankings of all the other top 10 cities have risen greatly. The bottom 10 cities are: Shenzhen (26), Shenyang (27), Nanning (28), Yinchuan

Table 4.1 Satisfaction Indexes of Living Standard in the 35 Chinese Cities

City	Score in 2013	Ranking in 2013	Places risen in 2013	Score in 2012	Ranking in 2012[4]	Ranking in 2011	Places risen in 2012
Haikou	56.46	1	2	54.75	3	1	-2
Qingdao	55.81	2	8	52.59	10	—	—
Xiamen	55.69	3	10	52.18	13	—	—
Xining	55.00	4	8	52.31	12	19	9
Fuzhou	54.64	5	-1	53.76	4	7	3
Ningbo	54.62	6	2	52.77	8	—	—
Hohhot	54.31	7	17	50.36	24	28	9
Jinan	54.29	8	9	51.43	17	5	-8
Hefei	54.14	9	-7	55.76	2	4	2
Hangzhou	54.10	10	-9	56.49	1	6	5
Urumqi	54.10	11	9	50.99	20	8	-8
Xi'an	53.88	12	19	48.79	31	21	-5
Guiyang	53.74	13	15	49.40	28	24	1
Changsha	53.44	14	11	50.29	25	9	-11
Chengdu	53.30	15	3	51.39	18	12	-2
Changchun	53.07	16	-11	53.74	5	14	9
Kunming	52.84	17	-6	52.32	11	16	7
Shanghai	52.59	18	-3	51.65	15	17	6
Nanjing	52.34	19	10	49.23	29	23	-1
Guangzhou	52.32	20	1	50.97	21	10	-7
Tianjin	52.24	21	-2	51.27	19	15	0
Beijing	52.19	22	1	50.37	23	11	-7
Nanchang	52.18	23	9	48.27	32	20	-7
Chongqing	52.11	24	-15	52.64	9	13	5
Shijiazhuang	51.79	25	-19	53.38	6	29	23
Shenzhen	51.65	26	-12	52.08	14	—	—
Shenyang	51.54	27	7	46.95	34	30	1
Nanning	51.48	28	-12	51.47	16	22	10
Yinchuan	51.10	29	-2	49.74	27	18	-4

024

Sub-Indexes of Quality of Life for the 35 Chinese Cities in 2013

Continued table

City	Score in 2013	Ranking in 2013	Places risen in 2013	Score in 2012	Ranking in 2012[4]	Ranking in 2011	Places risen in 2012
Taiyuan	50.42	30	3	48.27	33	26	-2
Wuhan	50.39	31	-5	49.95	26	27	6
Dalian	50.28	32	-10	50.69	22	—	—
Harbin	49.86	33	-3	48.89	30	3	-22
Lanzhou	49.72	34	1	46.88	35	2	-28
Zhengzhou	48.00	35	-28	52.86	7	25	18
National average	52.51			51.28		51.76	

(29), Taiyuan (30), Wuhan (31), Dalian (32), Harbin (33), Lanzhou (34) and Zhengzhou (35), including 3 eastern cities, 4 central cities and 3 western cities. Among them, rankings of Shenzhen, Nanning, Dalian and Zhengzhou have dropped dramatically.

Compared to last year, cities with a drastic rise are: Xi'an (19), Hohhot (17), Guiyang (15), Xiamen (10), Nanjing (10), Jinan (9), Urumqi (9), Xining (8) and Shenyang (7).[1] Cities with an obvious drop are: Zhengzhou (-28), Shijiazhuang (-19), Chongqing (-15), Shenzhen (-12), Nanning (-12), Changchun (-11) and Dalian (-10).[2] Among them, Zhengzhou and Shijiazhuang have experienced the greatest drops.

Satisfaction index of living standard comes from the weighted average of income status and income expectation indexes. Therefore, changes in the ranking of living standard satisfaction index can be explained by changes in the satisfaction with income status and income expectation. By asking interviewees about their satisfaction with the present income status and the income expectation, and assigning different values to their answers, we obtained the income status and the income expectation satisfaction indexes.

Tables 4.2 and 4.3 list the satisfaction indexes of income status and income

---

① Numbers in brackets stand for the places risen.
② Numbers in brackets stand for the places dropped.

Blue Book of Quality of Life in Cities

expectation in the 35 cities, along with their respective rankings and changes in places in 2012 and 2013.

Table 4.2   Satisfaction Indexes of Income Status in the 35 Chinese Cities

City	Score in 2013	Ranking in 2013	Places risen in 2013	Score in 2012	Ranking in 2012	Ranking in 2012[5]	Ranking in 2011	Places risen in 2012
Haikou	56.87	1	1	57.50	2	2	1	-1
Qingdao	56.58	2	8	53.18	10	—	—	—
Xiamen	56.39	3	12	52.03	15	—	—	—
Fuzhou	56.39	4	0	54.19	4	4	8	4
Hangzhou	56.25	5	-4	58.25	1	1	5	4
Ningbo	55.21	6	0	53.65	6	—	—	—
Changchun	54.52	7	-2	54.01	5	5	13	8
Xining	54.44	8	5	52.78	13	11	14	3
Hefei	54.42	9	-6	55.04	3	3	6	3
Urumqi	54.38	10	-1	53.29	9	8	3	-5
Jinan	54.15	11	3	52.11	14	12	7	-5
Chengdu	53.82	12	7	50.88	19	15	18	3
Hohhot	53.80	13	16	48.21	29	24	26	2
Nanjing	53.42	14	17	48.08	31	26	22	-4
Xi'an	53.25	15	13	48.30	28	23	24	1
Kunming	53.17	16	0	51.76	16	13	17	4
Guangzhou	52.94	17	4	50.57	21	17	9	-8
Changsha	52.62	18	12	48.10	30	25	11	-14
Shanghai	52.60	19	-2	51.43	17	14	15	1
Tianjin	52.15	20	0	50.79	20	16	21	5
Guiyang	51.98	21	11	47.86	32	27	16	-11
Shijiazhuang	51.85	22	-14	53.43	8	7	28	21
Shenyang	51.75	23	11	46.57	34	29	29	0
Beijing	51.65	24	-2	50.10	22	18	10	-8
Chongqing	51.38	25	-18	53.45	7	6	12	6

Sub-Indexes of Quality of Life for the 35 Chinese Cities in 2013

Continued table

City	Score in 2013	Ranking in 2013	Places risen in 2013	Score in 2012	Ranking in 2012	Ranking in 2012[5]	Ranking in 2011	Places risen in 2012
Yinchuan	51.37	26	-15	53.13	11	9	20	11
Nanning	51.20	27	-4	50.00	23	19	27	8
Nanchang	51.18	28	-2	48.58	26	21	19	-2
Shenzhen	51.12	29	-11	51.39	18	—	—	—
Dalian	50.46	30	-6	49.69	24	—	—	—
Wuhan	50.39	31	-6	49.68	25	20	23	3
Harbin	49.33	32	1	47.78	33	28	4	-24
Lanzhou	48.87	33	2	44.60	35	30	2	-28
Zhengzhou	48.42	34	-22	53.10	12	10	25	15
Taiyuan	48.32	35	-8	48.51	27	22	30	8
National average	52.54			51.20				

As it is shown in Table 4.2, the weighted average of income status indexes is 52.54 - higher than that of last year. Cities ranked top 10 are: Haikou (1), Qingdao (2), Xiamen (3), Fuzhou (4), Hangzhou (5), Ningbo (6), Changchun (7), Xining (8), Hefei (9) and Urumqi (10), including 6 eastern cities, 2 central cities and 2 western cities. Among them, Qingdao and Xiamen have a big rise, while Hangzhou and Hefei have a notable drop. The bottom 10 cities are: Yinchuan (26), Nanning (27), Nanchang (28), Shenzhen (29), Dalian (30), Wuhan (31), Harbin (32), Lanzhou (33), Zhengzhou (34) and Taiyuan (35), including 2 eastern cities, 5 central cities and 3 western cities. Among them, Yinchuan, Shenzhen, Dalian, Wuhan, Zhengzhou and Taiyuan have dropped remarkably.

Cities such as Nanjing (17), Hohhot (16), Xi'an (13), Xiamen (12), Changsha (12) and Shenyang (11) have seen a dramatic rise,[①] while cities like Zhengzhou (-22), Chongqing (-18), Yinchuan (-15) and Shijiazhuang (-14) have experienced a drastic

---

① Numbers in brackets stand for the places risen.

Blue Book of Quality of Life in Cities

drop.[1] Haikou has been among the leading ones for a couple of years, ranking No.1 in 2011 and No.2 in 2012.

Table 4.3 Satisfaction Indexes of Income Expectation in the 35 Chinese Cities

City	Score in 2013	Ranking in 2013	Places risen in 2013	Score in 2012	Ranking in 2012	Ranking in 2012[6]	Ranking in 2011	Places risen in 2012
Haikou	56.04	1	13	52.00	14	11	1	-10
Xining	55.56	2	16	51.85	18	14	24	10
Guiyang	55.51	3	20	50.95	23	18	26	8
Qingdao	55.04	4	9	52.00	13	—	—	—
Xiamen	55.00	5	7	52.33	12	—	—	—
Hohhot	54.82	6	4	52.50	10	9	27	18
Xi'an	54.50	7	22	49.27	29	24	17	-7
Jinan	54.43	8	16	50.75	24	19	3	-16
Changsha	54.26	9	2	52.49	11	10	5	-5
Ningbo	54.03	10	6	51.89	16	—	—	—
Hefei	53.85	11	-10	56.47	1	1	4	3
Urumqi	53.81	12	19	48.68	31	26	21	-5
Nanchang	53.18	13	20	47.97	33	28	23	-5
Fuzhou	52.90	14	-9	53.32	5	5	8	3
Chongqing	52.84	15	4	51.82	19	15	20	5
Chengdu	52.78	16	-1	51.90	15	12	6	-6
Beijing	52.74	17	8	50.63	25	20	11	-9
Shanghai	52.57	18	-1	51.88	17	13	22	9
Taiyuan	52.51	19	13	48.02	32	27	10	-17
Kunming	52.50	20	-13	52.88	7	7	15	8
Tianjin	52.34	21	-1	51.75	20	16	13	-3
Shenzhen	52.18	22	-14	52.78	8	—	—	—
Hangzhou	51.94	23	-21	54.72	2	2	9	7

---

① Numbers in brackets stand for the places dropped.

Sub-Indexes of Quality of Life for the 35 Chinese Cities in 2013

Continued table

City	Score in 2013	Ranking in 2013	Places risen in 2013	Score in 2012	Ranking in 2012	Ranking in 2012[6]	Ranking in 2011	Places risen in 2012
Nanning	51.76	24	-18	52.93	6	6	12	6
Shijiazhuang	51.74	25	-21	53.33	4	4	28	24
Guangzhou	51.71	26	-4	51.38	22	17	14	-3
Changchun	51.62	27	-24	53.48	3	3	18	15
Shenyang	51.33	28	6	47.34	34	29	30	1
Nanjing	51.26	29	-3	50.38	26	21	25	4
Yinchuan	50.82	30	5	46.35	35	30	16	-14
Lanzhou	50.56	31	-1	49.15	30	25	7	-18
Harbin	50.39	32	-4	50.00	28	23	2	-21
Wuhan	50.39	33	-6	50.21	27	22	29	7
Dalian	50.09	34	-13	51.69	21	—	—	—
Zhengzhou	47.58	35	-26	52.62	9	8	19	11
National average	52.48			51.36				

As it is shown in Table 4.3, the weighted average of income expectation indexes is 52.48 - slightly higher than that of last year. Except for Zhengzhou, the other 34 cities all score over 50 - 6 cities more than in 2012. However, Haikou the champion of 2013 scores 56.04, a bit lower than the champion of 2012 Hefei which scored 56.47. Cities ranked top 10 are: Haikou (1), Xining (2), Guiyang (3), Qingdao (4), Xiamen (5), Hohhot (6), Xi'an (7), Jinan (8), Changsha (9) and Ningbo (10), including 5 eastern cities, 2 central city and 3 western cities. Most of them have great improvements in the ranking. The bottom 10 cities are: Guangzhou (26), Changchun (27), Shenyang (28), Nanjing (29), Yinchuan (30), Lanzhou (31), Harbin (32), Wuhan (33), Dalian (34) and Zhengzhou (35), including 4 eastern cities, 4 central cities and 2 western cities. Among them, Changchun, Wuhan, Dalian and Zhengzhou have a big drop.

Cities such as Xi'an (22), Guiyang (20), Nanchang (20), Jinan (16), Urumqi (19),

Blue Book of Quality of Life in Cities

Xining (16), Haikou (13) and Taiyuan (13) have seen a dramatic rise, while cities like Zhengzhou (-26), Changchun (-24), Dalian (-13), Hangzhou (-21), Shijiazhuang (-21) and Nanning (-18) have experienced a drastic drop.

4.1.2 Objective Index (Social and Economic Data Index) of Living Standard

Table 4.4 lists the living standard objective indexes (social and economic data indexes) of the surveyed 35 cities, along with their respective rankings and changes in places. Same as last year, living standard objective index consists of two primary indicators (income level index and life improvements index) which are in turn made up of 6 secondary indicators: consumption rate, per capita wealth, per capita disposable income, per capita consumption growth, per capita wealth growth and per capita disposable income growth. The first 3 secondary indicators are used to evaluate income level index, and the last 3 to describe life improvements index.

Table 4.4   Objective Indexes of Living Standard in the 35 Chinese Cities

City	Score in 2013	Ranking in 2013	Places risen in 2013	Score in 2012	Ranking in 2012
Nanjing	80.00	1	5	66.33	6
Xiamen	79.22	2	21	52.40	23
Shenzhen	78.91	3	4	64.78	7
Xi'an	78.59	4	11	56.07	15
Beijing	77.84	5	-4	80.03	1
Shanghai	73.93	6	-4	77.84	2
Hangzhou	73.83	7	-4	76.79	3
Ningbo	72.47	8	-3	68.70	5
Jinan	72.27	9	3	57.43	12
Chengdu	72.13	10	1	58.80	11
Guangzhou	70.24	11	-7	72.14	4
Haikou	69.40	12	-2	59.80	10
Hohhot	68.67	13	3	55.87	16
Hefei	67.04	14	3	55.75	17
Lanzhou	65.59	15	17	46.30	32
Changchun	63.27	16	4	53.67	20

030

Sub-Indexes of Quality of Life for the 35 Chinese Cities in 2013

Continued table

City	Score in 2013	Ranking in 2013	Places risen in 2013	Score in 2012	Ranking in 2012
Fuzhou	61.51	17	-8	60.75	9
Zhengzhou	61.40	18	-4	56.11	14
Dalian	61.23	19	10	47.14	29
Changsha	60.91	20	4	50.97	24
Nanchang	60.59	21	10	46.60	31
Wuhan	60.51	22	3	50.81	25
Tianjin	60.42	23	-10	57.02	13
Yinchuan	60.00	24	9	45.55	33
Shijiazhuang	58.80	25	-4	53.09	21
Urumqi	58.61	26	2	47.54	28
Shenyang	57.82	27	-1	48.84	26
Qingdao	56.06	28	-20	64.76	8
Kunming	55.27	29	5	40.76	34
Xining	54.92	30	5	40.00	35
Taiyuan	52.32	31	-1	46.87	30
Guiyang	49.09	32	-5	47.86	27
Harbin	49.04	33	-15	55.47	18
Nanning	41.04	34	-12	52.98	22
Chongqing	40.00	35	-16	53.90	19
National average	63.39			56.28	

As it is shown in Table 4.4, the weighted average of living standard objective indexes is 63.39 - a big improvement than the national average of 56.28 in 2012. 5 cities score over 75, 24 over 60 and 31 over 50, which are respectively 2, 15 and 6 cities more than the record of 2012. Beijing, Guangzhou, Nanjing and Shenzhen have ranked among the top 5 for 2 years continuously, and Xining and Chongqing among the bottom 5 during the same period. Objective index of living standard has been obviously improved in general and in most of the cities.

Cities ranked top 10 are: Nanjing (1), Xiamen (2), Shenzhen (3), Xi'an (4), Beijing (5), Shanghai (6), Hangzhou (7), Ningbo (8), Jinan (9) and Chengdu (10), including 8 eastern cities and 2 western cities. Among them, Xiamen, Xi'an and Nanjing have

Blue Book of Quality of Life in Cities

a big rise. The bottom 10 cities are: Urumqi (26), Shenyang (27), Qingdao (28), Kunming (29), Xining (30), Taiyuan (31), Guiyang (32), Harbin (33), Nanning (34) and Chongqing (35), including 2 eastern cities, 3 central cities and 5 western cities. Among them, Qingdao, Harbin, Nanning and Chongqing have a notable drop. Generally speaking, eastern cities score higher than central or western cities in living standard index.

Cities such as Xiamen (21), Lanzhou (17), Xi'an (11), Dalian (10), Nanchang (10) and Yinchuan (9) have seen a dramatic rise, while cities like Fuzhou (-8), Tianjin (-10), Qingdao (-20), Harbin (-15), Nanning (-12) and Chongqing (-16) have experienced a drastic drop.[1]

4.2 Living Costs Index

Like other sub-indexes, living costs index also consists of a satisfaction index and an objective index (social and economic data index). The former was obtained through telephone survey by assigning values to survey answers, and the latter by calculating social and economic indexes of the 35 cities.

4.2.1 Subjective Satisfaction Index of Living Costs

Table 4.5 lists the satisfaction indexes of living costs in the 35 cities, along with their respective rankings. Same as in previous surveys, the higher the living costs index, the lower the living costs, and the higher the satisfaction among residents, and vice versa.

The weighted average of living costs satisfaction indexes is 31.22 - higher than the 2012 average of 28.91, but lower than the 2011 average of 32.70. Although improved, the living costs satisfaction index is still on the low side. The 35 cities all score below 40. Nevertheless, both the highest scorer Shijiazhuang (39.13) and the lowest scorer Shanghai (25.59) this year have performed better than the highest Hefei (35.43) and the lowest Beijing (23.06) last year. Cities ranked top 10 are:

---

① Numbers in brackets stand for the places risen or fallen.

032

Table 4.5 Satisfaction Indexes of Living Costs in the 35 Chinese Cities

City	Score in 2013	Ranking in 2013	Places risen in 2013	Score in 2012	Ranking in 2012	Ranking in 2012[7]	Ranking in 2011	Places risen in 2012
Shijiazhuang	39.13	1	3	34.27	4	4	8	4
Shenyang	36.31	2	5	31.73	7	7	12	5
Jinan	36.16	3	-1	35.39	2	2	9	7
Changchun	36.02	4	-1	34.36	3	3	1	-2
Zhengzhou	35.03	5	3	31.67	8	8	10	2
Hefei	34.40	6	-5	35.43	1	1	4	3
Taiyuan	34.22	7	4	30.94	11	11	7	-4
Haikou	33.96	8	21	26.00	29	26	26	0
Fuzhou	33.65	9	0	31.21	9	9	18	9
Nanning	33.45	10	14	27.16	24	23	15	-8
Tianjin	33.32	11	-6	32.62	5	5	6	1
Nanchang	33.18	12	2	28.66	14	14	17	3
Xi'an	33.03	13	-7	31.92	6	6	3	-3
Chongqing	32.94	14	-4	30.98	10	10	23	13
Chengdu	32.41	15	-3	30.92	12	12	16	4
Xiamen	32.36	16	-1	28.49	15	—	—	—
Harbin	32.06	17	0	28.38	17	16	2	-14
Wuhan	31.96	18	-5	30.57	13	13	13	0

Continued table

City	Score in 2013	Ranking in 2013	Places risen in 2013	Score in 2012	Ranking in 2012	Ranking in 2012	Ranking in 2011	Places risen in 2012
Changsha	31.08	19	2	27.63	21	20	27	7
Hohhot	30.85	20	8	26.43	28	25	11	-14
Nanjing	30.10	21	-2	27.95	19	18	22	4
Kunming	30.00	22	-4	28.04	18	17	19	2
Guiyang	29.38	23	7	25.71	30	27	5	-22
Hangzhou	29.10	24	-8	28.42	16	15	25	10
Ningbo	29.03	25	2	26.62	27	—	—	—
Xining	28.89	26	-3	27.31	23	22	14	-8
Qingdao	28.78	27	-2	27.12	25	—	—	—
Urumqi	28.53	28	6	24.67	34	29	20	-9
Guangzhou	28.46	29	-9	27.79	20	19	24	5
Lanzhou	27.82	30	-4	26.70	26	24	11	-13
Yinchuan	27.47	31	-9	27.60	22	21	21	0
Dalian	27.04	32	1	25.15	33	—	—	—
Shenzhen	26.56	33	-1	25.30	32	—	—	—
Beijing	26.13	34	1	23.06	35	30	28	-2
Shanghai	25.59	35	-4	25.45	31	28	30	2
National average	31.22			28.91			32.7	

Sub-Indexes of Quality of Life for the 35 Chinese Cities in 2013

Shijiazhuang (1), Shenyang (2), Jinan (3), Changchun (4), Zhengzhou (5), Hefei (6), Taiyuan (7), Haikou (8), Fuzhou (9) and Nanning (10), including 5 eastern cities, 4 central cities and 1 western city. The bottom 10 cities are: Xining (26), Qingdao (27), Urumqi (28), Guangzhou (29), Lanzhou (30), Yinchuan (31), Dalian (32), Shenzhen (33), Beijing (34) and Shanghai (35), including 6 eastern cities and 4 western cities. Low satisfaction with living costs in eastern large cities, such as Beijing, Shanghai, Shenzhen and Dalian, indicates that the living costs there must be high. The same conclusion can also be drawn from the following study on the objective indexes of living costs in which all these large cities rank low.

Cities such as Haikou (21), Nanning (14), Hohhot (8), Urumqi (6) and Guiyang (7) have seen dramatic improvements,[1] while cities like Yinchuan (-9), Hangzhou (-8), Xi'an (-7), Tianjin (-6) and Wuhan (-5) have experienced a drastic drop.[2] Rise in the satisfaction index of living costs indicates lower living costs and better satisfaction, and vise versa.

4.2.2 Objective Index (Social and Economic Data Index) of Living Costs

Living costs objective index consists of 3 secondary indicators: house price index, inflation rate and house-price-to-income ratio. Table 4.6 lists the living costs objective indexes of the 35 cities, along with their respective rankings.

Table 4.6 Objective Indexes of Living Costs in the 35 Chinese Cities

City	Score in 2013	Ranking in 2013	Places risen	Score in 2012	Ranking in 2012
Kunming	80.00	1	1	74.00	2
Hohhot	77.96	2	-1	79.97	1
Changsha	71.79	3	0	69.57	3
Shijiazhuang	66.75	4	0	64.74	4
Xining	66.05	5	5	60.51	10
Xi'an	65.27	6	3	61.38	9
Yinchuan	65.18	7	7	59.38	14

---

① Numbers in brackets stand for the places risen.
② Numbers in brackets stand for the places dropped.

Blue Book of Quality of Life in Cities

Continued table

City	Score in 2013	Ranking in 2013	Places risen	Score in 2012	Ranking in 2012
Nanchang	64.81	8	-3	63.36	5
Jinan	64.59	9	7	59.19	16
Qingdao	63.40	10	-2	62.34	8
Chongqing	63.36	11	-5	63.34	6
Shenyang	62.89	12	-1	60.11	11
Wuhan	62.61	13	0	59.68	13
Zhengzhou	62.30	14	-7	63.02	7
Chengdu	61.68	15	-3	60.06	12
Guiyang	61.67	16	1	58.21	17
Xiamen	60.70	17	-2	59.22	15
Nanning	60.61	18	1	54.24	19
Lanzhou	59.93	19	3	52.63	22
Changchun	59.57	20	0	53.58	20
Harbin	58.67	21	2	52.46	23
Urumqi	58.33	22	7	46.58	29
Hefei	58.17	23	3	51.49	26
Dalian	57.15	24	-6	56.00	18
Nanjing	55.70	25	-1	52.18	24
Fuzhou	55.43	26	1	51.01	27
Ningbo	55.19	27	3	46.16	30
Tianjin	54.63	28	-3	51.83	25
Taiyuan	53.84	29	2	46.09	31
Guangzhou	53.15	30	-9	53.24	21
Shanghai	50.00	31	1	44.50	32
Hangzhou	48.73	32	1	42.50	33
Shenzhen	45.82	33	-5	50.14	28
Beijing	45.17	34	0	40.80	34
Haikou	40.00	35	0	39.97	35
National average	58.67			56.10	

As it is shown in Table 4.6, the weighted average of living costs objective indexes is 58.67 - higher than the 2012 average of 56.10. 3 cities score over 70, 18 over 60 and 31 over 50, which are respectively 1, 6 and 3 cities more than the

Sub-Indexes of Quality of Life for the 35 Chinese Cities in 2013

record of 2012. Cities ranked top 10 are: Kunming (1), Hohhot (2), Changsha (3), Shijiazhuang (4), Xining (5), Xi'an (6), Yinchuan (7), Nanchang (8), Jinan (9) and Qingdao(10), including 3 eastern cities, 2 central cities and 5 western cities. The bottom 10 cities are: Fuzhou (26), Ningbo (27), Tianjin (28), Taiyuan (29), Guangzhou (30), Shanghai (31), Hangzhou (32), Shenzhen (33), Beijing (34) and Haikou (35), including 9 eastern cities and 1 central city. Generally speaking, living costs in eastern cities are higher than in central or western cities.

4.3 Human Capital Index

Human capital index consists of a satisfaction index and an objective index (social and economic data index). The former was obtained through telephone survey by assigning values to survey answers, and the latter by calculating social and economic indexes of the 35 cities.

4.3.1 Subjective Satisfaction Index of Human Capital

Table 4.7 lists the satisfaction indexes of human capital in the surveyed 35 cities, along with their respective rankings. The indexes were obtained by inquiring interviewees about their satisfaction with the education received by them or their children, then assigning different values to their answers.

Table 4.7 Residents' Satisfaction Indexes of Human Capital in the 35 Chinese Cities

City	Score in 2013	Ranking in 2013	Score in 2012	Ranking in 2012	Places risen
Qingdao	62.61	1	62.62	5	4
Jinan	61.99	2	62.20	7	5
Urumqi	61.86	3	61.18	10	7
Dalian	61.67	4	59.20	17	13
Zhengzhou	61.54	5	58.45	24	19
Hefei	61.37	6	59.71	13	7
Hohhot	60.96	7	61.07	11	4
Shanghai	60.35	8	58.79	22	14
Ningbo	60.14	9	64.19	1	-8

Blue Book of Quality of Life in Cities

Continued table

City	Score in 2013	Ranking in 2013	Score in 2012	Ranking in 2012	Places risen
Xining	60.09	10	58.80	21	11
Beijing	59.68	11	59.33	16	5
Guiyang	59.60	12	55.48	33	21
Fuzhou	59.60	13	62.72	4	-9
Tianjin	59.30	14	61.27	9	-5
Nanjing	59.29	15	59.36	15	0
Hangzhou	59.24	16	62.38	6	-10
Haikou	59.11	17	58.00	27	10
Xiamen	59.03	18	59.01	19	1
Changchun	58.90	19	63.37	2	-17
Shijiazhuang	58.86	20	63.31	3	-17
Nanning	58.73	21	58.18	25	4
Yinchuan	58.52	22	61.98	8	-14
Nanchang	58.45	23	56.10	32	9
Changsha	58.20	24	60.38	12	-12
Chengdu	58.17	25	59.14	18	-7
Shenyang	57.79	26	57.61	28	2
Chongqing	57.74	27	58.83	20	-7
Guangzhou	57.59	28	59.43	14	-14
Harbin	57.23	29	56.76	30	1
Lanzhou	57.20	30	58.52	23	-7
Wuhan	57.09	31	58.09	26	-5
Shenzhen	57.03	32	57.34	29	-3
Xi'an	56.65	33	56.19	31	-2
Kunming	54.33	34	55.45	34	0
Taiyuan	53.49	35	55.20	35	0
National average	58.89		59.42		

As it is shown in Table 4.7, the weighted average of human capital satisfaction indexes is 58.89 - lower than the 2012 average of 59.42. 10 cities score over 60 - 2 less than in 2012. The 35 cities all score over 50, generally on the high side. Cities ranked top 10 are: Qingdao (1), Jinan (2), Urumqi (3), Dalian (4), Zhengzhou (5), Hefei (6), Hohhot (7), Shanghai (8), Ningbo (9) and Xining (10), including 5 eastern

Sub-Indexes of Quality of Life for the 35 Chinese Cities in 2013

cities, 2 central cities and 3 western cities. The bottom 10 cities are: Shenyang (26), Chongqing (27), Guangzhou (28), Harbin (29), Lanzhou (30), Wuhan (31), Shenzhen (32), Xi'an (33), Kunming (34) and Taiyuan (35), including 3 eastern cities, 4 central cities and 3 western cities. Generally speaking, east regions have performed better than central or western regions. Cities such as Guiyang (21), Zhengzhou (19), Haikou (10), Nanchang (9) and Dalian (13) have seen a dramatic rise, while cities like Changchun (-17), Shijiazhuang (-17), Guangzhou (-14), Yinchuan (-14), Changsha (-12) and Hangzhou (-10) have experienced a drastic drop. [1]

4.3.2 Objective Index (Social and Economic Data Index) of Human Capital

Human capital objective index consists of two secondary indicators: one is educational provision index, and the other is ratio of education, culture and entertainment expenditures. Table 4.8 lists the human capital objective indexes in the 35 cities.

Table 4.8   Objective Indexes of Human Capital in the 35 Chinese Cities

City	Score in 2013	Ranking in 2013	Places risen	Score in 2012	Ranking in 2012
Guangzhou	80.00	1	0	80.01	1
Nanjing	79.73	2	0	79.52	2
Xi'an	72.94	3	0	79.42	3
Beijing	68.76	4	0	70.96	4
Changsha	66.65	5	6	58.80	11
Taiyuan	64.68	6	-1	69.05	5
Shanghai	63.03	7	-1	66.15	6
Changchun	61.79	8	13	54.72	21
Guiyang	61.65	9	-2	62.79	7
Wuhan	60.89	10	3	58.52	13
Hefei	60.28	11	-1	59.72	10
Ningbo	59.09	12	0	58.62	12
Hohhot	58.83	13	-5	61.75	8
Nanning	58.27	14	-5	60.93	9
Yinchuan	56.57	15	1	57.57	16

① Numbers in brackets stand for the places risen or dropped.

Blue Book of Quality of Life in Cities

Continued table

City	Score in 2013	Ranking in 2013	Places risen	Score in 2012	Ranking in 2012
Fuzhou	56.38	16	12	51.09	28
Kunming	56.19	17	0	57.20	17
Jinan	55.28	18	-3	57.66	15
Shijiazhuang	55.22	19	14	47.11	33
Shenyang	54.67	20	0	55.90	20
Lanzhou	53.68	21	2	54.33	23
Harbin	52.90	22	3	52.83	25
Hangzhou	52.89	23	1	53.38	24
Dalian	52.62	24	3	52.09	27
Nanchang	51.88	25	5	48.30	30
Chengdu	51.79	26	3	50.62	29
Tianjin	51.63	27	-9	56.58	18
Shenzhen	49.79	28	-6	54.43	22
Urumqi	49.17	29	-10	56.49	19
Chongqing	48.03	30	1	48.28	31
Zhengzhou	48.02	31	1	47.50	32
Haikou	46.39	32	-18	58.08	14
Qingdao	46.32	33	1	45.56	34
Xiamen	43.09	34	-8	52.32	26
Xining	40.00	35	0	39.99	35
National average	57.78			57.66	

As it is shown in Table 4.8, the weighted average of human capital objective indexes is 57.78 - higher than the 2012 average of 57.66. 27 cities score over 50 - 2 less than in 2012. Cities ranked top 10 are: Guangzhou (1), Nanjing (2), Xi'an (3), Beijing (4), Changsha (5), Taiyuan (6), Shanghai (7), Changchun (8), Guiyang (9) and Wuhan (10), including 4 eastern cities, 4 central cities and 2 western cities. The bottom 10 cities are: Chengdu (26), Tianjin (27), Shenzhen (28), Urumqi (29), Chongqing (30), Zhengzhou (31), Haikou (32), Qingdao (33), Xiamen (34) and Xining (35), including 5 eastern cities, 1 central city and 4 western cities. Rankings of the top 4 cities (Guangzhou, Nanjing, Xi'an and Beijing) remain unchanged. Cities such as Shijiazhuang (14), Changchun (13) and Fuzhou (12) have seen a

Sub-Indexes of Quality of Life for the 35 Chinese Cities in 2013

dramatic rise, while cities like Haikou (-18), Urumqi (-10), Tianjin (-9) and Shenzhen (-6) have experienced a drastic drop.[①]

4.4 Social Security Index

Social security index consists of a subjective satisfaction index and an objective index (social and economic data index).

4.4.1 Subjective Satisfaction Index

Satisfaction index of social security is measured with the satisfaction toward health care and urban security. First, we obtained the health care and the urban security indexes by inquiring interviewees about their satisfaction toward health care, elderly support and urban security (public order), and assigning different values to their answers. Then, we calculated the weighted average of the two indexes and get the social security (subjective) satisfaction index. Table 4.9 lists the survey results of the 35 cities along with their respective rankings.

Table 4.9 Satisfaction Indexes of Social Security in the 35 Chinese Cities

City	Score in 2013	Ranking in 2013	Score in 2012	Ranking in 2012	Places risen
Qingdao	61.87	1	62.26	7	6
Xiamen	61.25	2	62.79	4	2
Hangzhou	60.76	3	64.68	1	-2
Ningbo	60.52	4	63.65	2	-2
Yinchuan	60.03	5	62.24	8	3
Jinan	59.82	6	62.65	6	0
Xining	59.31	7	62.04	9	2
Nanjing	59.22	8	59.17	17	9
Beijing	58.94	9	61.27	12	3
Shanghai	58.04	10	58.71	18	8
Hefei	57.71	11	59.80	15	4
Changchun	57.59	12	62.83	3	-9

---

① Numbers in brackets stand for the places risen or dropped.

Blue Book of Quality of Life in Cities

Continued table

City	Score in 2013	Ranking in 2013	Score in 2012	Ranking in 2012	Places risen
Dalian	57.18	13	61.73	10	-3
Chengdu	57.05	14	61.33	11	-3
Shijiazhuang	56.64	15	61.24	13	-2
Taiyuan	56.63	16	58.66	19	3
Urumqi	56.57	17	58.06	22	5
Shenyang	56.40	18	57.04	25	7
Xi'an	56.27	19	59.65	16	-3
Fuzhou	56.23	20	58.60	20	0
Harbin	55.86	21	56.27	30	9
Zhengzhou	55.74	22	56.67	28	6
Lanzhou	55.65	23	57.67	23	0
Chongqing	55.61	24	62.78	5	-19
Tianjin	55.14	25	58.57	21	-4
Shenzhen	55.11	26	57.04	24	-2
Guangzhou	54.70	27	56.81	27	0
Nanchang	54.09	28	55.18	33	5
Changsha	54.09	29	56.14	31	2
Kunming	54.09	30	54.65	34	4
Haikou	53.86	31	55.75	32	1
Wuhan	52.64	32	56.83	26	-6
Hohhot	52.63	33	60.18	14	-19
Nanning	52.43	34	56.33	29	-5
Guiyang	51.98	35	52.26	35	0
National average	56.64		59.19		

As it is shown in Table 4.9, the weighted average of social security satisfaction indexes is 56.64 - lower than the 2012 average of 59.19, mainly due to the drop in urban security (public order) satisfaction.[1] The cities all score over 50, and 5 over 60 - 9 less than in 2012. Cities ranked top 10 are: Qingdao (1), Xiamen (2), Hangzhou (3), Ningbo (4), Yinchuan (5), Jinan (6), Xining (7), Nanjing (8), Beijing (9) and Shanghai (10), including 8 eastern cities and 2 western cities. The bottom 10 cities are: Shenzhen (26), Guangzhou (27), Nanchang (28), Changsha (29),

---

① Detailed analysis will be made in the following passages.

Table 4.10 Satisfaction Indexes of Health Care in the 35 Chinese Cities

City	Score in 2013	Ranking in 2013	Places risen in 2013	Score in 2012	Ranking in 2012	Ranking in 2012[8]	Ranking in 2011	Places risen in 2012
Xining	61.67	1	2	57.87	3	2	8	6
Ningbo	58.96	2	0	58.24	2	—	—	—
Lanzhou	58.33	3	20	52.27	23	18	1	-17
Qingdao	58.19	4	13	53.42	17	—	—	—
Beijing	57.29	5	7	55.71	12	10	5	-5
Guiyang	56.64	6	10	53.57	16	14	7	-7
Yinchuan	56.59	7	4	55.73	11	9	3	-6
Shijiazhuang	56.39	8	1	56.55	9	8	11	3
Urumqi	56.36	9	-5	57.57	4	3	6	3
Hangzhou	56.11	10	-9	58.37	1	1	4	3
Xi'an	55.96	11	-3	57.04	8	7	27	20
Xiamen	55.83	12	-2	56.40	10	—	—	—
Nanchang	55.64	13	15	51.63	28	23	30	7
Zhengzhou	54.82	14	8	52.38	22	17	12	-5
Chongqing	54.79	15	0	53.74	15	13	17	4
Nanjing	54.61	16	16	49.74	32	27	20	-7
Hohhot	54.53	17	-12	57.50	5	4	9	5
Kunming	54.42	18	9	51.76	27	22	29	7

Continued table

City	Score in 2013	Ranking in 2013	Places risen in 2013	Score in 2012	Ranking in 2012	Ranking in 2012[a]	Ranking in 2011	Places risen in 2012
Hefei	54.42	19	-6	55.58	13	11	16	5
Chengdu	54.40	20	-6	55.26	14	12	21	9
Shenyang	54.37	21	10	50.00	31	26	28	2
Jinan	54.24	22	4	51.96	26	21	10	-11
Taiyuan	54.05	23	-16	57.18	7	6	15	9
Fuzhou	53.75	24	6	51.30	30	25	14	-11
Haikou	53.11	25	9	49.50	34	29	2	-27
Changchun	52.90	26	-20	57.22	6	5	13	8
Harbin	52.47	27	6	49.52	33	28	18	-10
Changsha	52.45	28	-3	52.05	25	20	26	6
Guangzhou	52.37	29	0	51.38	29	24	22	-2
Dalian	52.13	30	-12	53.37	18	—	—	—
Nanning	52.11	31	-10	52.47	21	16	23	7
Shanghai	51.96	32	3	48.93	35	30	24	-6
Tianjin	51.64	33	-9	52.06	24	19	19	0
Shenzhen	51.23	34	-15	52.98	19	—	—	—
Wuhan	50.45	35	-15	52.52	20	15	25	10
National average		54.34			53.61		52.75	

Sub-Indexes of Quality of Life for the 35 Chinese Cities in 2013

Kunming (30), Haikou (31), Wuhan (32), Hohhot (33), Nanning (34) and Guiyang (35), including 3 eastern cities, 3 central cities and 4 western cities. Generally speaking, eastern cities have performed better than central or western cities. Cities such as Harbin (9), Nanjing (9), Shanghai (8), Shenyang (7) and Qingdao (6) have seen a dramatic rise, while cities like Hohhot (-19), Chongqing (-19), Changchun (-9) and Wuhan (-6) have experienced a drastic drop. [①]

As it is shown in Table 4.10, the weighted average of health care satisfaction indexes is 54.34 - slightly higher than that of 2012. 1 city (Xining) scores over 60 - a breakthrough compared to last year. The 35 cities all score over 50 - 4 more than in 2012. Cities ranked top 10 are: Xining (1), Ningbo (2), Lanzhou (3), Qingdao (4), Beijing (5), Guiyang (6), Yinchuan (7), Shijiazhuang (8), Urumqi (9) and Hangzhou (10), including 5 eastern cities and 5 western cities. The bottom 10 cities are: Changchun (26), Harbin (27), Changsha (28), Guangzhou (29), Dalian (30), Nanning (31), Shanghai (32), Tianjin (33), Shenzhen (34) and Wuhan (35), including 5 eastern cities, 4 central cities and 1 western city. Cities such as Lanzhou (20), Nanjing (16), Nanchang (15), Qingdao (13), Guiyang (10), Kunming (9), Zhengzhou (8) and Beijing (7) have seen a dramatic rise, while cities like Changchun (-20), Shenzhen (-15), Wuhan (-15), Dalian (-12), Nanning (-10) and Tianjin (-9) have experienced a drastic drop. [②]

Table 4.11 lists residents's satisfaction indexes of urban security (public order).

Table 4.11 Satisfaction Indexes of Urban Security (Public Order) in the 35 Chinese Cities

City	Score in 2013	Ranking in 2013	Places risen	Score in 2012	Ranking in 2012
Xiamen	66.67	1	5	69.19	6
Qingdao	65.55	2	1	71.11	3
Hangzhou	65.42	3	1	70.99	4
Jinan	65.41	4	-3	73.34	1
Shanghai	64.12	5	5	68.48	10
Nanjing	63.83	6	3	68.59	9
Yinchuan	63.46	7	1	68.75	8

① Numbers in brackets stand for the places risen or dropped.
② Numbers in brackets stand for the places risen or dropped.

Blue Book of Quality of Life in Cities

Continued table

City	Score in 2013	Ranking in 2013	Places risen	Score in 2012	Ranking in 2012
Changchun	62.29	8	3	68.45	11
Dalian	62.22	9	-4	70.09	5
Ningbo	62.08	10	-3	69.05	7
Hefei	61.00	11	8	64.03	19
Beijing	60.58	12	1	66.82	13
Chengdu	59.69	13	-1	67.40	12
Harbin	59.25	14	7	63.03	21
Taiyuan	59.22	15	16	60.15	31
Shenzhen	58.98	16	11	61.11	27
Fuzhou	58.71	17	-1	65.90	16
Tianjin	58.64	18	-1	65.08	17
Shenyang	58.43	19	-1	64.09	18
Guangzhou	57.02	20	4	62.25	24
Xining	56.94	21	-7	66.20	14
Shijiazhuang	56.89	22	-7	65.93	15
Urumqi	56.78	23	10	58.55	33
Zhengzhou	56.66	24	4	60.95	28
Xi'an	56.58	25	-2	62.26	23
Chongqing	56.43	26	-24	71.83	2
Changsha	55.73	27	2	60.23	29
Wuhan	54.83	28	-2	61.13	26
Haikou	54.61	29	-4	62.00	25
Kunming	53.75	30	4	57.53	34
Lanzhou	52.97	31	-11	63.07	20
Nanning	52.75	32	-2	60.19	30
Nanchang	52.55	33	-1	58.74	32
Hohhot	50.73	34	-12	62.86	22
Guiyang	47.32	35	0	50.95	35
National average	58.93			64.58	

As it is shown in Table 4.11, the weighted average of urban security (public order) satisfaction indexes is 58.93 - lower than the 2012 average of 64.58. 12 cities score over 60 - 19 less than in 2012. The drop in satisfaction indexes of

Sub-Indexes of Quality of Life for the 35 Chinese Cities in 2013

urban security (public order) has resulted in the fall of social security satisfaction indexes. Cities ranked top 10 are: Xiamen (1), Qingdao (2), Hangzhou (3), Jinan (4), Shanghai (5), Nanjing (6), Yinchuan (7), Changchun (8), Dalian (9) and Ningbo (10), including 8 eastern cities, 1 central city and 1 western city. The bottom 10 cities are: Chongqing (26), Changsha (27), Wuhan (28), Haikou (29), Kunming (30), Lanzhou (31), Nanning (32), Nanchang (33), Hohhot (34) and Guiyang (35), including 1 eastern city, 3 central cities and 6 western cities. Cities such as Taiyuan (16), Shenzhen (11), Hefei (8), Xiamen (5), Shanghai (5) and Urumqi (10) have seen a dramatic rise, while cities like Chongqing (-24), Lanzhou (-11), Hohhot (-12), Xining (-7) and Shijiazhuang (-7) have experienced a drastic drop.[1]

4.4.2 Objective Index (Social and Economic Data Index) of Social Security

Objective index of social security is measured by three secondary indicators: social security coverage, basic medical insurance coverage and unemployment insurance coverage. Table 4.12 lists the objective indexes of social security.

Table 4.12 Objective Indexes of Social Security in the 35 Chinese Cities

City	Score in 2013	Ranking in 2013	Places risen	Score in 2012	Ranking in 2012
Shenzhen	80.00	1	0	80.01	1
Beijing	77.24	2	0	71.82	2
Xiamen	74.37	3	0	71.43	3
Ningbo	72.36	4	4	56.19	8
Shanghai	67.23	5	-1	68.68	4
Guangzhou	66.71	6	-1	60.11	5
Hangzhou	63.84	7	0	58.36	7
Tianjin	63.13	8	-2	59.89	6
Shenyang	62.01	9	3	55.20	12
Changchun	59.84	10	7	48.23	17
Dalian	59.82	11	-2	55.67	9
Nanjing	58.11	12	-2	55.65	10
Urumqi	52.63	13	0	51.44	13

① Numbers in brackets stand for the places risen or dropped.

Blue Book of Quality of Life in Cities

Continued table

City	Score in 2013	Ranking in 2013	Places risen	Score in 2012	Ranking in 2012
Qingdao	52.34	14	2	48.63	16
Xi'an	52.15	15	-4	55.62	11
Yinchuan	51.93	16	2	47.15	18
Chengdu	50.84	17	5	45.00	22
Wuhan	50.48	18	-3	49.51	15
Taiyuan	49.08	19	-5	50.61	14
Jinan	47.36	20	0	46.08	20
Hohhot	46.91	21	0	45.68	21
Nanning	46.09	22	12	40.85	34
Changsha	45.97	23	4	43.07	27
Lanzhou	45.14	24	-5	46.35	19
Guiyang	44.95	25	-1	44.14	24
Chongqing	44.57	26	6	41.48	32
Fuzhou	44.06	27	4	42.17	31
Haikou	43.91	28	2	42.54	30
Hefei	43.72	29	-6	44.71	23
Nanchang	43.05	30	-5	43.46	25
Shijiazhuang	41.77	31	2	40.86	33
Harbin	41.73	32	-6	43.21	26
Kunming	41.21	33	-4	42.85	29
Zhengzhou	40.98	34	-6	42.99	28
Xining	40.00	35	0	39.98	35
National average	55.26			50.85	

As it is shown in Table 4.12, the weighted average of social security objective indexes is 55.26 – higher than the 2012 average of 50.85. 18 cities score over 50 - 4 more than in 2012. The 35 cities all score over 40. Cities ranked top 10 are: Shenzhen (1), Beijing (2), Xiamen (3), Ningbo (4), Shanghai (5), Guangzhou (6), Hangzhou (7), Tianjin (8), Shenyang (9) and Changchun (10), including 9 eastern cities and 1 central city. The bottom 10 cities are: Chongqing (26), Fuzhou (27), Haikou (28), Hefei (29), Nanchang (30), Shijiazhuang (31), Harbin (32), Kunming (33), Zhengzhou (34) and Xining (35), including 3 eastern cities, 3 western cities and 4 central cities. Through comparison, we find that the indexes of eastern cities

048

Sub-Indexes of Quality of Life for the 35 Chinese Cities in 2013

are obviously higher than those of central or western cities. Cities such as Nanning (12), Changchun (7), Chongqing (6) and Chengdu (5) have seen a dramatic rise, while cities like Hefei (-6), Harbin (-6), Zhengzhou (-6) and Nanchang (-5) have experienced a drastic drop. [1]

4.5　Living Experience Index

Living experience index consists of a satisfaction index and an objective index (social and economic data index) as well.

4.5.1　Subjective Satisfaction Index

Satisfaction index of living experience is made up of pace of life and living convenience satisfaction indexes. First, we obtained the two satisfaction indexes by inquiring interviewees about their satisfaction with the pace of life and the living convenience in their cities, then assigning different values to their answers. In the end, we calculated the weighted average of the two indexes for the results of living experience satisfaction indexes.

Table 4.13 lists the survey results of the 35 cities along with their respective rankings.

Table 4.13　Satisfaction Indexes of Living Experience in the 35 Chinese Cites

City	Score in 2013	Ranking in 2013	Score in 2012	Ranking in 2012	Places risen
Yinchuan	58.24	1	59.90	1	0
Xining	57.76	2	57.41	7	5
Nanjing	57.54	3	58.08	5	2
Hangzhou	57.05	4	58.25	3	-1
Tianjin	56.75	5	56.63	13	8
Xiamen	56.67	6	59.01	2	-4
Chongqing	56.66	7	56.18	16	9
Ningbo	56.56	8	55.34	19	11
Qingdao	56.20	9	56.96	11	2
Fuzhou	56.20	10	56.72	12	2

[1]　Numbers in brackets stand for the places risen or dropped.

049

Blue Book of Quality of Life in Cities

Continued table

City	Score in 2013	Ranking in 2013	Score in 2012	Ranking in 2012	Places risen
Changchun	56.14	11	58.22	4	-7
Jinan	56.13	12	57.23	8	-4
Shanghai	56.10	13	56.58	14	1
Zhengzhou	56.09	14	54.17	25	11
Chengdu	56.06	15	57.86	6	-9
Xi'an	55.96	16	55.46	18	2
Haikou	55.63	17	55.75	17	0
Taiyuan	54.75	18	53.84	28	10
Shijiazhuang	54.43	19	57.11	9	-10
Dalian	54.35	20	55.06	22	2
Shenyang	54.21	21	55.33	20	-1
Hefei	54.09	22	55.31	21	-1
Harbin	53.95	23	53.62	31	8
Changsha	53.94	24	57.02	10	-14
Beijing	53.87	25	53.30	32	7
Nanchang	53.84	26	53.86	27	1
Wuhan	53.29	27	54.31	24	-3
Guiyang	53.18	28	53.81	29	1
Hohhot	53.07	29	52.68	34	5
Shenzhen	53.07	30	54.02	26	-4
Guangzhou	52.99	31	53.67	30	-1
Nanning	52.96	32	54.86	23	-9
Lanzhou	52.47	33	50.00	35	2
Kunming	52.40	34	53.13	33	-1
Urumqi	50.85	35	56.25	15	-20
National average	55.07		55.63		

As it is shown in Table 4.13, the weighted average of living experience satisfaction indexes is 55.07 - lower than the 2012 average of 55.63. The 35 cities all score between 50 and 60, up to the satisfaction level, - a generally stable result compared to that of last year. Cities ranked top 10 are: Yinchuan (1), Xining (2), Nanjing (3), Hangzhou (4), Tianjin (5), Xiamen (6), Chongqing (7), Ningbo (8), Qingdao (9) and Fuzhou (10), including 7 eastern cities and 3 western cities. The

Sub-Indexes of Quality of Life for the 35 Chinese Cities in 2013

bottom 10 cities are: Nanchang (26), Wuhan (27), Guiyang (28), Hohhot (29), Shenzhen (30), Guangzhou (31), Nanning (32), Lanzhou (33), Kunming (34) and Urumqi (35), including 2 eastern cities, 2 central cities and 6 western cities. Cities such as Ningbo (11), Taiyuan (10), Chongqing (9), Harbin(8) and Beijing (7) have seen a dramatic rise, while cities like Urumqi (-20), Changsha (-14), Shijiazhuang (-10) and Chengdu (-9) have experienced a drastic drop.[①] Changes in the scores and the rankings of living experience satisfaction indexes can be further explained by analyzing the pace of life and the living convenience satisfaction indexes. Table 4.14 lists the pace of life satisfaction indexes in the 35 cities along with their respective rankings.

As it is shown in Table 4.14, the weighted average of pace of life satisfaction indexes is 42.97 - roughly the same as the previous two surveys. The fact that all the 35 cities score below 50 indicates a widespread worry over the crazy pace among city dwellers. Cities ranked top 10 are: Changchun (1), Xining (2), Haikou (3), Chengdu (4), Lanzhou (5), Zhengzhou (6), Guiyang (7), Hangzhou (8), Taiyuan (9) and Yinchuan (10), including 2 eastern cities, 3 central cities and 5 western cities. The bottom 10 cities are: Dalian (26), Changsha (27), Harbin (28), Shenyang (29), Urumqi (30), Beijing (31), Qingdao (32), Shanghai (33), Guangzhou (34) and Shenzhen (35), including 7 eastern cities, 2 central cities and 1 western city. Cities such as Lanzhou (20), Zhengzhou (12), Jinan (8), Tianjin (8) and Hohhot (11) have seen a dramatic rise, while cities like Changsha (-21), Urumqi (-20), Xiamen (-15), Shijiazhuang (-11), Nanchang (-9), Yinchuan (-9), Nanning (-8) and Wuhan (-7) have experienced a drastic drop.[②] Survey results show that the widespread worry is worse in eastern cities than in central or western cities.

Table 4.15 lists the satisfaction indexes of living convenience in the 35 cities, along with their respective rankings.

---

① Numbers in brackets stand for the places risen or dropped.
② Numbers in brackets stand for the places risen or dropped.

051

Table 4.14 Satisfaction Indexes of Pace of Life in the 35 Chinese Cities

City	Score in 2013	Ranking in 2013	Places risen in 2013	Score in 2012	Ranking in 2012	Ranking in 2012[9]	Ranking in 2011	Places risen in 2012
Changchun	49.88	1	4	45.72	5	5	19	14
Xining	47.95	2	2	47.22	4	4	2	-2
Haikou	47.25	3	0	47.50	3	3	21	18
Chengdu	47.22	4	-2	48.39	2	2	22	20
Lanzhou	46.47	5	20	41.48	25	24	29	5
Zhengzhou	46.27	6	12	42.98	18	17	13	-4
Guiyang	45.90	7	0	45.48	7	7	10	3
Hangzhou	45.83	8	0	44.93	8	8	4	-4
Taiyuan	45.11	9	6	43.32	15	14	11	-3
Yinchuan	45.05	10	-9	50.00	1	1	1	0
Jinan	45.02	11	8	42.92	19	18	5	-13
Tianjin	44.95	12	8	42.70	20	19	7	-12
Kunming	44.90	13	3	43.27	16	15	8	-7
Fuzhou	44.90	14	7	42.49	21	20	20	0
Hohhot	44.74	15	11	41.43	26	25	17	-8
Nanjing	44.62	16	1	43.21	17	16	3	-13
Xi'an	44.32	17	7	42.23	24	23	16	-7
Hefei	44.27	18	5	42.27	23	22	15	-7

Continued table

City	Score in 2013	Ranking in 2013	Places risen in 2013	Score in 2012	Ranking in 2012	Ranking in 2012[9]	Ranking in 2011	Places risen in 2012
Nanning	44.23	19	-8	44.44	11	10	25	15
Chongqing	44.01	20	2	42.34	22	21	18	-3
Wuhan	43.69	21	-7	43.49	14	13	14	1
Nanchang	43.62	22	-9	43.90	13	12	23	11
Shijiazhuang	43.11	23	-11	44.35	12	11	12	1
Xiamen	43.06	24	-15	44.77	9	—	—	—
Ningbo	42.99	25	3	40.54	28	—	—	—
Dalian	42.87	26	5	39.57	31	—	—	—
Changsha	42.81	27	-21	45.61	6	6	6	0
Harbin	42.54	28	2	39.96	30	27	26	-1
Shenyang	41.81	29	-2	40.86	27	26	9	-17
Urumqi	41.81	30	-20	44.74	10	9	27	18
Beijing	39.32	31	2	37.11	33	29	30	1
Qingdao	39.22	32	-3	40.09	29	—	—	—
Shanghai	38.20	33	1	37.05	34	30	24	-6
Guangzhou	36.67	34	-2	38.12	32	28	28	0
Shenzhen	34.93	35	0	35.81	35	—	—	—
National average	42.97			42.87		42.67		

Sub-Indexes of Quality of Life for the 35 Chinese Cities in 2013

Table 4.15 Satisfaction Indexes of Living Convenience in the 35 Chinese Cities

City	Score in 2013	Ranking in 2013	Places risen in 2013	Score in 2012	Ranking in 2012	Ranking in 2012[10]	Ranking in 2011	Places risen in 2012
Shanghai	73.993	1	0	76.12	1	1	9	8
Qingdao	73.179	2	0	73.82	2	—	—	—
Yinchuan	71.429	3	13	69.79	16	11	5	-6
Shenzhen	71.205	4	1	72.22	5	—	—	—
Nanjing	70.461	5	-1	72.95	4	2	10	8
Xiamen	70.278	6	-3	73.26	3	—	—	—
Ningbo	70.139	7	5	70.14	12	—	—	—
Chongqing	69.313	8	5	70.01	13	8	2	-6
Guangzhou	69.307	9	9	69.23	18	13	20	7
Tianjin	68.551	10	0	70.56	10	7	15	8
Beijing	68.419	11	6	69.50	17	12	16	4
Hangzhou	68.264	12	-6	71.58	6	3	3	0
Xi'an	67.590	13	6	68.69	19	14	22	8
Xining	67.565	14	9	67.59	23	18	19	1
Fuzhou	67.493	15	-7	70.95	8	5	13	8
Jinan	67.251	16	-9	71.54	7	4	1	-3
Shenyang	66.604	17	-2	69.80	15	10	8	-2
Zhengzhou	65.907	18	8	65.36	26	21	14	-7

Continued table

City	Score in 2013	Ranking in 2013	Places risen in 2013	Score in 2012	Ranking in 2012	Ranking in 2012[10]	Ranking in 2011	Places risen in 2012
Dalian	65.833	19	-8	70.55	11	—	—	—
Shijiazhuang	65.751	20	-6	69.86	14	9	21	12
Harbin	65.359	21	4	67.28	25	20	17	-3
Changsha	65.068	22	-2	68.42	20	15	23	8
Chengdu	64.901	23	1	67.32	24	19	6	-13
Taiyuan	64.385	24	5	64.36	29	24	26	2
Nanchang	64.059	25	7	63.82	32	27	27	0
Haikou	64.011	26	4	64.00	30	25	12	-13
Hefei	63.910	27	-6	68.35	21	16	7	-9
Wuhan	62.887	28	0	65.13	28	23	30	7
Changchun	62.392	29	-20	70.72	9	6	11	5
Nanning	61.690	30	-3	65.28	27	22	29	7
Hohhot	61.404	31	0	63.93	31	26	28	2
Guiyang	60.452	32	2	62.14	34	29	24	-5
Kunming	59.904	33	0	62.98	33	28	25	-3
Urumqi	59.887	34	-12	67.76	22	17	18	1
Lanzhou	58.475	35	0	58.52	35	30	4	-26
National average		67.18			68.39		56.24	

Blue Book of Quality of Life in Cities

As it is shown in Table 4.15, the weighted average of living convenience satisfaction indexes is 67.81. It is generally on the high side, but lower than the 2012 average of 68.39. Cities ranked top 10 are: Shanghai (1), Qingdao (2), Yinchuan (3), Shenzhen (4), Nanjing (5), Xiamen (6), Ningbo (7), Chongqing (8), Guangzhou (9) and Tianjin (10), including 8 eastern cities and 2 western cities. The bottom 10 cities are: Haikou (26), Hefei (27), Wuhan (28), Changchun (29), Nanning (30), Hohhot (31), Guiyang (32), Kunming (33), Urumqi (34) and Lanzhou (35), including 1 eastern city, 3 central cities and 6 western cities. Cities such as Yinchuan (13), Guangzhou (9), Xining (9), Zhengzhou (8), Nanchang (7), Beijing (6) and Xi'an (6) have seen a dramatic rise, while cities like Changchun (-20), Urumqi (-12), Dalian (-8), Hefei (-6) and Hangzhou (-6) have experienced a drastic drop.[①] The rankings of Shanghai, Qingdao, Tianjin, Wuhan, Hohhot, Lanzhou and Kunming remain unchanged. Survey results show that governmental investments in infrastructure have greatly improved the living convenience of city dwellers. Because the infrastructure in eastern cities is more advanced than in central or western cities, the satisfaction indexes of living convenience there are generally higher.

4.5.2 Objective Index (Social and Economic Data Index) of Living Experience

Objective index of living experience consists of 3 primary indicators: living convenience, eco-environment and perception of income disparities. The primary indicators are in turn made up of 6 secondary indicators: transportation capacity, number of cinemas and theaters per 10,000 residents, medical care capacity, per capita green area, air quality and the Gini coefficient. Table 4.16 lists the objective indexes of living experience in the 35 cities.

As it is shown in Table 4.16, the weighted average of living experience objective indexes is 53.67 - higher than the 2012 average of 51.89. 22 cities score over 50 - 5 more than in 2012. Cities ranked top 10 are: Beijing (1), Shenzhen (2),

---

① Numbers in brackets stand for the places risen or dropped.

Sub-Indexes of Quality of Life for the 35 Chinese Cities in 2013

Table 4.16 Objective Indexes of Living Experience in the 35 Chinese Cities

City	Score in 2013	Ranking in 2013	Places risen	Score in 2012	Ranking in 2012
Beijing	80.00	1	0	80.01	1
Shenzhen	65.12	2	0	71.86	2
Guangzhou	64.16	3	4	58.88	7
Shenyang	62.56	4	1	62.90	5
Wuhan	60.15	5	-2	64.52	3
Nanjing	59.70	6	2	58.24	8
Hohhot	58.74	7	6	54.50	13
Hangzhou	58.41	8	-4	64.43	4
Haikou	57.80	9	3	55.45	12
Kunming	57.57	10	0	55.61	10
Taiyuan	57.34	11	10	48.10	21
Harbin	56.98	12	8	48.25	20
Qingdao	55.68	13	6	48.97	19
Yinchuan	54.74	14	0	52.58	14
Shanghai	54.71	15	-6	56.45	9
Hefei	54.46	16	15	42.91	31
Xi'an	54.32	17	-6	55.46	11
Urumqi	54.20	18	5	46.58	23
Changchun	53.70	19	-3	51.25	16
Xiamen	52.07	20	-14	58.95	6
Lanzhou	51.76	21	-4	50.77	17
Shijiazhuang	51.39	22	0	46.63	22
Ningbo	48.24	23	1	46.35	24
Dalian	47.37	24	-6	49.07	18
Tianjin	47.28	25	0	46.20	25
Changsha	46.47	26	2	45.23	28
Fuzhou	45.93	27	-12	51.84	15
Xining	45.51	28	-1	45.60	27
Guiyang	44.89	29	3	41.91	32
Nanchang	44.81	30	0	43.40	30
Jinan	44.71	31	-5	45.72	26
Nanning	43.97	32	-3	44.47	29
Chengdu	43.35	33	1	41.30	34
Chongqing	43.18	34	1	40.02	35
Zhengzhou	40.00	35	-2	41.65	33
National average	53.67			51.89	

057

Blue Book of Quality of Life in Cities

Guangzhou (3), Shenyang (4), Wuhan (5), Nanjing (6), Hohhot (7), Hangzhou (8), Haikou (9) and Kunming (10), including 7 eastern cities, 1 central city and 2 western cities. The bottom 10 cities are: Changsha (26), Fuzhou (27), Xining (28), Guiyang (29), Nanchang (30), Jinan (31), Nanning (32), Chengdu (33), Chongqing (34) and Zhengzhou (35), including 2 eastern cities, 3 central cities and 5 western cities. Cities such as Hefei (15), Taiyuan (10), Harbin (8) and Qingdao (6) have seen a dramatic rise, while cities like Xiamen (-14), Fuzhou (-12), Shanghai (-6) and Xi'an (-6) have experienced a drastic drop.[1] The rankings of Beijing, Shenzhen, Kunming, Yinchuan, Shijiazhuang, Tianjin and Nanchang remain unchanged.

4.6   Primary Indicator Radar Charts of QLICC

The following radar charts show the primary indicators of the subjective or objective indexes in the 35 cities. It can be easily discerned that living costs is a key factor which pulls down subjective or objective QLI.

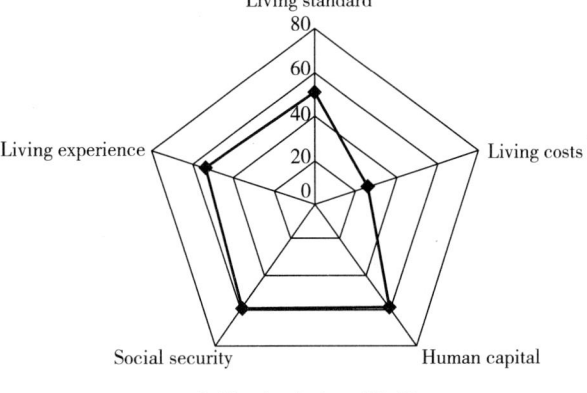

Subjective index of Beijing

――――――――――――

[1]   Numbers in brackets stand for the places risen or dropped.

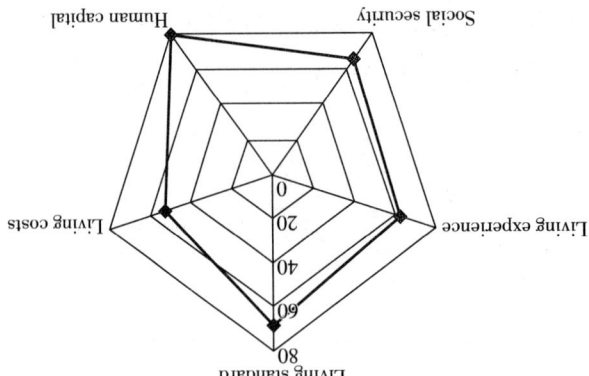

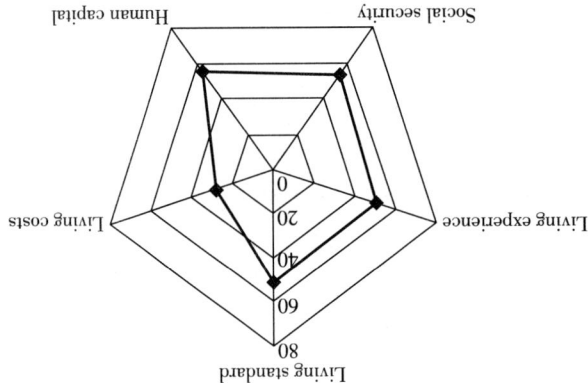

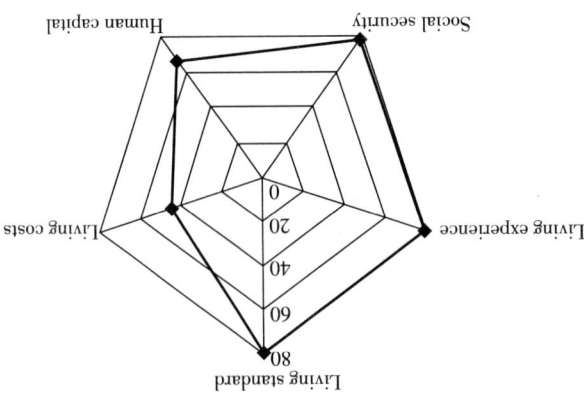

Sub-Indexes of Quality of Life for the 35 Chinese Cities in 2013

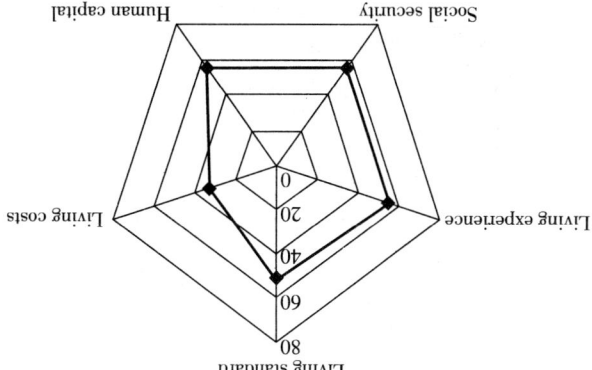

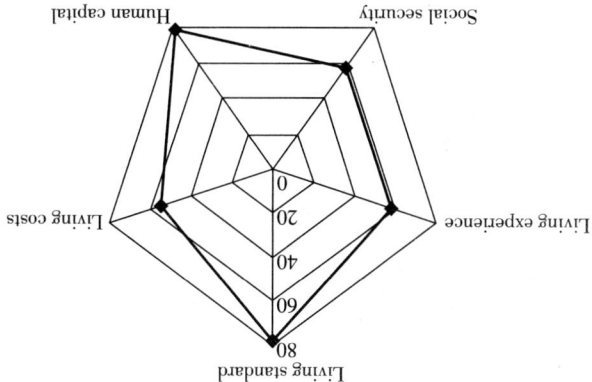

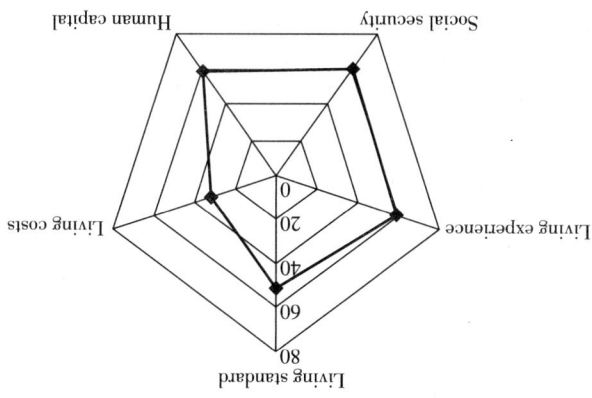

Sub-Indexes of Quality of Life for the 35 Chinese Cities in 2013

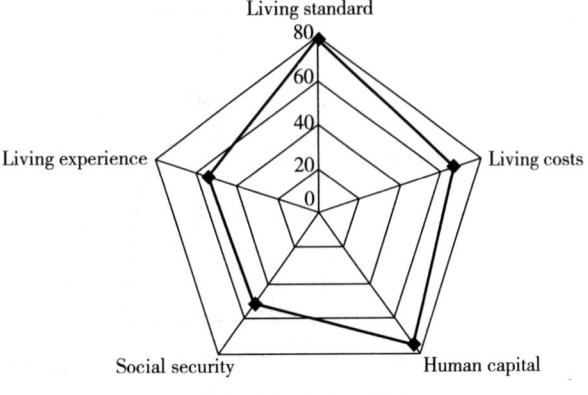

Objective index of Xi'an

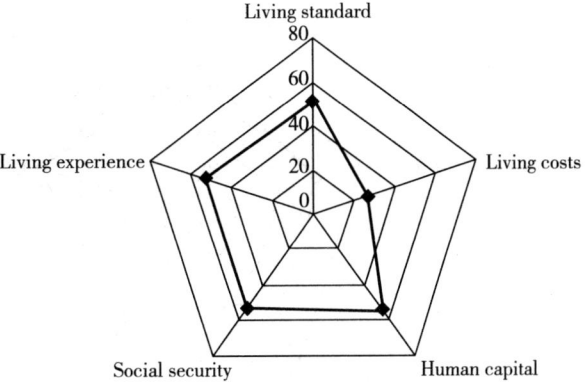

Subjective index of Shenzhen

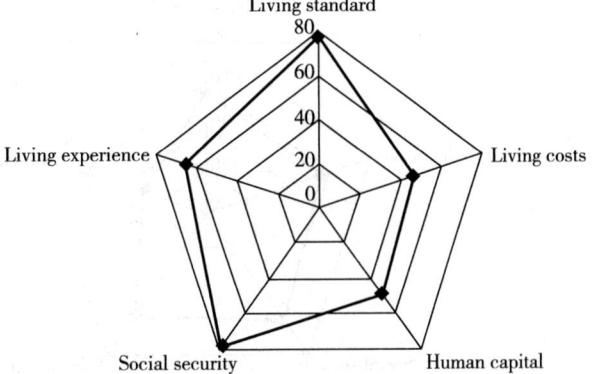

Objective index of Shenzhen

Blue Book of Quality of Life in Cities

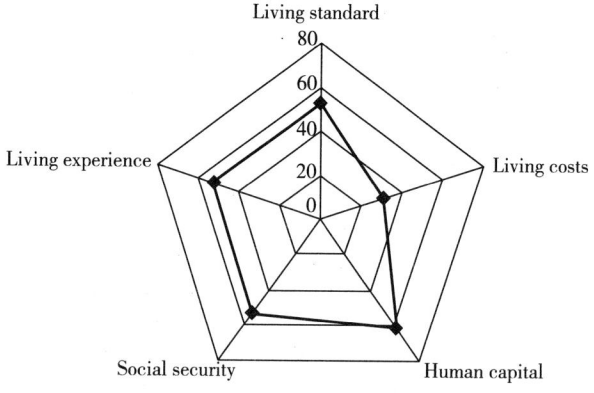

Subjective index of Hohhot

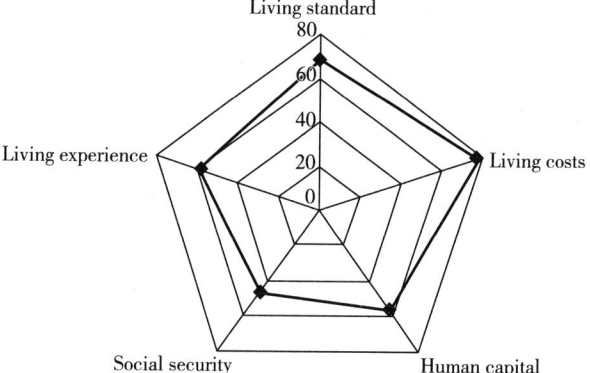

Objective index of Hohhot

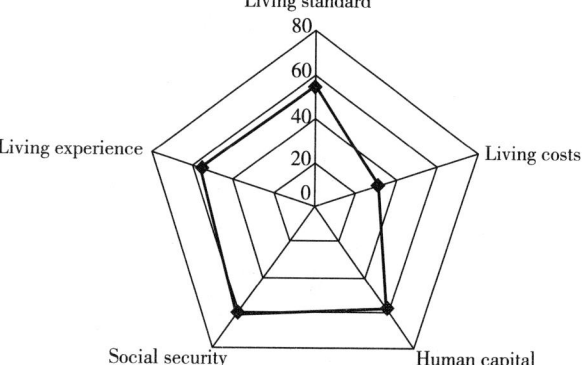

Subjective index of Xiamen

Sub-Indexes of Quality of Life for the 35 Chinese Cities in 2013

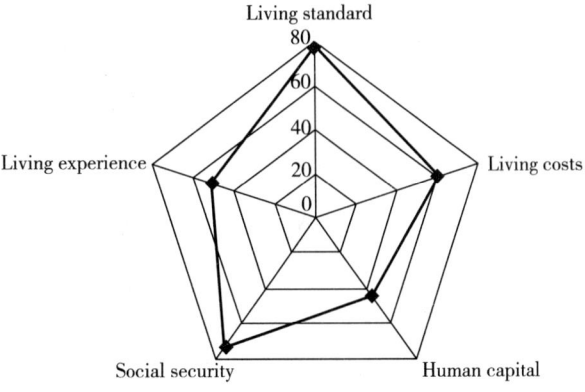

Objective index of Xiamen

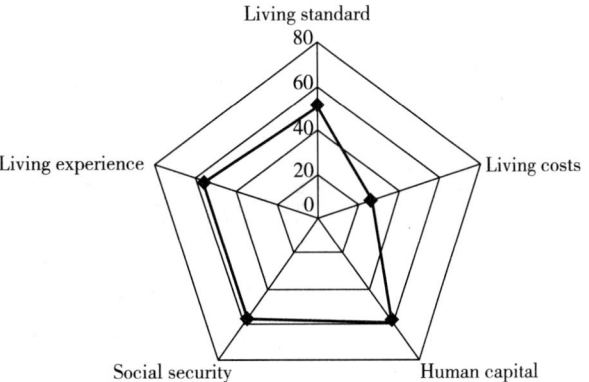

Subjective index of Shanghai

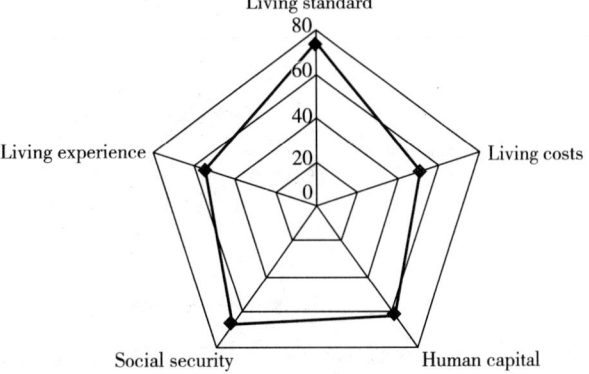

Objective index of Shanghai

Blue Book of Quality of Life in Cities

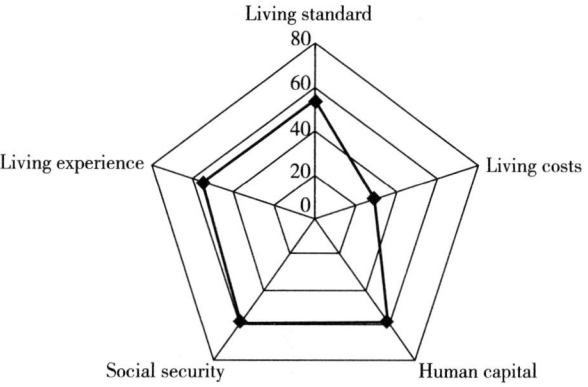

Subjective index of Ningbo

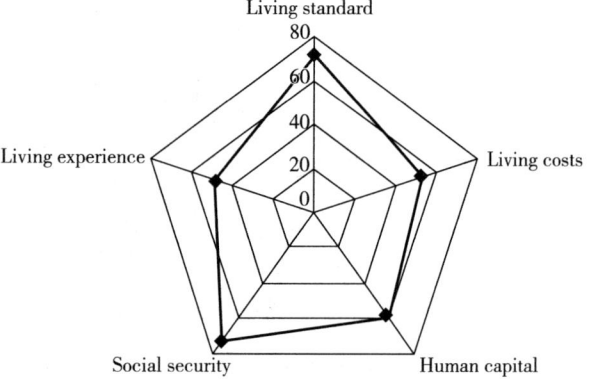

Objective index of Ningbo

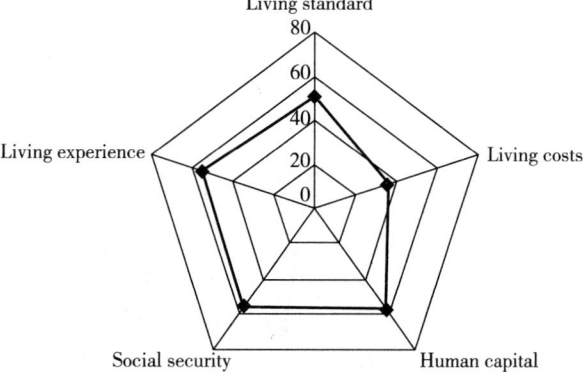

Subjective index of Shenyang

Sub-Indexes of Quality of Life for the 35 Chinese Cities in 2013

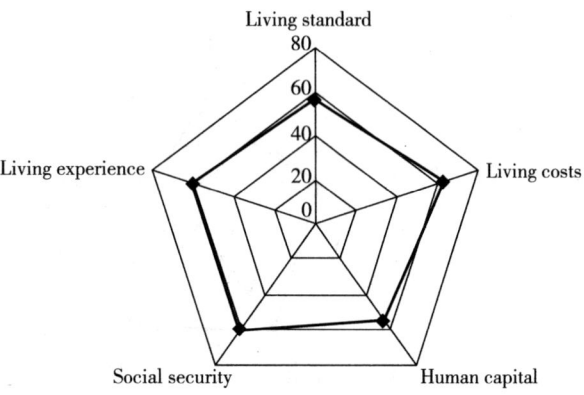

Objective index of Shenyang

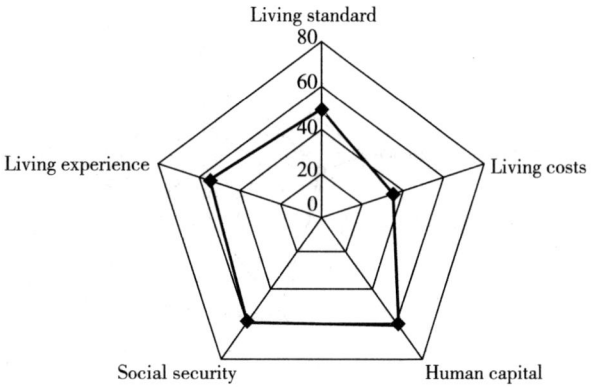

Subjective index of Changchun

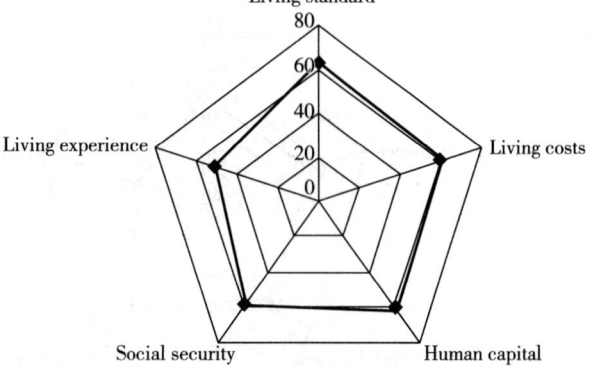

Objective index of Changchun

065

Blue Book of Quality of Life in Cities

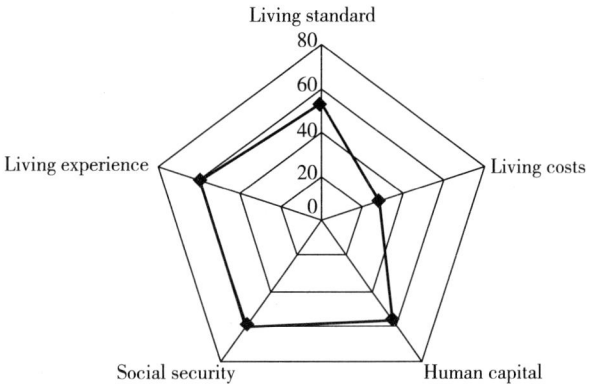

Subjective index of Hangzhou

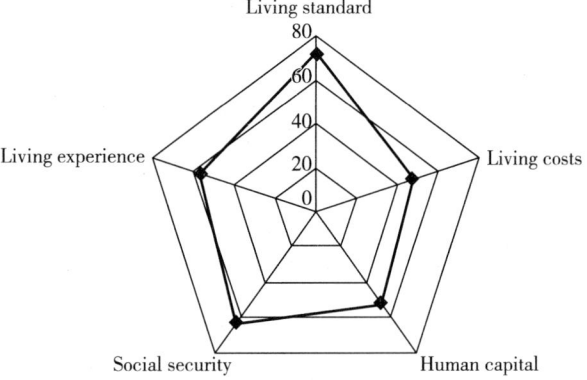

Objective index of Hangzhou

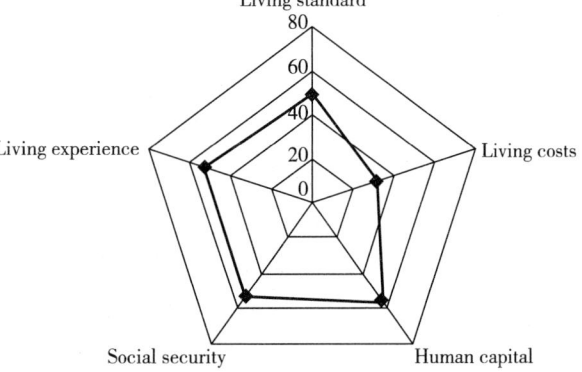

Subjective index of Wuhan

Sub-Indexes of Quality of Life for the 35 Chinese Cities in 2013

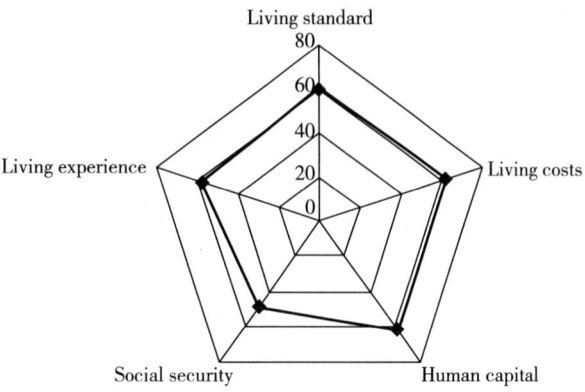

Objective index of Wuhan

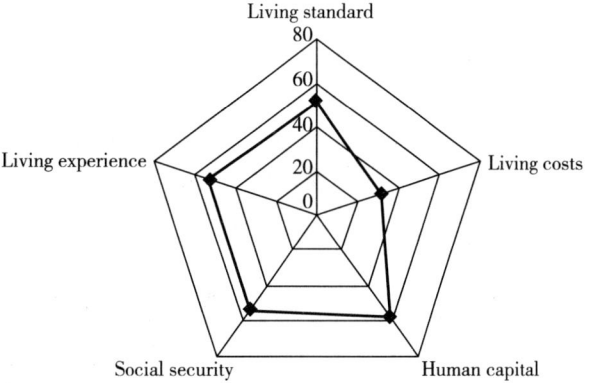

Subjective index of Changsha

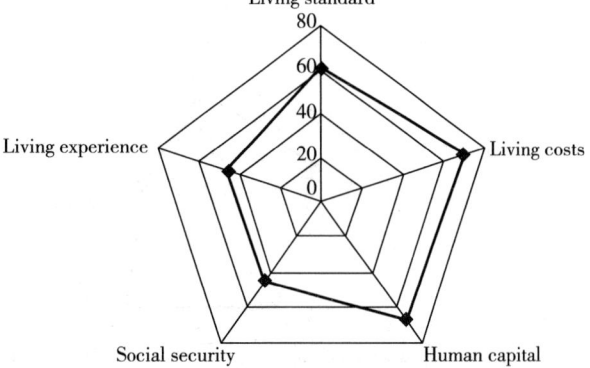

Objective index of Changsha

Blue Book of Quality of Life in Cities

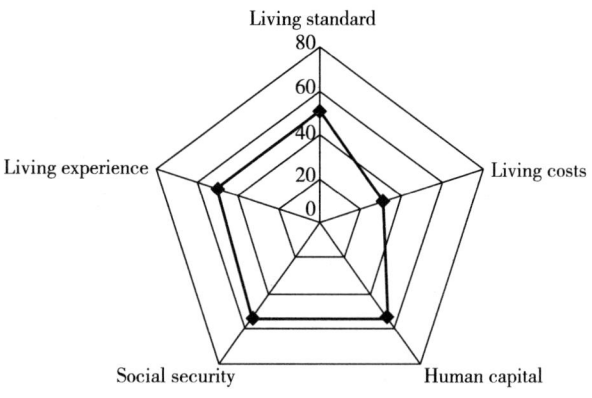

Subjective index of Kunming

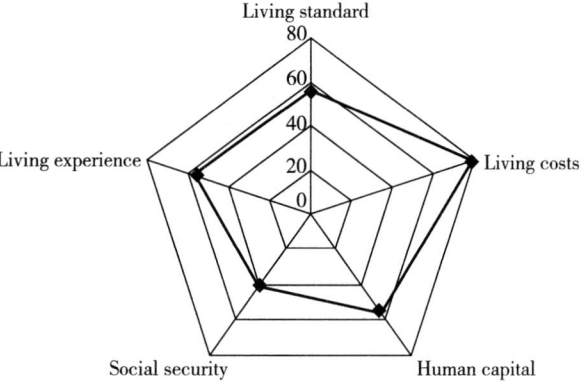

Objective index of Kunming

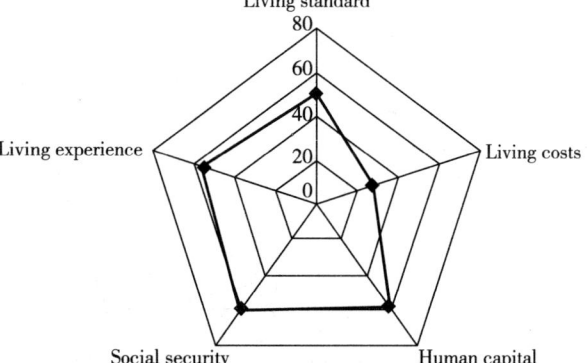

Subjective index of Yinchuan

Sub-Indexes of Quality of Life for the 35 Chinese Cities in 2013

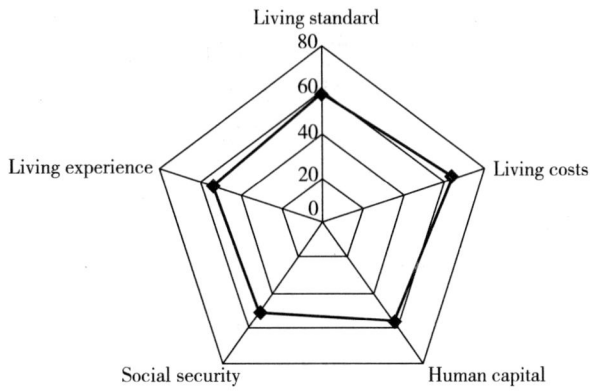

Objective index of Yinchuan

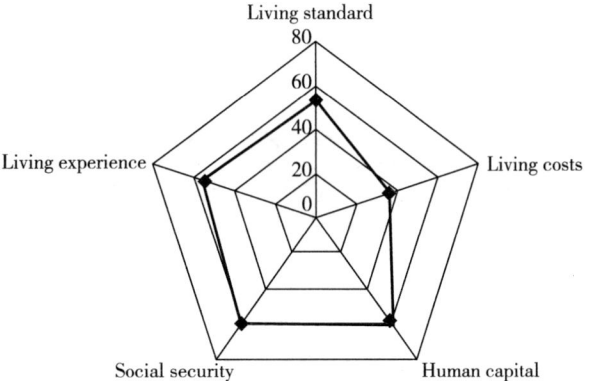

Subjectiue index of Jinan

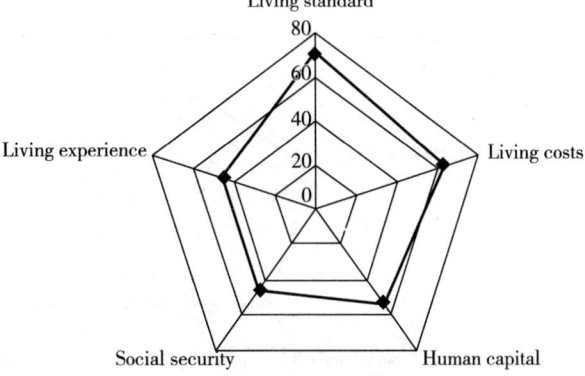

Objective index of Jinan

Blue Book of Quality of Life in Cities

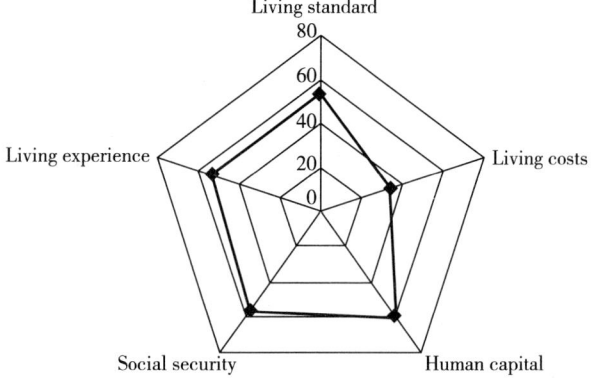

Subjective index of Hefei

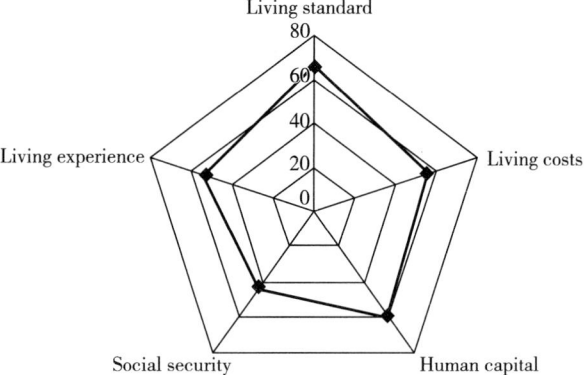

Objective index of Hefei

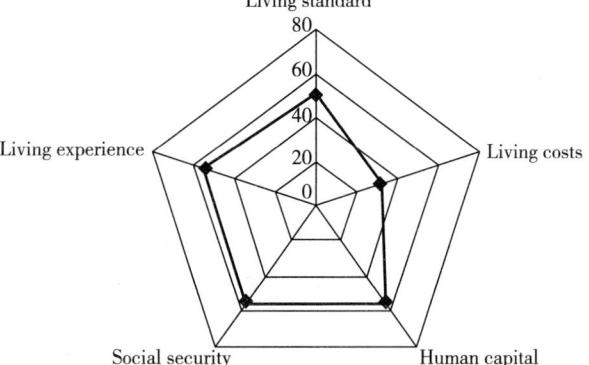

Subjective index of Chengdu

Sub-Indexes of Quality of Life for the 35 Chinese Cities in 2013

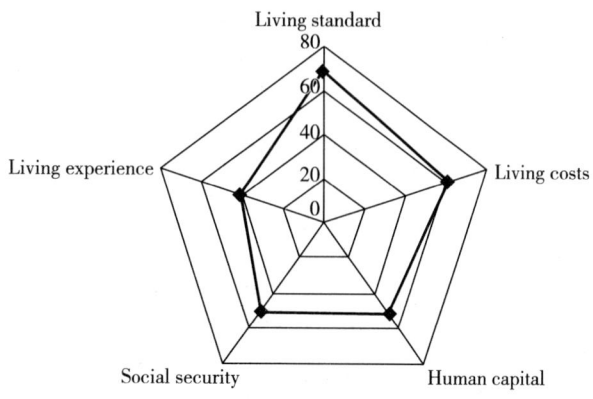

Objective index Chengdu

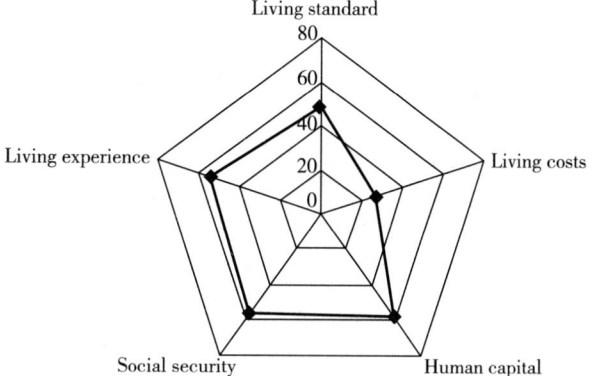

Subjective index of Dalian

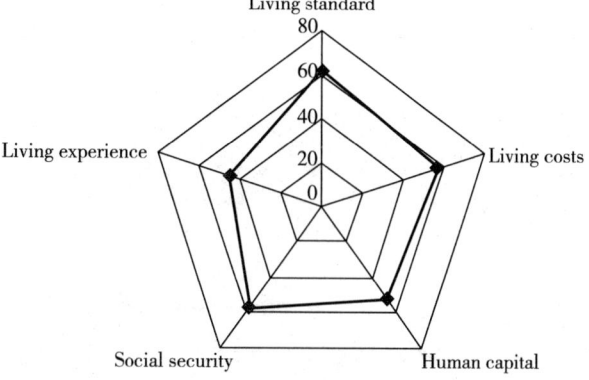

Objective index of Dalian

071

Blue Book of Quality of Life in Cities

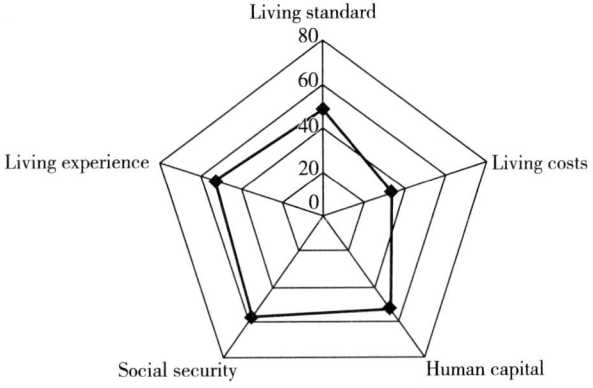

Subjective index of Taiyuan

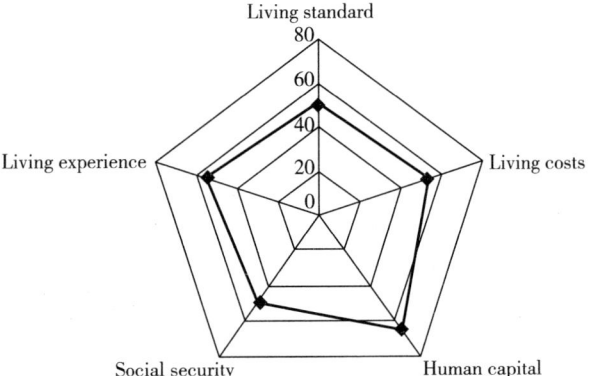

Objective index of Taiyuan

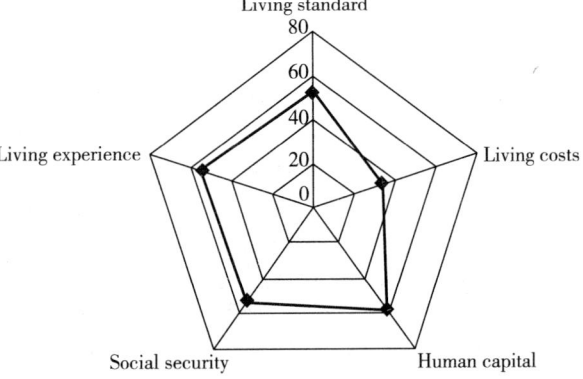

Subjective index of Tianjin

Sub-Indexes of Quality of Life for the 35 Chinese Cities in 2013

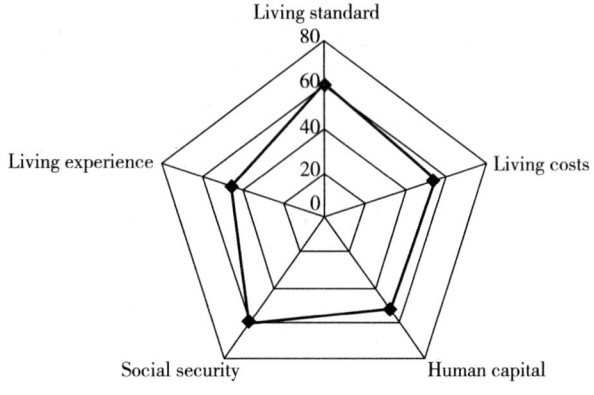

Objective index of Tianjin

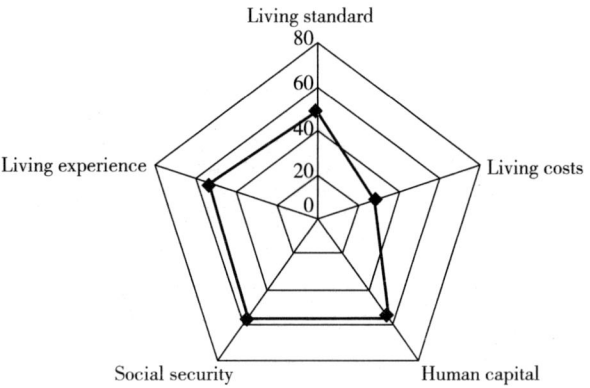

Subjective index of Lanzhou

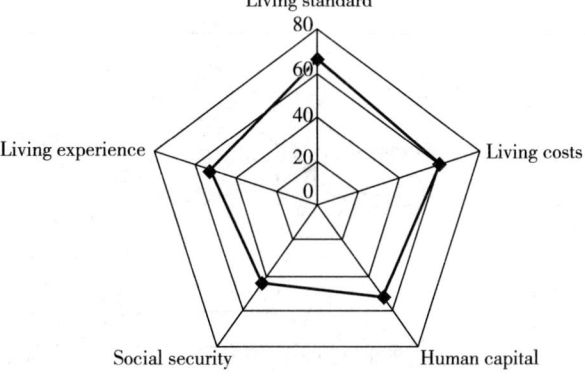

Objective index of Lanzhou

073

Blue Book of Quality of Life in Cities

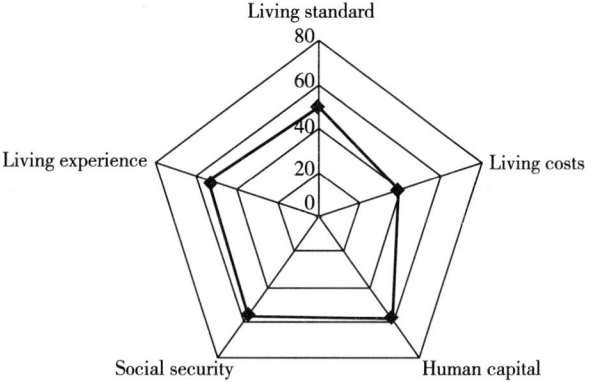

Subjective index of Shijiazhuang

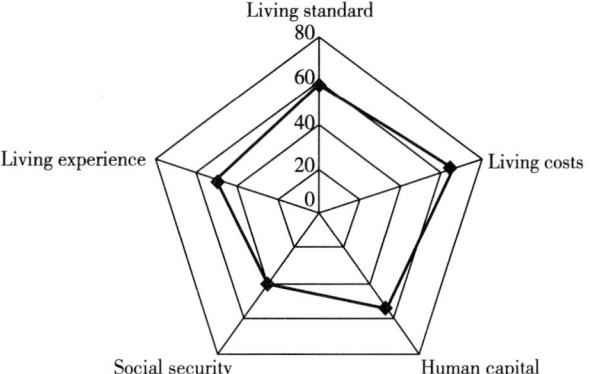

Objective index of Shijiazhuang

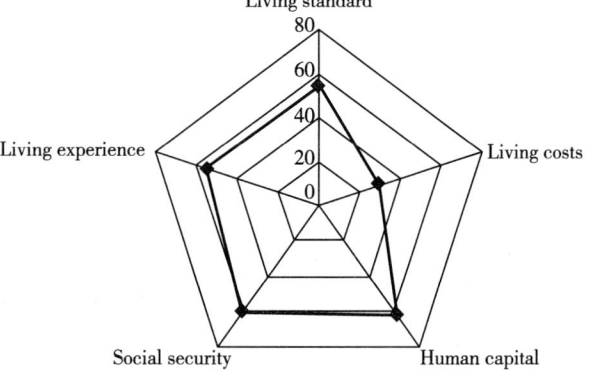

Subjective index of Qingdao

Sub-Indexes of Quality of Life for the 35 Chinese Cities in 2013

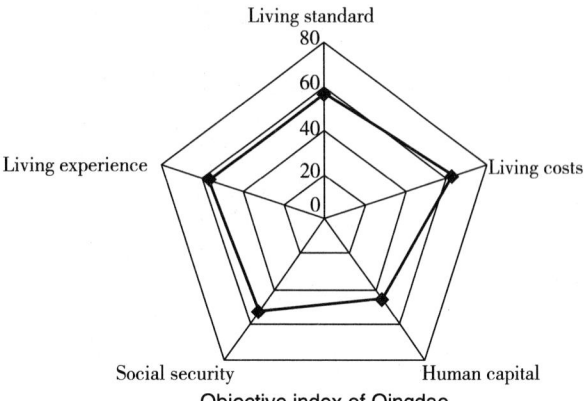

Objective index of Qingdao

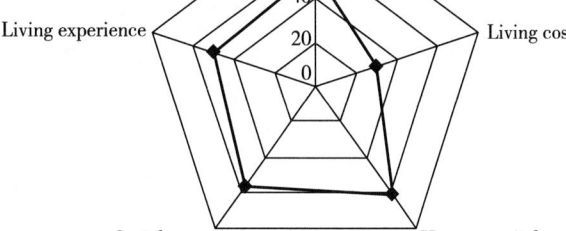

Subjective index of Urumqi

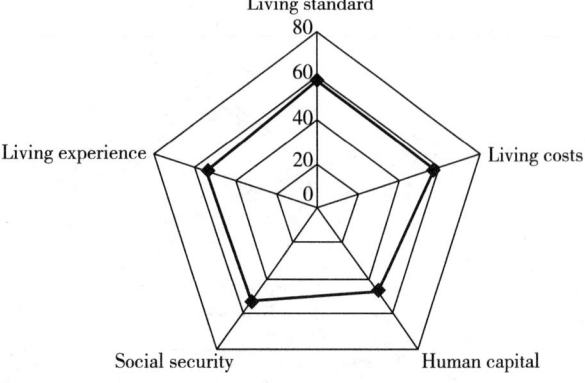

Objective index of Urumqi

075

Blue Book of Quality of Life in Cities

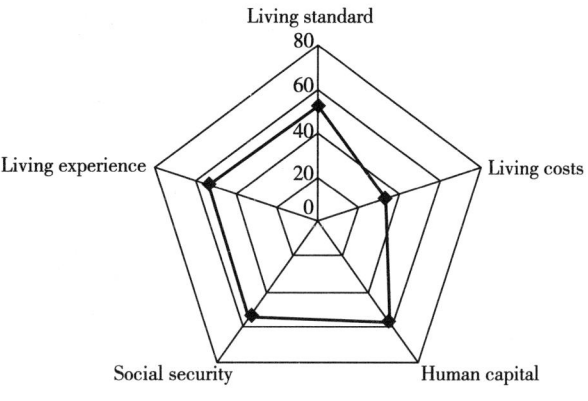

Subjective index of Nanchang

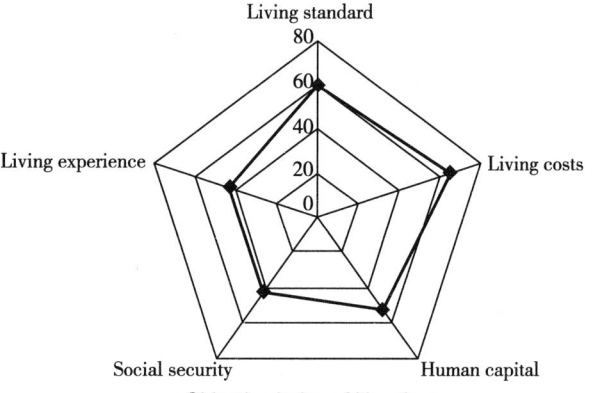

Objective index of Nanchang

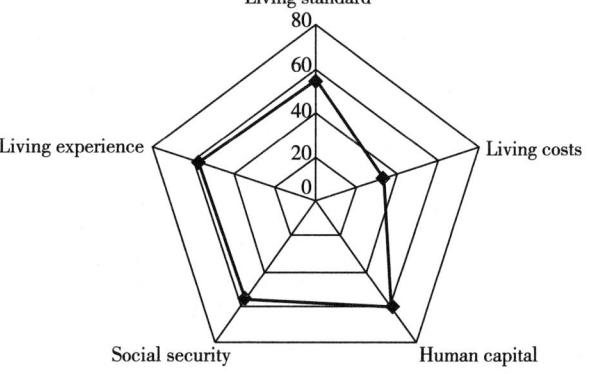

Subjective index of Fuzhou

Sub-Indexes of Quality of Life for the 35 Chinese Cities in 2013

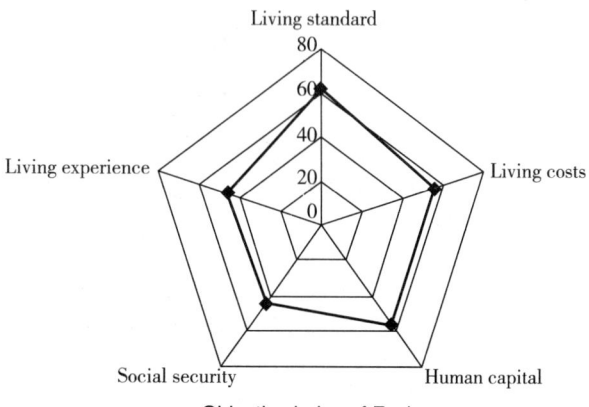

Objective index of Fuzhou

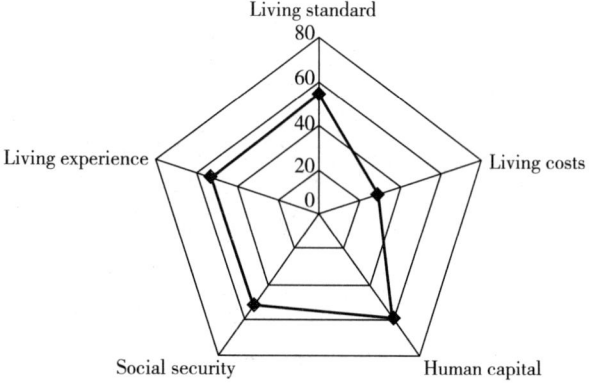

Subjective index of Guiyang

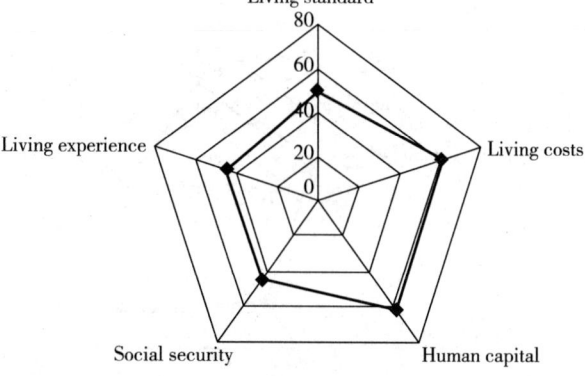

Objective index of Guiyang

Blue Book of Quality of Life in Cities

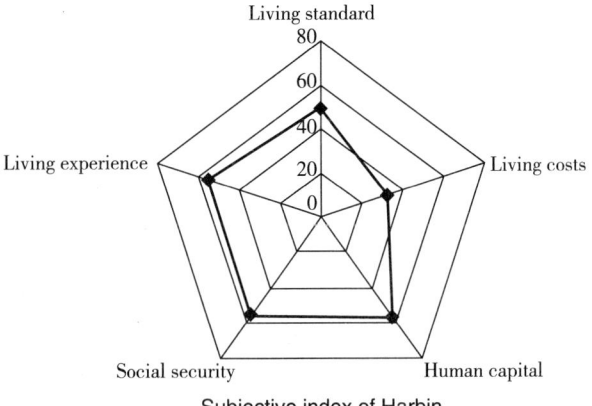

Subjective index of Harbin

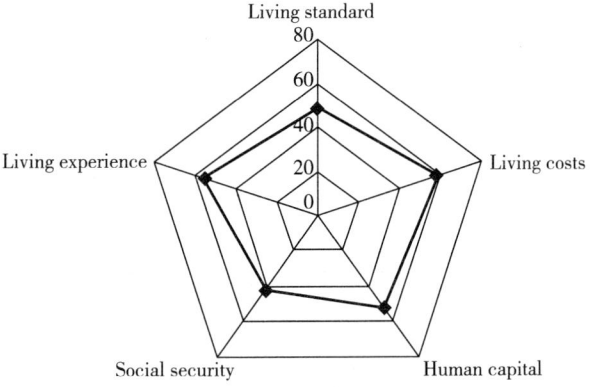

Objective index of Harbin

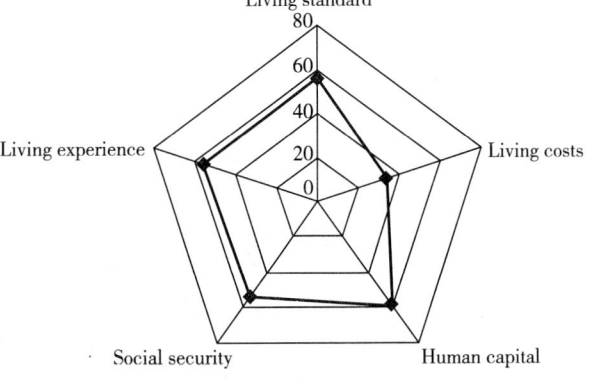

Subjective index of Haikou

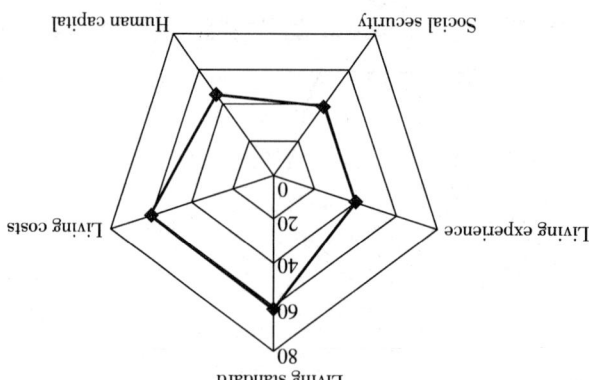

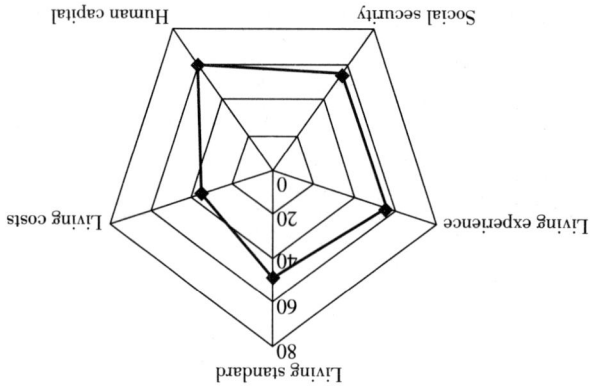

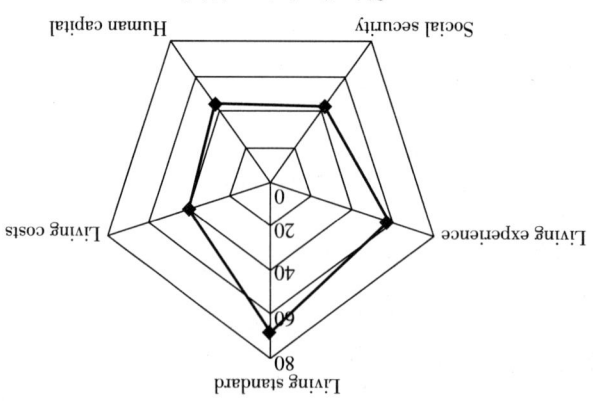

Sub-Indexes of Quality of Life for the 35 Chinese Cities in 2013

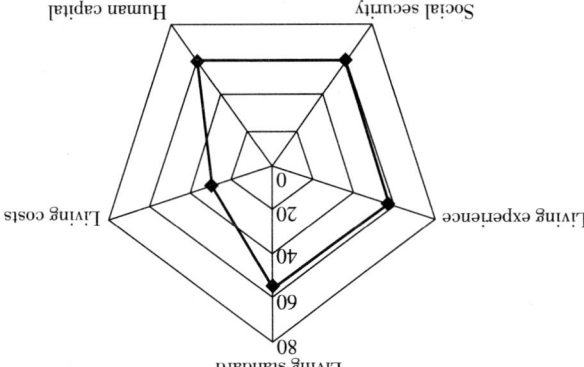

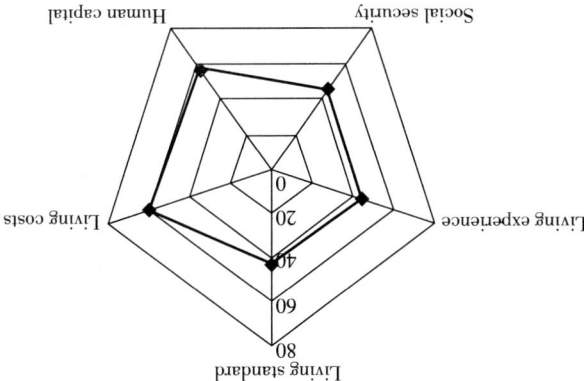

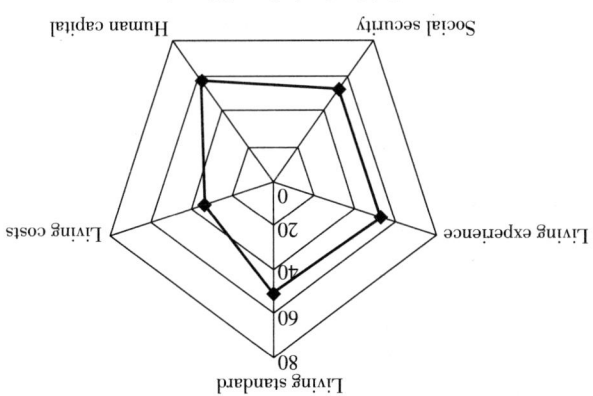

Sub–Indexes of Quality of Life for the 35 Chinese Cities in 2013

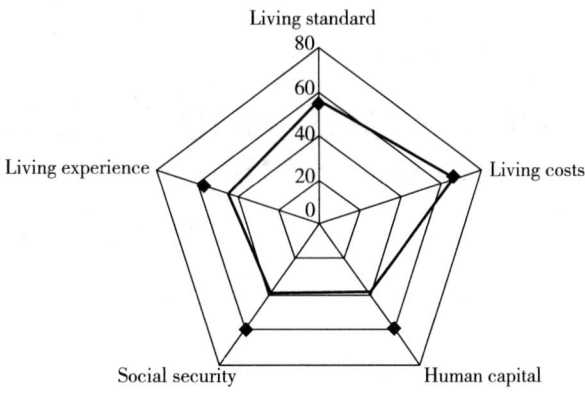

Objective index of Xining

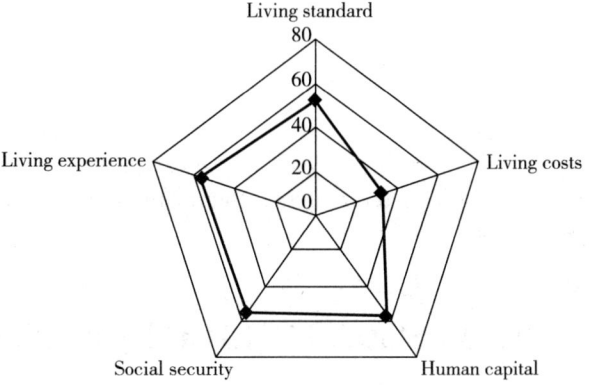

Subjective index of Chongqing

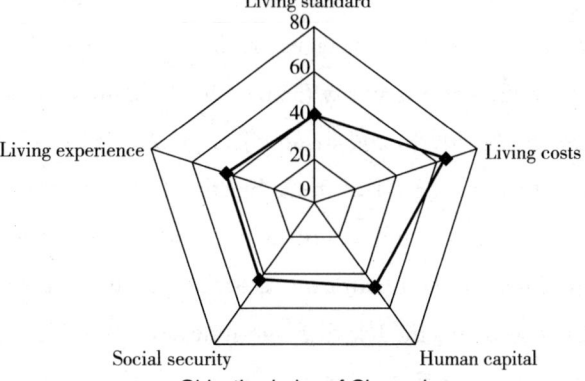

Objective index of Chongqing

Conclusions and Policy Suggestions

B.5

Conclusions and Lessons

The following conclusions and enlightenment can be drawn or obtained from the survey.

5.1 Overall Status of QLICC Remaining Stable

According to the 2013 survey, the subjective satisfaction QLI is 50.87 - a squeak up to the satisfaction level, approximately the same as in 2012. The objective QLI is 57.75 - higher than the 2012 score of 54.56. The satisfaction index is specified with 5 sub-indexes whose weighted averages are from the highest to the lowest: human capital (58.89, 59.42), social security (56.64, 59.19), living experience (55.07, 55.63), living standard (52.51, 51.28) and living costs (31.22, 28.91) - same as the order in 2012. Compared to that of 2012, the subjective QLI remains roughly unchanged, with rises in the satisfaction indexes of living standard and living costs, and drops in the satisfaction indexes of human capital, social security and living experience. The objective QLI is also specified with 5 sub-indexes, whose 2013 weighted averages are from the highest to the lowest: living standard (63.39, 56.28), living costs

Conclusions and Lessons

(58.67, 56.10), human capital (57.78, 57.66), social security (55.26, 50.85) and living experience (53.67, 51.89)[①] - all improved but in a different order than in 2012. Generally speaking, the subjective and the objective QLIs have remained stable in comparison with those of 2012.

5.2 Two Remaining Contrasts

According to the 2011 and the 2012 surveys, there existed "Two Contrasts" despite the rapid economic growth in China. Whether the "Two Contrasts" still exist in 2013 became the focus of our attention. Since the reform and opening-up policy was introduced, Chinese economy had been growing rapidly at an annual average rate of nearly 10%. In recent years, the economic growth has gradually slowed down to a rate of 7.8% in 2012 and 7.7% in the first quarter of 2013 - below expectation but still on the high side. Nevertheless, rapid economic growth did not lead to great improvements in QOL. The satisfaction index has barely squeaked up to the satisfaction level, while the objective index has scored below 60. It shows the first contrast still exists.

Moreover, the satisfaction index (50.87) is lower than the objective index (57.75), with the gap between them widening continuously, especially in large cities. For example, the objective index rankings of Beijing, Guangzhou, Shenzhen and Shanghai are respectively No.1, No.2, No.5 and No.8, while their satisfaction index rankings are No.24, No.31, No.34 and No.20. Further analysis shows, in 31 out of the 35 cities (6 more than in 2012), the subjective index is lower than the objective index. It indicates that the second contrast does exist and is getting worse.

5.3 High Living Costs – the Key Factor Pulling Down QOL Satisfaction

Among the 5 satisfaction sub-indexes, living costs remains the lowest (31.22)

---

① The first value in brackets is the national average in 2013,while the second is the national value in 2012.

083

Blue Book of Quality of Life in Cities

despite its improvement compared to that of 2012. High living costs is still the key factor which pulls down QOL satisfaction. It is even more obvious when it comes to specific cities. Cities ranked low in satisfaction indexes of living costs, such as Urumqi (28, 21), Guangzhou (29, 31), Lanzhou (30, 35), Yinchuan (31, 18), Dalian (32, 26), Shenzhen (33, 34), Beijing (34, 24) and Shanghai (35, 20), have low scores in subjective QLIs, too. On the contrary, cities ranked high in satisfaction indexes of living costs, such as Shijiazhuang (1, 8), Jinan (3, 1), Changchun (4, 4), Zhengzhou (5, 15), Hefei (6, 5) and Haikou (8, 11), have high scores in subjective QLIs as well.[1] Large cities like Beijing, Shanghai, Shenzhen and Guangzhou still score low in the satisfaction index of living costs.

Viewed by objective indexes, the weighted average of living costs objective indexes is 58.67 - higher than the 2012 average of 56.10. Urban living costs have dropped, but still on the high side. Living costs objective index is measured with three secondary indicators, namely house price index, inflation rate and house-price-to-income ratio. In our opinion, the slight drop in living costs index may have resulted from the fall of inflation rate caused by the slowdown of economic growth. The annual Consumer Price Index (CPI) of 2012 had increased by 2.6% compared to that of 2011. It was a slower increase than before, but to an extent, it has lowered people's expectation of inflation. Despite all this, we are still facing pressures from problems such as high money stock, rising food prices and imported inflation. Considering the tough situation of commodity prices, the Government will still need to adopt a prudent monetary policy, and take into account both economic growth and price stability.

5.4 Strong HPA Expectation

As it is shown in the 2013 subjective satisfaction survey on HPA expectation, the weighted average of house price expectation indexes is 64.65—9.66 higher than

---

[1] The first value in brackets is subjective satisfaction index of living costs, while the second is subjective satisfaction QLI.

Conclusions and Lessons

that of 2012, which indicates stronger HPA expectation among city dwellers. The rise of actual house prices in almost all the major cities in 2012 was consistent with our survey results of house price expectation obtained during March and April, 2012. A basic principle in economics was once again testifies: actual inflation is a function of expected inflation.

Will the 2013 survey results of HPA expectation lead to further rises in house prices this year? It has become not only a universal worry among residents, but also a severe challenge to governmental macroeconomic control over real estate prices. It is worth noting that, despite strict macroeconomic control, administrative control and suppressing policies, Chinese real estate prices still went up in the past few years, accompanied by a widespread HPA expectation among residents in the 35 cities. Therefore, the series of regulatory policies on real estate prices are virtually of no avail. Indeed, all the policies to control real estate prices may eventually fail without institutional changes and economic transition or without fundamental reduction in regional governments' dependence on "land finance".

House prices have direct impact on not only the subjective feelings of QOL among city dwellers, but also their actual quality of life. Meanwhile, run-ups in house prices may bring negative influences on further urbanization and healthy economic development. Thus, despite all the difficulties, it is high time for institutional changes and economic transition, and for the construction of a reasonable and long-effective system to control real estate prices on the basis of market mechanism.

5.5 Tough Situation of Food Safety

Although food safety is not included in the QLICC system, it is still a problem which directly influences residents' living experiences. Therefore, the satisfaction with food safety can greatly impact the satisfaction with QOL. The weighted average of food safety satisfaction indexes is only 41.67, which is below the satisfaction level and consistent with the food safety situation in China.

085

Blue Book of Quality of Life in Cities

In our opinion, low satisfaction with food safety among city dwellers is caused by the rampant food safety problems exposed in recent years. Incidents such as tainted milk, hogwash oil, dead pig and fake mutton, have seriously damaged consumers' trust in food safety. The situation of food safety is already a problem beyond dispute. However, at the same time, consumers find it difficult to safeguard their rights of food safety, because of difficulties in providing evidences and making complaints or claims. The ever-emerging food safety incidents have exposed the defects in the food safety supervision system along with other problems. It is a big challenge for the Government as to how to improve residents' satisfaction with food safety, and how to create a safe consumption environment for consumers.

5.6   Accelerating Economic Transition and Improving overall QOL

According to the survey results, the quality of life in Chinese cities is generally on the low side. HPA expectation is growing stronger. Food safety problem becomes a matter of repeated occurrence. Air quality and public order are worrying. Facing all this, we have no choice but to accelerate the transition and institutional reform of Chinese economy, with the latter being the premise of the former. Economic transition means not only transformation of growth patterns, but also improvement of people's QOL; not only sustainable growth of people's actual income, but also better social security and beautiful living environment, as well as the enjoyment of clean air, clear water and safe food. Our cities must become places where people could lead fulfilling lives in dignity, good health, safety, happiness and hope. [1]

To carry out economic transition and to upgrade Chinese economy, governments at all levels should not only have a sense of urgency, but also take active measures and solve major problems in front of them. Thus, the following

---

[1]   *The Istanbul Declaration on Human Settlement*, June 14, 1996.

Conclusions and Lessons

adjustments would be necessary. One, we should not be over-dependent on the traditional mode of economic growth, and should transit from element-driven and investment-driven to innovation-driven and consumption-driven, from over-depended population bonus and land bonus to system bonus generated through reform. Two, we should plan well, carry out economic transition and upgrade, raise residents' QOL, increase investments, and improve the ecological environment. Three, we should continue implementing life-improving projects and bettering social security systems.

Subject Report

B.6

Dynamic Comparison of Real Estate Prices in China and Other Countries

By Zhang Ping, Wu Wei, Wang Hongju*

According to data released by National Bureau of Statistics, the national cumulative average of commodity house prices increased by 9% in September 2013, compared to that of the same period last year, including the prices of completed houses and forward delivery houses which rose by 12% and 8% respectively. However, the rising or falling of prices varied greatly in different cities. Compared to that of the same month last year, prices of new commodity houses (excluding indemnificatory housing) dropped in only 1 out of the 70 large or medium-sized cities while rose in all the other 69 cities. In the year-based price comparison of this September and last September, Beijing had the highest rise (20.6%), while Wenzhou had the lowest (-1.8%). The problem of HPA has already gained wide attention. The article is

---

* Zhang Ping, Institute of Economics under Chinese Academy of Social Sciences, deputy director, research fellow; Wu Wei, Research Division of AVIC Securities, research fellow; Wang Hongju, Institute of Economics under Chinese Academy of Social Sciences, research fellow.

Dynamic Comparison of Real Estate Prices in China and Other Countries

intended to understand the present stage of Chinese real estate industry and to find out proper development strategies by discussing the evolution of real estate prices at different stages of economic growth. In the process, equilibrium house prices are calculated through the construction of the macro land price model and the user cost model. Historical trends in China and in other countries or regions, such as USA, Germany, Korea, Japan and Singapore, are also comparatively analyzed, with the help of indexes like house-price-to-income ratio, monthly-mortgage-to-income ratio, household debt ratio and houses in stock.

6.1   Real Estate Price Fluctuation Synchronizing with GDP and Money Supply

6.1.1   International House Prices Synchronizing with GDP and Quantity of Money

By comparing the trends of real estate industry in China and in other countries,we find that real estate prices synchronize with GDP fluctuation.The uncertainty of real estate prices results from three factors: economic slowdown, drop in domestic demand for houses and strict monetary condition. Only under the joint effect of the three can big influences happen. The following conclusions can be drawn from the comparison of international cases:

1) Generally speaking, economic growth synchronizes with the trend of house prices. In other words, economic growth determines the range of HPA. We compared the trends of house prices and the GDPs in USA, Japan, Korea, Hong Kong and Thailand, and concluded that house prices synchronize largely with GDP, but have greater degrees of fluctuation (See Figure 6.1);

2) Drop in domestic demand for houses is affected by many long-term factors. As for short-term factors, the most influential one is monetary condition, namely money supply. If money supply is stable, house prices will be roughly stable, too. Money supply is the leading indicator of house prices (See Figure 6.2).

089

Blue Book of Quality of Life in Cities

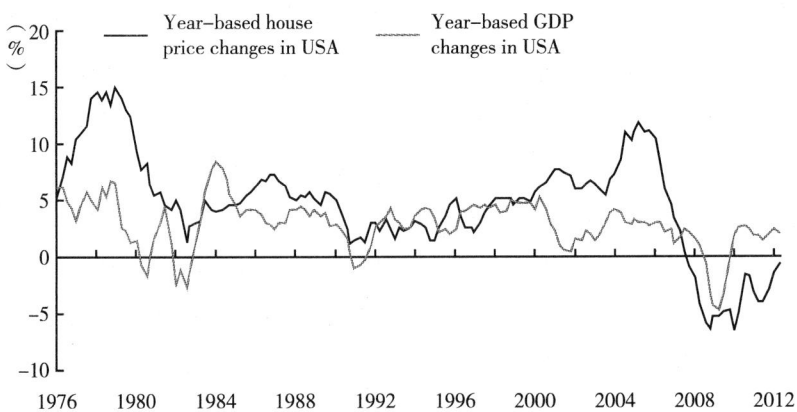

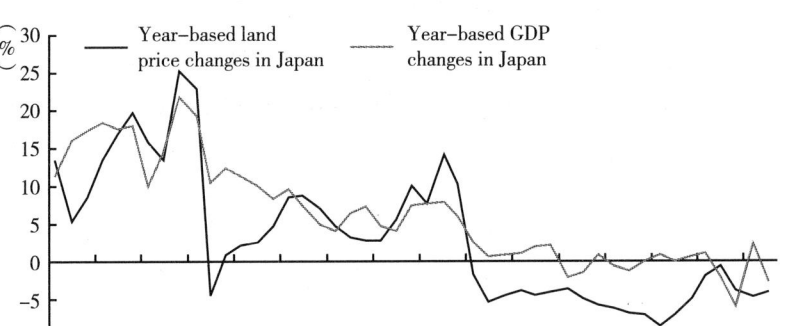

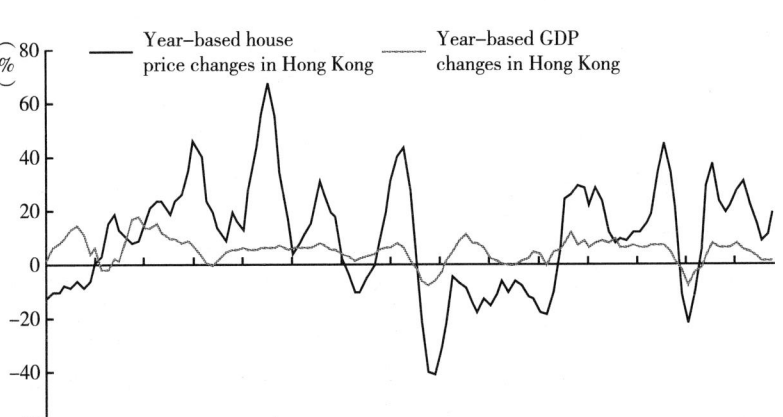

Dynamic Comparison of Real Estate Prices in China and Other Countries

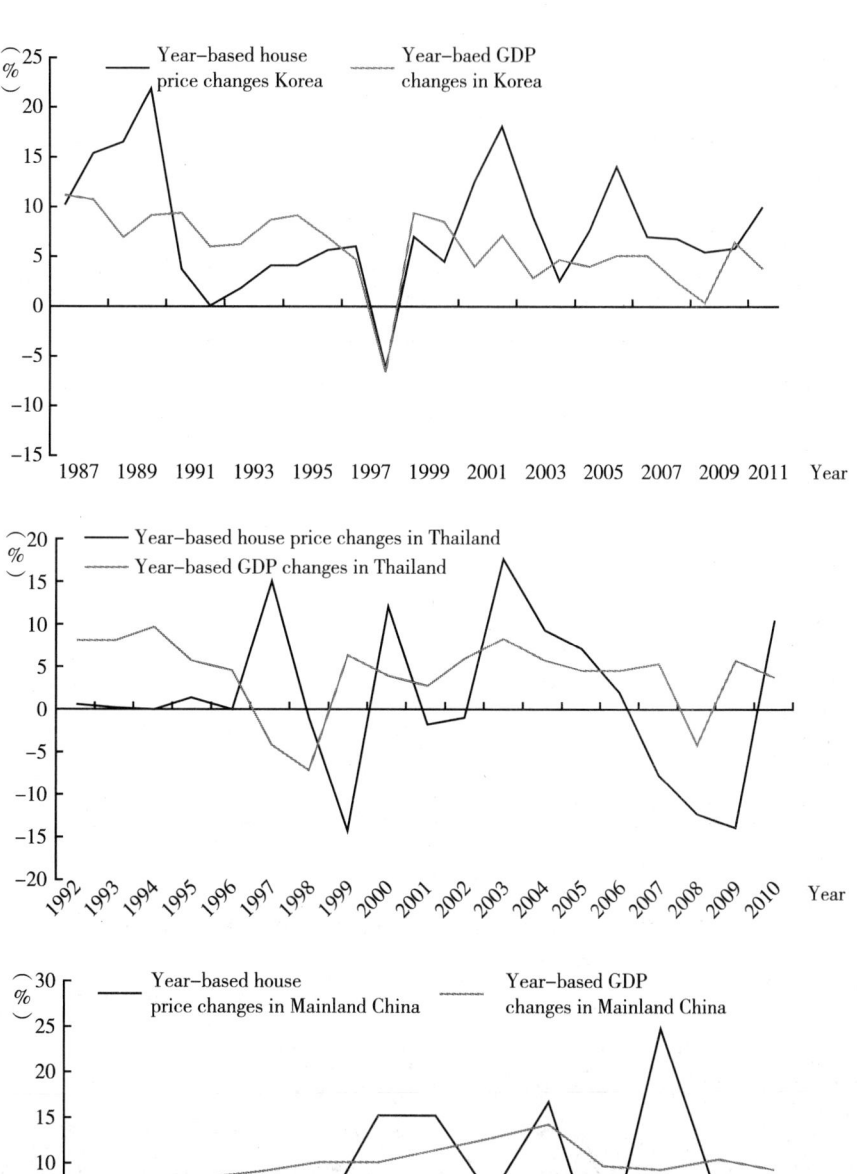

Figure 6.1　Comparison of Year–based House Prices and GDP

Source: CEIC, wind, Financial Research Division of AVIC Securities.

Blue Book of Quality of Life in Cities

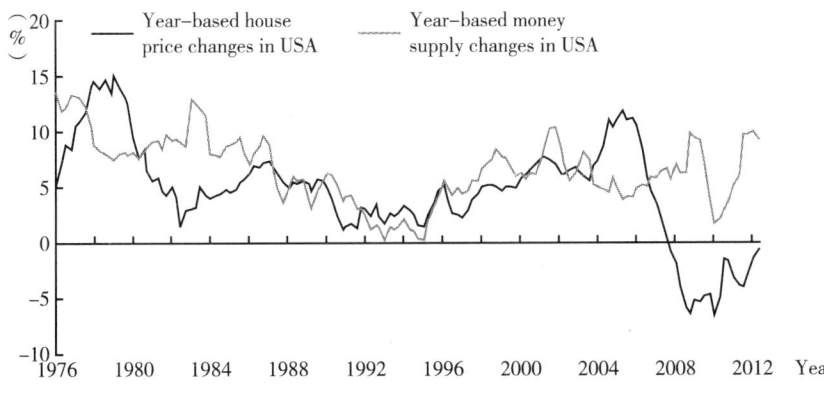

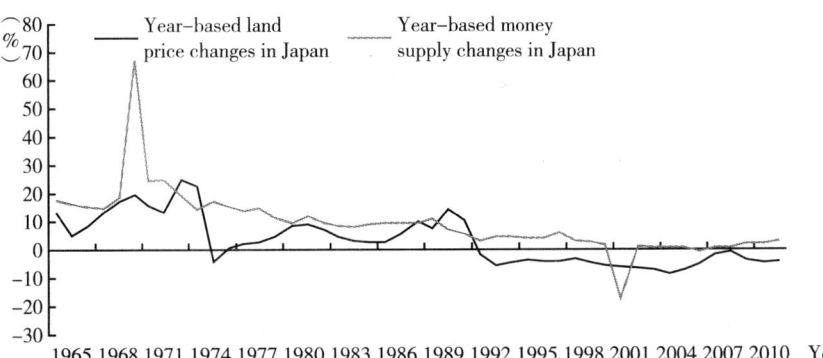

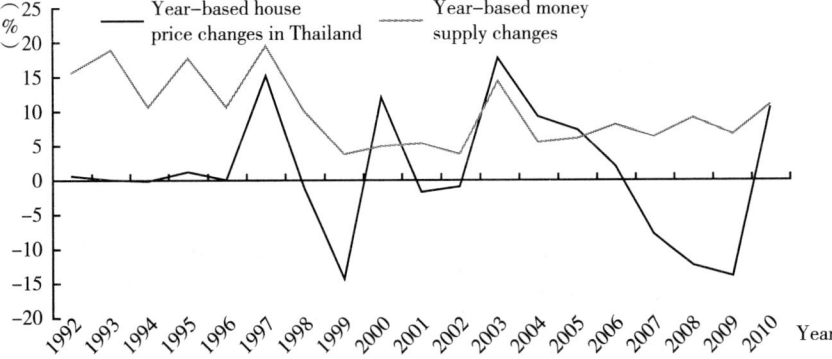

Dynamic Comparison of Real Estate Prices in China and Other Countries

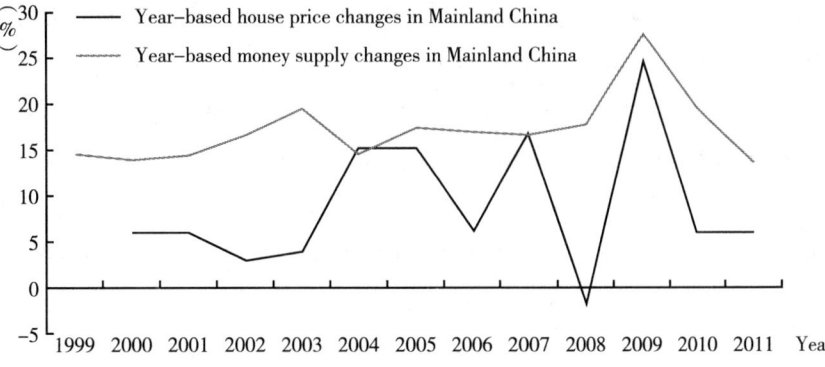

Figure 6.2 Comparison of House Prices and Money Supply

Source: CEIC, wind, Financial Research Division of AVIC Securities.

6.1.2 Three Stages in the Development of Chinese Real Estate Industry

The real estate market in China has been developing quickly, thanks to rapid urbanization, RMB appreciation, housing system reform and the fast increase in resident incomes. The development can be divided into three stages. The first is the stage of adjustments (1999-2005). Before 1998, land allocation was strictly planned.Price of the land element was constrained for a very long time. From 1999 to 2005, adjustments were made to the real estate market. People in China came to realize the value of real estates. The second is the stage of element revaluation (2005-2007), featured by rapid economic growth and the correction of suppressed exchange rate and land prices. In 2005, the exchange rate reform was launched. International capitals started to flow in for arbitrage. It was a stage of revaluation for all sorts of properties such as stock rights, creditor's rights, real estate and collections. The Housing Price Index of 70 large or medium-sized cities increased by up to 25% compared to that of the same period in the previous year. In first-tier cities like Beijing, Shenzhen, Shanghai and Hangzhou, the range of HPA was even greater, resulting in changes in residents' expectation of future house prices. Long-constrained land prices were then freed. Three, stage of property valuation (2007~). As Chinese economy slows down and stabilizes, pressure on RMB appreciation decreases. Revaluation of element prices is accomplished. The influence of

093

Blue Book of Quality of Life in Cities

exchange rate on property prices weakens. According to Eichengreen (2011), 2007 was a turning point for Chinese economic growth. On one hand, after the adjustments of exchange rate, labor costs in China were close to that of America under the same productivity. On the other hand, China's potential economic growth rate had reached the limit. Based on the study of the World Bank, China's economic growth rate would slow down to 5% in the long run. Owing to economic slowdown and rises in both property prices and inflation caused by the anti-crisis policies in 2008, the Chinese real estate market moved quickly into the valuation stage.

6.1.3 Chinese Real Estate Prices Synchronizing with GDP and Quantity of Money

From a macro point of view, national real property value is the net present value of future GDP discounted according to the expected rate of return. Given fixed capital costs and future long-term GDP growth rate, the short-term equilibrium price of real properties shall be determined by the initial GDP, while real property prices shall grow at the same rate as GDP. In the past 13 years, the nationwide growth rate of housing price index has been far lower than the rate of GDP. If we take the data in 1997 as the fixed base of 100, then in June 2012, the house prices index would have been 199. The Nominal GDP index would have been 508. The Nominal GDP index in USD would have been 641. Only in June 2010 was the year-based growth rate of quarterly real estate sales index higher than that of Nominal GDP. Therefore, booming HPA around China since 2005 was no overdraft of future economic growth, but merely a natural result of rapid economic growth.

According to Shiller in "Long-Term Perspectives on the Current Boom in Home Prices", the essence of house price is in the long run a monetary phenomenon. Money supply is one of the key influent factors of house prices. We conducted regression analysis based on single variable on China's M2 and actual house prices from 1999 till now, and found that M2 had remarkable influence on Chinese real estate prices and could account for most of the house price changes. In 2007 and

Dynamic Comparison of Real Estate Prices in China and Other Countries

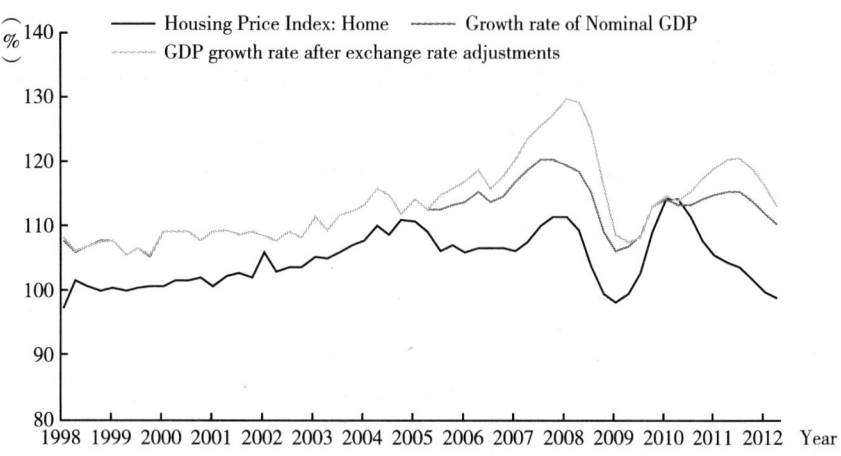

Figure 6.3   Comparison of Chinese GDP and HPA

Source: wind.

2009, the actual house prices deviated somewhat from the equilibrium house price which was determined by money supply. However, due to the 2008 economic crisis and the regulatory policies implemented since 2010, the actual house price deviated much less, and is at present lower than the equilibrium house price which is determined by money supply.

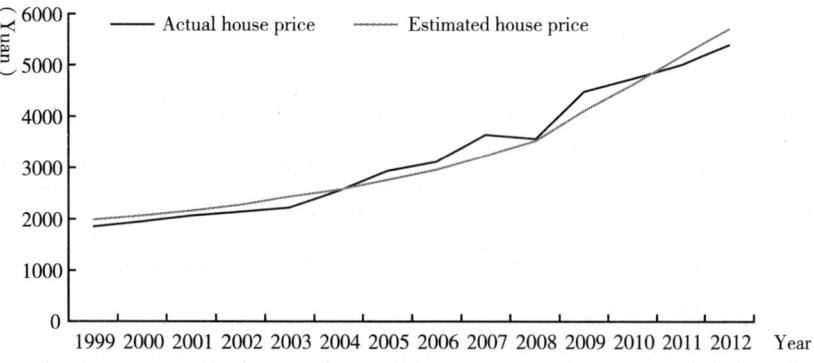

Figure 6.4   Actual House Prices in China Synchronizing with Money Supply

Source: wind, Financial Research Division of AVIC Securities.

Therefore, we can conclude that Chinese real estate prices generally synchronize with GDP growth and money supply. There is no overdraft of the future.

095

Blue Book of Quality of Life in Cities

6.2 Measuring of Estate Price Fluctuation – Overheated, Reasonable or Low: Construction of the Equilibrium Value Deviation Model

Real estate price fluctuation should synchronize with GDP growth and money supply. Just like economy may overheat or decline, money supply may be swollen or tight, real estate prices fluctuation may also be too high (bubble), too low or reasonable. How could we quantify real estate price fluctuation? There are many ways of measurement. Compared to house-price-to-income ratio or house-price-rental ratio, the user cost model can reflect not only interest rate changes, but also the influence of house price growth rate on local house prices in different areas, which enablea better prediction of future house price changes. Himmelberg et al. (2005) had analyzed the house prices in 46 American urban agglomerations of the past 25 years based on this model. Cities with a high deviation degree of house prices in the 1980's all encountered large house price fluctuation later. The user cost model is based on the non-arbitrage hypothesis of the Asset Pricing Model. In areas with adequate credit market and leasing market, the leasing cost should be equal to the holding cost during the same period. If the holding cost is too high, then the user could easily turn to the leasing market, and vice versa. Eventually, actions of the user will influence supply and demand in the leasing market and the trading market, and in turn affect the final house price and the final leasing price, until the holding cost balances with the leasing cost.

House holding cost is influenced mainly by risk-free interest rate, mortgage interest rate, house depreciation, taxation, expected HPA rate and risk premium. Leasing cost is mostly rent. The model can be demonstrated by the mathematical formula below, in which r_t refers to unit rent, u_t to use cost rate, P_t to housing unit price, r_{ft} to risk-free interest rate, r_{mt} to mortgage rate, d_t to

Dynamic Comparison of Real Estate Prices in China and Other Countries

house depreciation rate, $\bar{P}_{t-1}/P_t$ to expected HPA rate and r_p to other risks of holding a house.

$$r_t = u_t \times P_t$$
$$u_t = r_{ft} + r_{mt} + d_t - \bar{P}_{t-1}/P_t + r_p$$

The user cost model was constructed to measure the price level of houses in China. In July 2012, the deviation degree of actual house price in China was 39%, while the deviation degrees of USA (1990), Germany (1995), Hong Kong (1997), Japan (1990) and Korea (1991) right before the real estate bubble burst were 73%, 131%, 152%, 488% and 876% respectively. Therefore, the deviation degree in China was still comparatively low. In addition, the mortgage interest rate in China is relatively high - 47% higher than that of 2008, and far higher than that of USA, Japan or Hong Kong. If China resumes its 15% discount policy of mortgage rate, the deviation degree will drop to 11%. Consequently, we consider present house prices in China reasonable, with no much overdraft of the future.

Table 6.1 Comparison of Deviation Degrees of Actual House Prices in Different Countries

	2011	Maximum	Minimum	Average	Median	Standard Deviation
USA	-14%	73%(1990)	-70%(2003)	8%	9%	38%
Germany	-78%	131%(1995)	-78%(2011)	2%	-7%	56%
Hong Kong	-103%	152%(1997)	-106%(2004)	-2%	8%	80%
Japan	-72%	488%(1990)	-86%(1998)	27%	-43%	158%
Korea	-18%	876%(1991)	-48%(2003)	284%	238%	289%
Singapore	-11%	21%(2006)	-20%(2008)	-1%	-5%	13%
China	48%	63%(2007)	-41%(2003)	8%	4%	31%

Source: CEIC, Financial Research Division of AVIC Securities.

Blue Book of Quality of Life in Cities

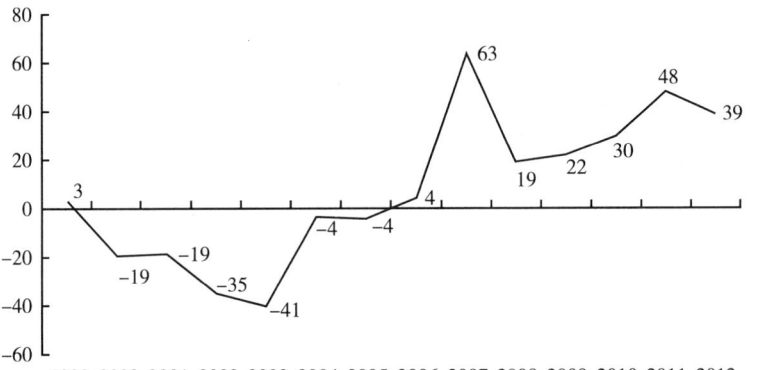

Figure 6.5   Deviation Degrees of House prices in China

Source: Financial Research Division of AVIC Securities, wind, National Bureau of Statistics, Google.

6.3   Comparison of the Factors Influencing the Trends of Real Estate Price Fluctuation in China

6.3.1 View on Chinese House Prices with Reference to GDP Changes

GDP growth determines long-term HPA expectation in the future. The World Bank predicted that Chinese economic growth would gradually slow down to 8.9% between 2011 and 2015, then to 7.0% between 2016 and 2020, to 5.9% between 2021 and 2025, and to 5% between 2026 and 2030. The expected growth rate of national average house price would drop as well. Suppose in 2012 the expected growth rate falls to 7%, then the deviation degree will reach 67%, close to that of USA at the peak of its bubble, but still far lower than that of Korea, Japan, Hong Kong and Germany at their respective peaks. If the GDP continues to grow at a rate of 8% to 9%, then the deviation degree will drop to 14%. In China, economic growth and urbanization stage vary greatly in different regions, so is the real estate market. Therefore, there still exist plenty of investment opportunities in some regional markets.

098

Dynamic Comparison of Real Estate Prices in China and Other Countries

Table 6.2   Analysis on the Sensitive Relations between GDP Growth and House Price Deviation Degree

Expected HPA Rate (GDP growth)	House price deviation degree in 2012
8.90%	14%
8%	39%
7%	67%
5.90%	97%
5%	122%

Source: Financial Research Division of AVIC Securities.

6.3.2   House Prices and Credit Relations

Real estate bubbles usually come with the overdevelopment of credit. Ideally, the household leverage ratio in China is still on the low side. In 2011, the ratio of mortgage outstanding to National Disposable Income (NDI) was 43% in China, and 84%, 101%, 92%, 103%, 32% and 46% in USA, Germany, Korea, Japan, Singapore and Hong Kong respectively. However, we should be aware that the outstanding of mortgages in China has started to increase rapidly since 2009, with the ratio of mortgage outstanding to NDI growing from 30% to 43%. It shows that large-scale credit expansion is behind the upsurge of real estate in these 3 years, and that given the chance, Chinese residents can raise the household debt ratio instantly which will in turn become a support to the development of the real estate market.

Value of houses in stock can be used to measure real estate bubbles. However, the values of different countries are hardly comparable, owing to differences in house depreciation, location, relevant taxation and financial systems. In our estimation, China's houses in stock was worth about RMB 44.9 trillion, accounting for 95% of the 2011 GDP, while that of USA, Germany, Japan and UK made up 160%, 250%, 200% and 350% of their respective GDP in 2006. It means that China's house values still have much room for growth. However, in China there are already about 150 million units of urban houses in stock, including 60 million units (5.58 billion square meters) completed since 1998 and the existing 90 million units

099

Blue Book of Quality of Life in Cities

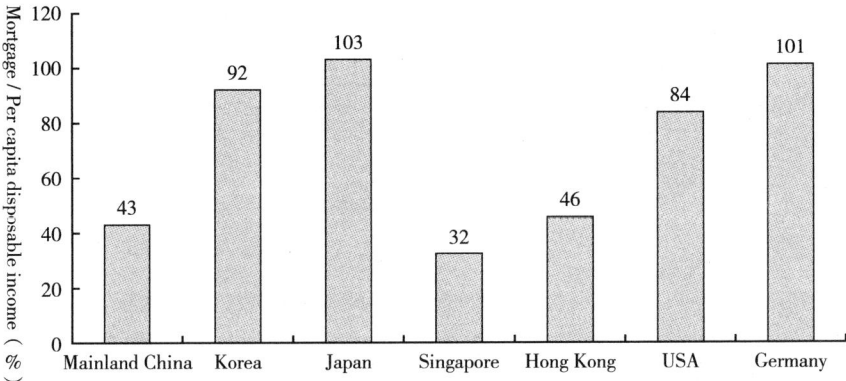

Figure 6.6   Comparison of Mortgage–to–income Ratios in Different Countries

Source: wind, Financial Research Division of AVIC Securities.

constructed before 1999. The stock is high compared to the 2011 urban household number of 220 million. Therefore, makeup construction of the housing problem left over by history is already coming to an end.

6.3.3 View on Real Estate Prices in Chinese Cities with Reference to House–price–to–income Ratio and Monthly–mortgage–to–income Ratio

House price and the house-price-to-income ratio, the monthly-mortgage-to-income ratio derived from it are indexes of measuring real estate bubbles. The national house-price-to-income ratio of China was 7.4 in 2011 - relatively high compared to that of certain developed countries such as USA, UK or Germany, but quite reasonable comparing with that of Hong Kong, Korea or Japan whose ratios were above 20 times at the peaks of their bubbles. Considering the similarity of Chinese culture and East Asian culture, we regard Hong Kong, Korea and Japan better reference objects for China. In addition, besides the rapid increase of Chinese resident incomes, it was average household income that was used in the calculation of Chinese house-price-to-income ratio, while actual house buyers were mostly urban upper- or middle-class families. The house-price-to-income ratio calculated with the amount earned by the top 20% income groups is between 4 to 5 times - close to the international normal level of 4 to 6 times. Therefore,

100

Dynamic Comparison of Real Estate Prices in China and Other Countries

a nationwide bubble of house price is unlikely. Nevertheless, the house-price-to-income ratios of first-tier cities such as Beijing, Shanghai and Hangzhou are relatively higher compared to that of other international metropolises around the world. At present, a unit in Tokyo, London, New York, Sydney or Paris is usually worth around RMB 3 to 4 million in total. The absolute house prices in Beijing and Shanghai have already reached the international level, next only to that of Singapore or Hong Kong. House prices in first-tier cities tend to be under the threat of a bubble.

Table 6.3 Comparison of House–price–to–income Ratios

| | House-price-to-income Ratio | | |
	2011	Peak of bubble	Peak Period
China	7.4	—	—
USA	3.1	5	2006
Germany	5.21	7.0	1994
UK	5	6.0	2007
Hong Kong	12.6	22.3	1997
Korea	11.65	25	1991
Japan	18.89	39.5	1991
Singapore	5.8	6	Relatively stable

Source: CEIC, wind, Financial Research Division of AVIC Securities.

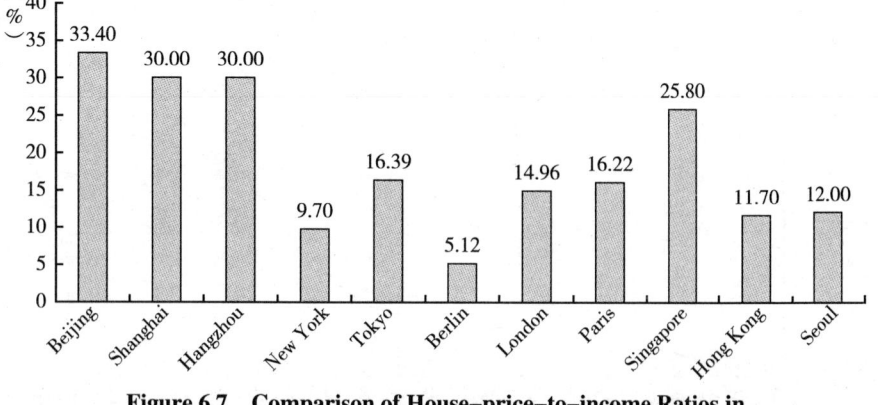

Figure 6.7 Comparison of House–price–to–income Ratios in International Metropolises in June 2012

Source: numbeo.com.

101

Blue Book of Quality of Life in Cities

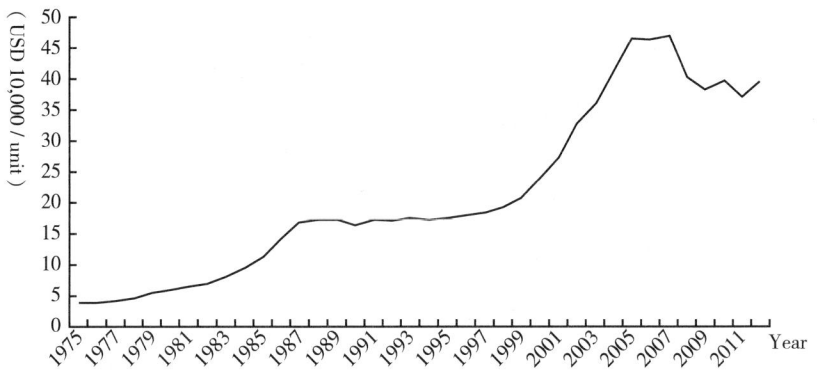

Figure 6.8   History of House Price Fluctuation in New York

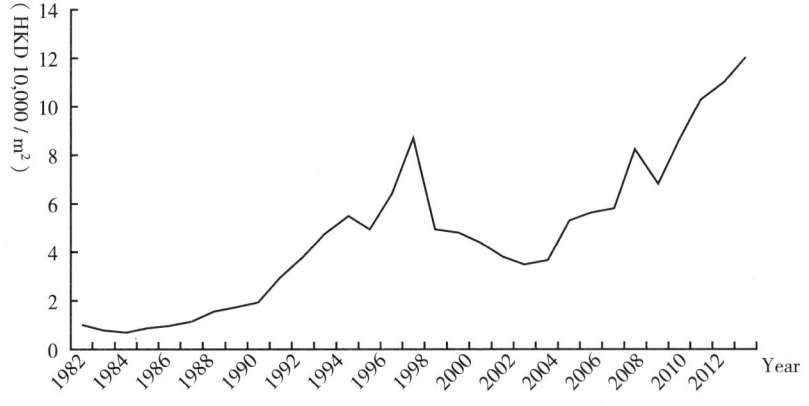

Figure 6.9   History of House Price Fluctuation in Hong Kong

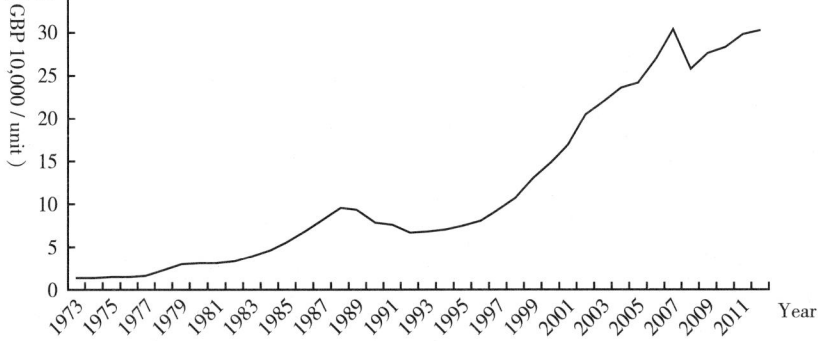

Figure 6.10   History of House Price Fluctuation in London

Dynamic Comparison of Real Estate Prices in China and Other Countries

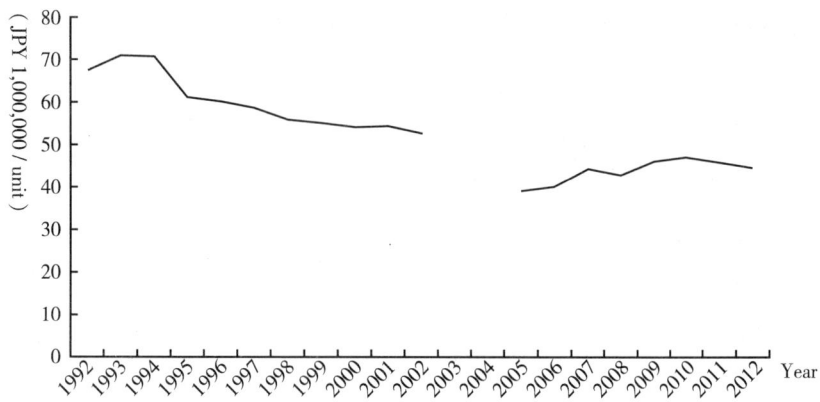

Figure 6.11   History of House Price Fluctuation in Tokyo

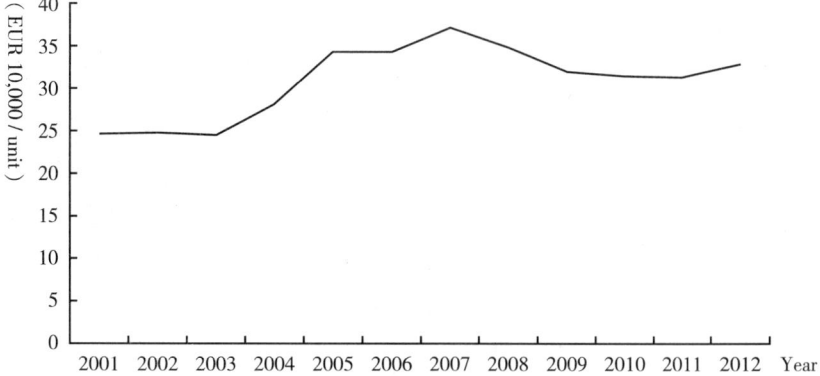

Figure 6.12   History of House Price Fluctuation in Paris

Source of the above 5 figures: CEIC, FHFA, Japan Real Estate Institute, Rating Department of Hong Kong.

Same conclusion was drawn from the comparison of monthly-mortgage-to-income ratios. There is no nationwide bubble of real estate prices, but in some areas especially in first-tier cities, house prices are under the threat of a bubble. The weighted average of monthly-mortgage-to-income ratios in first-tier cities reached 110% in June 2012. The average house price was 29% higher than the maximum house price which rigid demands could support. Taking into account the expectation of income rise and interest rate cut, the average house price was still 20% higher. In second-tier cities, the weighted average of monthly-mortgage-to-

103

income ratios was 51%. The average house price was 9% higher than the maximum house price that rigid demands could support. Allowing for expectation factors, the average house price was still 4% higher. As for third- or fourth-tier cities, the house prices were roughly within the limit of rigid demands.

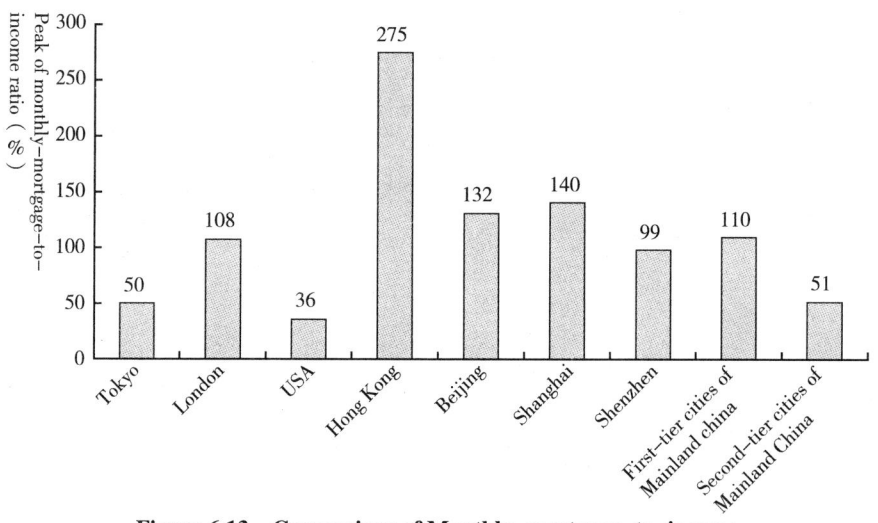

Figure 6.13   Comparison of Monthly–mortgage–to–income Ratios in Major Regions

Source: Beta Fact, Financial Research Division of AVIC Securities.

Note: The monthly-mortgage-to-income ratios of foreign cities are the peak values in their respective histories, while that of China is the value in June 2012.

6.3.4   Adverse Factors

In the long run, we should be aware of all the adverse factors that the real estate industry may face, and should seize the opportunity of business transition.

1) Weakening of population bonus. As the experiences of OECD countries show, dependency ratio of population has negative correlation with house prices. When dependency ratio increases by 1%, house prices will drop by 3% to 4%. In China, their correlation was not clearly observed. However, in the stage of property valuation, fundamental factors will have more obvious influence on China's house prices. It was estimated that the dependency ratio of population would drop to as

Dynamic Comparison of Real Estate Prices in China and Other Countries

low as 38.3% and then bounce back. UN (2009) predicted that China's dependency ratio of population would rise to 40.3% in 2020. If so, suppose all the other factors remain unchanged, house prices will drop by 6% to 8%. Weakening of the population bonus also means the rapid increase in resident incomes which will hedge against the negative impact of population bonus on the real estate market. Meanwhile, as the aging population grows, residents will need more houses for the aged, thus creating development opportunities for certain market segments.

2) End of RMB appreciation and real estate market's entering into property valuation stage. Since capitals can flow freely around the world, exchange rate fluctuation has major impact on short-term house prices. According to a study (Zhang Ping, 2007), if exchange rate appreciates by 1% annually, short-term house valuation will push house price up by 10%. However, the fluctuation of exchange rate is highly uncertain. The most important function of exchange rate is to influence money supply.

3) Institutional changes. In China, we cannot avoid the influence of governmental policies on the real estate market. The housing reform in 1998 raised the curtain of a 10-year golden age for the Chinese real estate market. In the next decade, the collection of property taxes and the 36 million indemnificatory housing units brought to the market will also have great impacts on the development of the real estate market. Property tax will add to using cost, and will in theory lower equilibrium house price. Suppose the property tax rate is 1%, then the national equilibrium house price is estimated to drop by 16.7%. However, if individuals with only 1 unit are not taxed, property tax will have much less influence over equilibrium house price.

4) Increase of houses in stock due to indemnificatory housing. After the completion of 36 million indemnificatory housing units (can satisfy the needs of 5.2% of the urban population), houses in stock in all the Chinese cities are estimated to reach a number of 186 million units which can satisfy the needs of 85% of the urban households. Indemnificatory housing will meet the need of many buyers with rigid demands, and create pressure for real estate prices to go down. After the 1988 Seoul Olympic Games, Korea launched a project of 2 million

indemnificatory housing units (could satisfy the needs of 4.7% of the population). In 1992, the year of house delivery, the house prices there dropped by 6.4%. Till 1995, Korean house prices had decreased by 14.6% cumulatively. Nevertheless, it should also be noted that Korea was having a serious real estate bubble at the time. Therefore, the drop in house prices was the result of multiple reasons.

Major influent factors over the real estate industry in the next decade are shown in the table below based on our study. The market as a whole still has much room for development, but the real estate industry has to seize opportunities and carry out business transition, so as to survive and thrive in the development changes of future stages.

Table 6.4 Major Factors Affecting the Real Estate Market in the Next Decade

Favorable factors	Adverse factors
Urbanization moving into stage two	Slowdown of GDP potential growth rate
Fast increase of resident incomes	Weakening of population bonus
Rapid development of tertiary industry	Institutional changes such as indemnificatory housing and property tax
Room for development in resident leverage ratio	Decrease of RMB appreciation expectation

Source: Financial Research Division of AVIC Securities.

6.4 Urbanization and Segmentation of the Real Estate Market during the Property Valuation Stage

McKinsey released the report "Preparing for China's urban billion" in 2008. According to the report, by 2025, China's urban population would hit the one billion mark, and China would have 221 cities with one million–plus inhabitants (compared with 35 cities of this size in Europe then), including 15 super cities with an average population of over 25 million or 11 urban agglomerations of more than 60 million people. "World Development Report 2009: Reshaping Economic

Dynamic Comparison of Real Estate Prices in China and Other Countries

Geography" of the World Bank said, the most effective policies of promoting long-term economic growth were the ones favoring geographic concentration and economic integration.It also pointed out that urbanization was a key method of increasing returns to scale, and that concentrated integration and functional development of future urban agglomerations were important strategies of urbanization.

In 2012, Chinese GDP per capita reached USD 6100, with an urbanization rate of over 52%. According to the universal law of urban development, when the urbanization rate is between 30% and 70%, there will be a period of rapid urbanization growth. Between 30% and 50%, there will be a period of accelerated growth when urbanization flourishes everywhere. Between 50% and 70%, urbanization will slow down, and its development will tend to be concentrated around urban agglomerations. However, the slowdown point of urbanization growth varies greatly in different countries. The turning point of China might be 56%, happening in approximately 2017, according to international experiences and digital simulation results. Laws of real estate development show that real estate prices are usually higher and stable in urban agglomerations where there are much more developer-owned properties. In the GDP composition of USA, home development (Home Building) belongs to the building industry, while developer-owned property (Real Estate) belongs to the financial service industry. In 2011, the building industry accounted for only 3.5% of the current dollar GDP, while Real Estate and relevant leasing business made up 12.6%. In the GDP composition of China, the real estate industry is mostly home building, which makes up 5.6% of the GDP. Viewed by investments, 4.4 trillion was invested in home building in 2011, while only 255.9 billion and 742.4 billion were invested in respectively office building and mercantile occupancy development. Total of the latter two items equaled to mere 22.5% of the amount invested in home building. After China passes the slowdown point of urbanization, the proportion of developer-owned properties will rise remarkably. In around 2025, Chinese GDP per capita will exceed USD 13,000, with an urbanization rate of over 65%. By then, it will be the

developer-owned properties that take the lead.

From 1994 to 2011, the compound annual growth rate (CAGR) of Chinese urban population was 4.2%. By 2011, the urbanization rate had exceeded 50%, with an urban population of 690 million. According to McKinsey Institute, by 2025 Chinese urban population would increase by 926 million. From 2011 to 2025, the CAGR would be 2.1%. Urbanization would slow down, but its pace might vary in different types of cities. Megacities and medium-sized cities (with a population of 1.5-5 million) would grow even quicker in the next two decades. From 2005 to 2011, they might develop at an estimated CAGR of 6.9% and 3.4% respectively. Shenzhen, Guangzhou, Tianjin, Wuhan, Chengdu and Chongqing would follow the steps of Beijing and Shanghai and become megacities with a population of over 10 million.

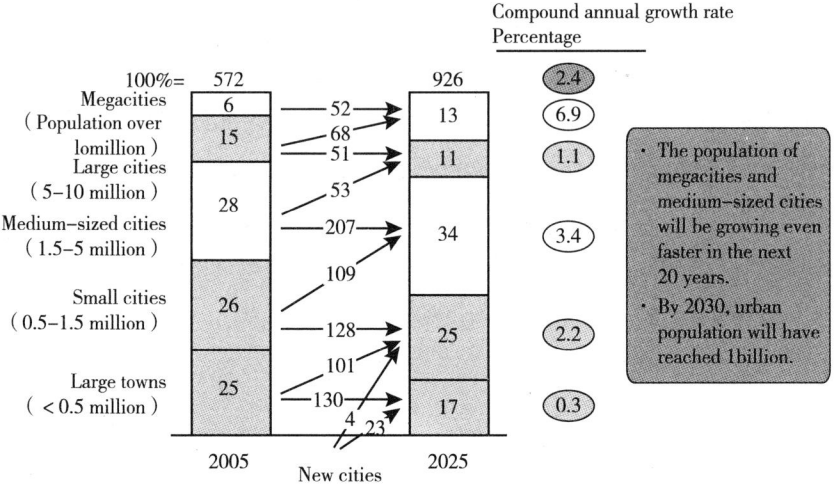

Figure 6.14 Prediction about China's Urbanization

Source: McKinsey Institute.

As we move into the metropolitanization stage, most new cities will appear in the vicinity of existing cities, and relative economic circles will come into being. The Twelfth Five Year Plan contains a strategic structure of "2 latitudinal and 3

Dynamic Comparison of Real Estate Prices in China and Other Countries

longitudinal lines". As the economy of different economic zones grows rapidly, real estate developers will have more choices, besides the existing Pearl River Delta, Yangtze River Delta and Beijing-Tianjin-Hebei economic zones. Our updated area selection model now assesses the real estate potential of different regions from 5 aspects, namely urbanization rate, dependency ratio, loan growth, loan/deposit ratio and monthly-mortgage-to-income ratio. Viewed by urbanization potential and population bonus, regions such as Henan, Sichuan, Xinjiang, Qinghai, Hebei, Shaanxi, Hunan, Shanxi and Hubei have more latent capacity. Viewed by financial resources, provinces such as Ningxia, Qinghai, Guizhou, Chongqing, Hainan, Guangxi, Fujian, Anhui, Inner Mongolia, Zhejiang and Jiangsu fit better into the picture. Compared to the 2009 results, Tianjin and Hubei are already out of the game, while Fujian, Guizhou, Qinghai and Hainan are new on the list. Zhejiang, Jiangsu, Chongqing, Anhui, Guangxi, Inner Mongolia and Ningxia have still performed well in financial resources. Viewed by monthly-mortgage-to-income ratio, markets in cities such as Chengdu, Harbin, Haikou, Hangzhou, Hefei, Hohhot, Jinan, Nanjing, Shenyang, Shijiazhuang, Taiyuan, Yinchuan, Zhengzhou and Chongqing, are still healthy. Same as the 2009 results, the three indexes do not tell exactly the same story. However, we can still conclude that Sichuan province (Chengdu) of the central/western region has performed well in all the three indexes, while Hubei province (Wuhan) on the 2009 list has lost it place due to lack of financial resources and excessive monthly-mortgage-to-income ratio.

During the property valuation stage, regional markets will be further segmented. Market segmentation of different product types will also accelerate. Different from the element revaluation stage, now multiple factors will influence the real estate market and will interact with each other, resulting in different market performances of different product types in different area at different time. Owing to the 2010 regulation of the housing market, house sales dropped remarkably, while the sales of office buildings and mercantile occupancies perked up. After the population bonus weakened due to population aging, the economy slowed down, but residents' needs for well-equipped "homes for three generations" rose instead. Therefore,

Blue Book of Quality of Life in Cities

adverse factors like the slowdown of potential GDP growth rate and the weakening of population bonus do have some impacts on the housing market as a whole, but they can also promote the product demands in certain market segments. Product segmentation in the future market will accelerate. Therefore, diversified development will be needed in order to cope with market fluctuation.

In conclusion, market in the future may be affected by various factors, and product segmentation may accelerate. Enterprises should pay attention to their clients and the demands of different market segments, so as to seize opportunities and avert risks. By category, to hedge against the influences of frequent real estate regulation on corporate cash flow, developer-owned mercantile property is the inevitable choice of corporate strategies. Developer-owned properties require enterprises to have longer-term financial resources. Financial innovation will be necessary, if the proportion of developer-owned properties is to reach 50%. By international experiences, return on net rent has to be above 5%. In USA, the return of Equity REITs dividends is about 6.1% during this decade. The reasonable return of global REITs has been about 6.4% since 2001. As for home building, enterprises should tailor their product lines to customer needs, in order to establish their own brands and core competences.